A Devotional Guide for Every Day of the Year

Daily Bread

Editors: Richard A. Brown
Cheryll L. Peterman

2004

Community of Christ
Herald Publishing House
Independence, Missouri

Bible Reference Code

IV	—Inspired Version
RSV	—Revised Standard Version
NRSV	—New Revised Standard Version
NIV	—New International Version
LB	—Living Bible
TEV	—Today's English Version
KJV	—King James Version
REB	—Revised English Bible
NEB	—New English Bible
NAB	—New American Bible
CEV	—Contemporary English Version
NLT	—New Living Translation
NCV	—New Century Version
TM	—The Message

Copyright © 2003
Herald Publishing House
Independence, Missouri
Printed in the United States of America

Library of Congress has cataloged this serial publication as follows:

Daily Bread
Independence, Mo., Herald Publishing House

v.17 cm

Annual.
"A devotional guide for every day of the year."
Key Title: Daily Bread, ISSN 0092-7147.
1.Devotional calendars
BV4810.D23 242'.2   74-640475   MARC-S

Library of Congress 74 [8205]

ISBN 0-8309-1024-7

Introduction

A relationship with God and others in community grounded in scripture provides the foundation for a spiritual life. That calls for daily nurture, which requires both time and intention. For more than a half century Herald House has been providing *Daily Bread* for just that reason.

These inspirational devotionals are written by members and friends of a worldwide faith community: the Community of Christ. The Spirit of Jesus Christ flows through the personal testimonies, selected scriptures, hymn selections, and prayer thoughts. We hope they will bring comfort, challenge, and inspiration to those who use this book.

Hymns are selected from the three hymnals published by Herald House: *Hymns of the Saints* (1981), *Sing for Peace* (1994), and *Sing a New Song* (1999). Author and scripture indexes appear at the end. Scripture selections are drawn from the three texts held sacred by the Community of Christ: the Bible, the Book of Mormon, and the Doctrine and Covenants.

Approximately 120 gifted authors share their personal reflections in this year's edition, and we are sincerely grateful for their talent, dedication, and enthusiasm. The work of many on the publishing house staff is required, as well, to produce, publish, and distribute this book each year.

If you've read *Daily Bread* before you will no doubt recognize many familiar names along with discovering several new ones. Next year your name could appear here, too, and we sincerely invite your participation. Please note the general format for style, content, and length. Deadline is May 3, 2004, with submissions sent to one of the following addresses:

Regular mail:	*Daily Bread* Editors
	Herald House Editorial Services
	Community of Christ Temple
	1001 West Walnut Street
	Independence, MO 64050-3652
	USA
By e-mail:	*dailybread@CofChrist.org*
By fax:	(816) 521-3043

Richard A. Brown
Cheryll L. Peterman
Editors

4

January 2004

S	M	T	W	T	F	S
				1	2	3
4	5	6	7	8	9	10
11	12	13	14	15	16	17
18	19	20	21	22	23	24
25	26	27	28	29	30	31

"'But I am trusting you, O Lord,' I said. 'You alone are my God; my times are in your hands.'"

—Psalm 31:14–15 TLB

The day I've dreaded has arrived at last. For years, friends and family have encouraged me to start the process of placing my son, Alex, in an appropriate facility. It was assumed that he would be on a waiting list for a very long time. Truthfully, I didn't want to hear it. I could not imagine "abandoning" my precious boy. "God will let me know when it's time, and God will open the right doors," was always my response.

Alex is severely autistic. He's also 200 pounds and prone to violent outbursts. I've had to accept the fact that my husband and I are no longer able to give him the care he needs. It is time to move Alex into a home designed for developmentally disabled adults.

If Alex is to continue going to the school he has attended since he was three years old, he will have to continue living in either Mason or Lake County. There is just one facility available, the Alternative to Institutional Settings (AIS) home in Scottville, and they have an opening. Community Mental Health is working with the home's director to ease us through the process. They plan to take Alex and his future roommate out to lunch once a week so they may get acquainted. An aide from Alex's school will accompany them and suggest strategies that work.

As I toured the AIS home, my orange tabby begged to go outside. I did a double-take and saw that it was a look-alike.

"I didn't know you had a cat," I said.

"We have two cats," my guide answered.

I remember thinking, *Wouldn't it be weird if....*

"Is the other one black?" I asked.

"Why, yes, it is."

Alex's new home has cats that look like his own two pets. I took that as a sign!

I am astounded and greatly comforted. Everything is falling into place, as I knew it would. God has opened those doors, and Alex will move into his "grown-up" home when he turns eighteen this summer.

Hymns of the Saints: No. 137, "My Times Are in Thy Hand"

Prayer Thought: Help us, loving God, to seek your will in all of life's difficult decisions and trust you to open the doors.

Friday **2** January	**A Friendly Voice** By Mark E. Megee East Windsor, New Jersey	

"And we know that all things work together for good to them that love God, to them who are the called according to his purpose."—Romans 8:28

At times in our lives it may truly seem like everyone has disappeared. Most recently I went through a divorce, lost my job, recovered from a mini-stroke, and got custody of my two children. Except for getting my two kids, things seemed pretty bleak. Financial resources were at a low. Family and friends were unsure of what was going on, so they kept their distance. I spent many nights alone, crying and praying for discernment as to what God's plan was.

It was during one of these times that I felt very alone. Despite the famous poem, I saw no footsteps in the sand, and it almost seemed as if the storm had washed them away. Family and friends were always so busy. And I had put on a brave face for most people to see. But inside, my stomach and heart were in upheaval. I felt very alone.

Then one day, I checked my e-mail. Tired of bills, jokes, and offers for free things, I found a note from someone who had read one of my *Daily Bread* submissions and just wanted to see how I was doing. It was a friendly voice from someone I had never met. You see, someone had reached out to a stranger and touched someone. I don't know which one of us did, but I know I was touched by someone caring enough to check on me. One of Christ's disciples cared enough to reach out and touch another.

Hymns of the Saints: No. 369, "Bear Each Other's Burdens"

Prayer Thought: Holy Comforter, free us from our reluctance to seek after the welfare of others. Teach us to be burden-bearers.

Saturday **3** January	**What Grandma Knew** By Janice Townsend Spokane, Washington	

"Jesus then said...'You will know the truth, and the truth will make you free.'"—John 8:31–32 LB

Head bowed, eyes closed, hands clasped firmly together, my grandmother offered her usual blessing on our evening meal. My adolescent heart grew hard and tight as I heard the same old words Grandma prayed each night: "Give us courage, Lord, to face what's before us."

How negative, I thought. How depressing. How *old*. Grandma sounds like an old lady who sees only the sad, discouraging things of life and doesn't expect much joy to come her way.

Many years have passed since then, and now, if I could, I would tell my grandmother that I have come to understand and appreciate what she said. "Grandma," I would say, "you knew things I didn't even suspect! Your life contained times of sadness and discouragement, yet you never stopped believing in the power of God to get you through. You didn't expect your life to be always smooth and happy. You knew that every life has its negative moments. But your faith held fast at all times, Grandma, and I love you for it."

My hope is that the heritage of faith I received from my grandmother, and from my mother, whom Grandma raised in the gospel, will continue in me and be passed on to my children and grandchildren.

Hymns of the Saints: No. 273, "I Know That My Redeemer Lives"

Prayer Thought: Thank you, God, for all the steadfast souls whose lives have touched our own. May their wisdom and courage inspire us to faithfully face the challenges of life.

Tell Your Story!
By Steve Calvarese
Tulsa, Oklahoma

"If you will move out in faith and confidence to proclaim my gospel my Spirit will empower you and there will be many who respond, even in places and ways which do not now seem clear."—Doctrine and Covenants 154:7a

During our congregational prayer-and-testimony Communion service held the first Sunday of 2003, Brenda testified that she had been sharing her enthusiasm, from a renewed church life over the past seven years, with Michelle, one of her co-workers. This co-worker, inactive in her own church for many years, did not respond immediately, but over time became interested in attending a church near her home in Locust Grove.

Over a number of years, Brenda continued to share her enthusiasm and encouraged Michelle to begin attending church with Brenda's parents, despite Michelle's husband's unwillingness. Gradually, Michelle caught the spirit of Brenda's testimonies and became more and more active in Brenda's church. Eventually, her husband also began attending.

Recently, Michelle shared her decision to be baptized and thanked Brenda for all her encouragement. Michelle's husband, Brent, also decided to follow Jesus into the waters of baptism. Brenda had simply humbly told her story of discipleship and renewal, as she grew in Christ through congregational worship and ministry. The result of listening to and following God's voice is that two souls were brought to Christ.

Hymns of the Saints: No. 473, "I Love to Tell the Story"

Prayer Thought: May we be vibrant witnesses, Lord, faithfully planting the seed of the gospel yet leaving the results in your hands.

Monday **5** January	**Encouragement in Unexpected Places** By Donna Needham Carnation, Washington	

"The Lord is my strength and my shield; my heart trusted in him, and I am helped; therefore my heart greatly rejoiceth; and with my song will I praise him."
—Psalm 28:7 IV

Last year was a Spirit-filled one for me. So the contrast between that and the current barren year has been significant and very discouraging at times. Then I found something I had written for a friend during my Spirit-filled year and her barren year. Here's how that writing ended:

"Life ebbs and flows. I don't know why sometimes we are keenly aware of the Spirit and are so filled that it flows in, around, and out of us to others. I don't know why sometimes we feel like a barren wasteland. I just know that life ebbs and flows like the tide. It may be out now, but it will eventually come in. Because of that I am encouraged to go with the instinct and longing that compels me to continue to be drawn to the source of all love."

I certainly didn't expect to find encouragement in something I had written in a previous year for someone else, but I am grateful that God finds unexpected ways to reach me in my need.

Hymns of the Saints: No. 168, "Draw Thou My Soul, O Christ"

11

Prayer Thought: God, who knows all our needs, it is with humble gratitude that we thank you for the unexpected ways you encourage and draw us to you.

| Tuesday **6** January | **Creations of Love**
By Shirley Botting
Wiarton, Ontario, Canada | |

"For we are his workmanship, created in Christ Jesus unto good works, which God hath before ordained that we should walk in them."—Ephesians 2:10

My friend Jean asked me if I would like to help a group of women tie quilts. This group belongs to the I.O.D.E. (Imperial Order of the Daughters of the Empire). Although I was not a member, I said yes because they do so many wonderful things for people in need.

On this particular day I went to the church where they were meeting to tie the quilts. There were many quilt tops that they had sewn, some for single beds and others for double ones. There was batting to put in the middle, and lots of varied material for the backing, plus a great many colors of yarn. We tried to match the colors of the backing and yarn to the quilt tops; then we used darning needles to tie the blocks every so far apart.

I helped them all morning but left at noon. The quilts were for needy people, such as those who had lost all their belongings in a house fire.

Seeing all those quilt tops gave me an idea. I decided to make one of my own, but using smaller squares. We cut the material and I used my sewing machine to join the squares together. When I finished the top, we got a quilt frame and stretched my quilt on it. I ended up with a wonderful double-size quilt.

There is always something we can do for others, that although it might seem small to us, to others can be quite big.

Hymns of the Saints: No. 441, "In Nature's Voice We Hear You, Lord"

Prayer Thought: Lord, we thank you for the joy we feel when we make something beautiful, whether to bless our own home or that of someone else.

| Wednesday
7
January | **Weave Us Together**
By Melba Jean Dixon
Farwell, Michigan | |

"There was no contention in the land because of the love of God which dwelt in the hearts of the people."
—IV Nephi 1:17

After his retirement my husband took on what we refer to as a "fun job." He provides transportation for a group of young Amish carpenters. Thus, we have become good friends with many people in the Amish community. On several occasions we have received invitations to marriage ceremonies. These weddings typically begin at 8 a.m. and continue until after noon. The number of wedding guests may reach as many as 300.

They often travel from several states by bus or van. Residents from surrounding areas come by horse and buggy. As they gather in a large building, the men are seated on one side of the room, while the women sit on the opposite side. Children may be with their parents on either side. The greater portion of the service consists of advice and readings given by the bishop, spoken in a "low" German dialect and presented in a solemn tone. The bride and groom remain standing throughout the service. At times, hymns are sung in a sort of chanting style. Singing is primarily done by the men.

Following the ceremony guests are invited to a banquet where the finest Amish fare is served and enjoyed. Prayers and table grace are offered in silence. During one of these receptions each guest was given a copy of a hymn to sing together. As I attempted to sing from the printed page in German, I recognized that we were singing the tune to "Weave Us Together." No matter where our origins may be, or the diversity of our customs, Christian love weaves us together into one great human family.

Sing a New Song: No. 51, "Weave"

Prayer Thought: Lord of the universe, we are grateful for experiences that open our eyes to a greater appreciation of all people.

Thursday **8** January	**Fed by _Daily Bread_** By Luther M. Beal Beals Island, Maine	

"As each one has received a gift, minister to one another, as good stewards of the manifold grace of God."
—I Peter 4:10 NIV

All too often we take for granted our brief but enormously important opportunities to worship and commune. No matter how many times I am reminded of this, I still allow the human nature in me to permit it to happen again.

My wife, Alice, and I just returned from an incredible opportunity to see more of God's wondrous creation. After a flight to London with several days spent there,

14

we went to Dover to board a ship for the transatlantic crossing to Boston. We viewed the magnificent White Cliffs of Dover as our ship left the harbor. The words of hope from the World War II song "When Bluebirds Fly Over the White Cliffs of Dover" flooded my mind as tears filled my eyes. Although written for a different era, the words still bring hope to a world suffering the shock of the event of September 11, 2001.

Our luxurious vessel afforded us many comforts as we traveled to France, Ireland, Scotland, Iceland, Newfoundland, and Nova Scotia. We were happy to see favorite places and were filled with awe as we viewed new splendors of God's creation. We met many wonderful, helpful people on shore and aboard ship. Excursions and activities filled our time, but a few minutes of each day seemed empty because of my neglect.

As I packed for the voyage, I planned to put *Daily Bread* in my carry-on bag. I almost did this a day early to be certain not to forget, but I wanted to read it the morning of our departure. I didn't think of it again until our plane left the ground. A rabbi and Roman Catholic priest performed services aboard ship, and there was an occasional Protestant service on the TV in our stateroom. Nevertheless, each day I missed the minutes traditionally spent with my *Daily Bread*.

I am grateful for the wonderful, enriching experiences that we enjoyed during the past three weeks. However, I am grateful too for the painful reminder of how much the Community of Christ and the quiet moments with *Daily Bread* mean to me.

Hymns of the Saints: No. 180, "Take Time to Be Holy"

Prayer Thought: Remind us, Lord, of our worldwide church family through these pages of shared testimony. Connect us daily through the power of words and prayer.

15

Friday **9** January	**Speak Boldly for Justice** By Eileen Turner Portland, Oregon

"Finally, brethren, whatever is true, whatever is honorable, whatever is just, whatever is pure, whatever is lovely, whatever is gracious, if there is any excellence, if there is anything worthy of praise, think about these things."
—Philippians 4:8 RSV

On a recent January evening, the Oregon Symphony performed Shostakovich's Symphony no. 11, *The Year 1905*. The historical significance of this composition centered on what was later referred to as "Bloody Sunday," January 9, when the troops of Czar Nicholas II opened fire on a crowd of unarmed civilians demonstrating in front of the Winter Palace in St. Petersburg, Russia

Although Shostakovich gave it this title, *1905* was composed in the aftermath of the Soviet invasion of Hungary much later in the century. The universal nature of people pleading for peace, justice, equality, food, and relief from poverty was expressed in this musical-historical painting. The gifted composer wrote a rich, full-bodied, pleading, heavy, mournful piece that might be interpreted two ways: palace guards firing on innocent, pleading civilians; or Soviet tanks roaring through the streets of Budapest. The latter of these was so clear to the composer's son that he whispered to Shostakovich during the dress rehearsal, "Papa, what if they hang you for this?"

Sometimes one has to speak out, find ways to provoke thought, and promote dialogue on issues of serious importance. Shostakovich found a way, through his music, to represent the pain, suffering, and stories of the oppressed. He captured it so soulfully that on this evening there were four standing ovations by the audience for James Depriest, conductor, and the Oregon Symphony's rendition.

Each of us in our own way needs to give thought to how we can bring about peace and justice in our little corner of the world. Although our gifts may not be as magnificent as this composer's, we may be able to make a difference in some small way.

Hymns of the Saints: No. 322, "O How Blessed Are the Poor in Spirit"

Prayer Thought: Lord, give us the courage to speak boldly on issues of peace and justice.

Saturday **10** January	**Trust in His Perfect Will** By Shirley Dauzvardis Blue Springs, Missouri	

"Peace I leave with you, my peace I give unto you; not as the world giveth, give I unto you. Let not your heart be troubled, neither let it be afraid."—John 14:27

Osteosarcoma, rhabdomyosarcoma—cancer. I was stunned and speechless as I heard my son relate his diagnosis to me that day on the phone. How could this be happening to an otherwise healthy young man? Christopher was only twenty years old. My nursing experience told me that his prognosis was not good. In the days that followed, I fervently prayed and fasted that Chris's life might be spared.

As Chris grew progressively worse, I felt that my prayers had gone unheard, unanswered. The one thing in my life that I couldn't bear to think about was happening—the loss of one of my children. I again went to the Lord in prayer and laid this terrible burden at his feet, asking that his perfect will might be done. In the days that followed, I experienced a strength and peace that could only have come from God.

Chris died after three years of extensive surgery, radiation, and chemotherapy. We were blessed with this precious child for twenty-three years, and my faith in God's promises is stronger than ever. We will see our loved ones again in heaven—a place of unspeakable beauty and joy. Praise be to God.

Hymns of the Saints: No. 126, "I Know Not What the Future Hath"

Prayer Thought: Nurture in us a profound trust, Lord, that carries us beyond our earthly understanding of your will.

Sunday **11** January	**Country Tours** By Susan L. Berg Gladstone, Michigan	

"Let brotherly love continue. Be not forgetful to entertain strangers."—Hebrews 13:1–2

Over the past several years, our small congregation has been blessed with the opportunity to serve lunch to tour buses traveling around Lake Michigan. From May to October our small dining room is filled with smiles and laughter and the fellowship of people from all across America. What an awesome experience.

The blessings I have received while helping with the country tours are immeasurable. Yes, it is a great fund-raiser for our congregation, but the personal rewards far outreach the financial. Our guests so appreciate a home-cooked meal and an at-home atmosphere that by the time they are ready to leave us, they have full stomachs, stories to share, and smiles from ear to ear.

I am truly thankful to be able to serve them, providing food and drink and sharing in conversation with them, while serving God in the process. And I am filled with a heart overflowing with joy each and every time, no matter how weary I become, because I work in honor of the Lord.

Hymns of the Saints: No. 407, "Yesu, Yesu, Fill Us with Your Love"

Prayer Thought: Lord, we thank you for opportunities to serve you by serving others and for the blessings of joy we receive from our efforts.

Monday **12** January	**Timely Blessing** By Dorothy Troyer Plainfield, Illinois	

"Seek the Lord and his strength, seek his presence continually."—I Chronicles 16:11 NRSV

It was Sunday evening. My husband, Clarence, had had back surgery seven days before. His recovery seemed slow and we were both discouraged. Visiting hours were over and I prepared to leave the hospital. It was January, cold and snowy, and I had an hour's drive to an empty house. Seeing how reluctant I was to leave, Clarence said, "Let's have prayer before you go." We asked for strength and comfort and for God's Spirit to be with both of us.

I kissed him good-bye and started out of the room, only to be met by the doctor coming in. When Clarence saw the doctor the first thing he said was, "When can I go home?" The doctor checked a couple of charts and then said, "Right now, if you want to." We were elated! It had taken only the doctor's six words to change our attitude completely, but if we hadn't stopped to pray, I wouldn't have been there when the doctor came.

Hymns of the Saints: No. 155, "Sometimes a Light Surprises"

Prayer Thought: Almighty Creator, we give thanks for unexpected blessings that cheer us in time of need.

Tuesday **13** January	**Just a Minute, Lord** By Dorene Kilburn St. Paul's Station, Ontario, Canada

"My Spirit is reaching out to numerous souls even now and there are many who will respond if you, my people, will bear affirmative testimony of my love and my desires for all to come unto me."—Doctrine and Covenants 153:9b

I am a procrastinator and have been all my life, always intending to change but never making much of an effort. Sometimes procrastination pays off—maybe what I had planned to do, but put off, turned out to be the wrong thing to do, and I would have been sorry if I'd acted immediately. But that rarely happens. All too often I sense the Lord prompting me to do something, and all too often I say, "Just a minute, Lord." There's something else I need to finish—and maybe it's just a crossword puzzle! Because I put off making that phone call, someone may be sitting alone and in tears, wanting so much to have someone to talk to. Because I don't stop and spend some time in my "quiet corner" of the house, where I go to talk to Jesus, I miss out on insights and guidance.

There is no good reason why I can't respond to the Lord's call, only excuses. I deprive myself of so many blessings through procrastination. When I respond to the promptings of the Spirit, and don't keep the Lord waiting, I always receive more than I give. And caring can lead to sharing, I've found. Sharing Christ's love, bringing weary and hurting souls to him, is what we are called to do. He will give us opportunities, if we listen to his voice, calling us to feed his sheep.

Hymns of the Saints: No. 424, "Send Me Forth, O Blessed Master"

Prayer Thought: Lord, forgive us for those times when we have not responded to someone in need. We would listen more carefully to your voice, that we might not miss an opportunity to reach out to someone who is discouraged, fearful, or lonely.

Wednesday **14** January	**My Angel** By Bridget Dinger Thompsonville, Michigan	

"In this was manifested the love of God toward us, because that God sent his only begotten Son into the world, that we might live through him. Herein is love, not that we loved God, but that he loved us, and sent his Son to be the propitiation for our sins."—I John 4:9–10 IV

I had been dating John for five months when he broke it off. I didn't understand. We had so much fun hanging out, and we had gotten along great. I was devastated and spent almost three months being depressed, trying to figure out what went wrong. It just didn't make sense.

I had shut God out of my life four years before, but never understood why. I suppose I was afraid I wasn't good enough. I didn't want to be a disappointment, but I knew I needed God. I prayed day and night, until finally I asked God to either let me know that John was going to come back or give me a way to let him go. I knew I could no longer go on like this. Two days later I learned he was seeing someone else, but to my surprise I was not upset about it.

I realized that the real attachment had been to his two-year-old son, Logan. Logan had opened my eyes. He showed me all the good in my life, and I was no longer afraid of being a disappointment to God. I knew it was time for me to go back to Michigan and that I would have to let Logan go. I wish I'd been able to be there for Logan like he was for me, but I know that God will be there for him. God never forgets his "angels," and neither will I.

Hymns of the Saints: No. 156, "Children of the Heavenly Father"

Prayer Thought: Touch our hearts through the innocence of children, Lord. May they show us a new way of seeing ourselves.

Thursday **15** January	**Surrounded and Protected** By Ruth Andrews Vreeland Albuquerque, New Mexico	

"'Have faith in God,' Jesus answered. 'I tell you the truth, if anyone says to this mountain, "Go, throw yourself into the sea," and does not doubt in his heart but believes that what he says will happen, it will be done for him. Therefore I tell you, whatever you ask for in prayer, believe that you have received it, and it will be yours.'"—Mark 11:22–24 NIV

We bought a house for our growing family and suffered major consequences: for five years we lived in the most horrible neighborhood possible. Our last year there, we realized we were caught in the middle of an explosive neighborhood war that was escalating out of control. Our property was constantly vandalized or stolen, and our children's lives were threatened daily. Even the police advised our family to sell the house and move to a different neighborhood across town, if we valued the safety of our children. We put the house on the market a few weeks later.

During that time I feared for my children's lives in a way I never thought I would. I got down on my knees several times a day to pray through a storm of anguished tears that God would send every available angel he had to guard our home and protect us during the time we had left there. I prayed for angels to literally surround our home like a shield, and that God would not allow *any* harm to come to my young children. I had much faith that he would honor my prayer.

One day my ten-year-old son, Scott, coasted out of our open garage door on his bicycle and down our inclined driveway, where he could coast out onto the street, as was his custom. As he got to the end of the driveway, the bicycle came to an abrupt halt, as if meeting an invisible shield. He did not have hand brakes and had not braked with his foot, yet the bicycle stopped moving. Just then, a huge semi-truck rounded the corner and went roaring past Scott, only a foot or so away. He had not seen it coming, and he told me later he knew instantly he would have been killed if "something" had not stopped his bicycle. He didn't know what that something could be until I shared with him what I had been praying for.

I knew my son's life had been saved that day. Our home was truly surrounded by the protection of heavenly beings, in answer to my urgent prayers.

Hymns of the Saints: No. 142, "A Mighty Fortress Is Our God"

Prayer Thought: Faithful God, we pour out our thanks for those times when we have experienced your protection.

Friday **16** January	**Confidence** By Ina G. Beggs Goodwood, Ontario, Canada	

"I can do all things through Christ which strengtheneth me."—Philippians 4:13

Recently, a great nephew asked me to do something for him, and my response was, "Oh, Curtis, I couldn't do that." He looked at me with disappointment and a little reproach and said, "Auntie Ina, you have to believe in yourself and have confidence. You can do it!" Words of wisdom from a five year old.

I thought how I must have disappointed my heavenly Father many times as I have thought or answered, "I couldn't do that" when approached to serve in some way. With this attitude we are limiting the God-given potential placed in each of us.

Just as Curtis believed in me so does the Lord believe in us. Next time may our answer be, "Yes, Lord, we will try to do the tasks that come our way, remembering to believe and have confidence in ourselves and your promise that with you all things are possible."

Hymns of the Saints: No. 409, "Touch Me, Lord, with Thy Spirit Eternal"

Prayer Thought: Lord, may we prayerfully seek the support that will give us strength to serve you better.

| Saturday **17** January | **He Knows My Name!** By Judy Oetting Levasy, Missouri | |

"However, do not rejoice that the spirits submit to you, but rejoice that your names are written in heaven."

—Luke 10:20 NIV

I volunteer as a naturalist for the Missouri Conservation Department and am often privileged to present bird or wildflower programs for area nursing homes. The attendees are in varying degrees of health, lucidity, and alertness. I try to learn their names quickly, because I've noticed that when I call them by name they become more attentive. But at one nursing home the chaplain who brought them to me had learned something of greater importance. My heart was touched as he introduced them to me and told me who they were. For example, "This is Mary. She is a pilot." "This is Everett. He is a trucker." As a result, I could see them hold their heads a little higher.

Too often we tend to dismiss our elderly loved ones as of no value when they can no longer function as they once did. This chaplain understood a basic need of all humankind: the need to feel worthy, to know that we still are who we have worked hard to be, and that someone knows our name.

The Bible is full of accounts of the importance of a name. God knows our name and who we are. In God's eyes we are of value and he has written our name on his heart. As we all grow older may we not forget how important we will always be to our heavenly Father.

Sing a New Song: No. 32, "Lord, I Give You"

Prayer Thought: Lord, we are humbled by the realization

of how deep and wondrous your love must be to know and record forever our names and who we are.

Sunday **18** January	**With Whom Can I Share My Fears?** By Diane Brunner Jones Anton, Colorado

"Now, however, that you have come to know God, or rather to be known by God, how can you turn back again to the weak and beggarly elemental spirits?"

—Galatians 4:9 NRSV

Our fifteen-year-old son, Morgan, was invited to a classmate's birthday party on a Saturday night. Earlier in the day his dad, Randy, had taken him to his friend Webb's house to ride dirt bikes. Later in the day Morgan called to ask if he could just go to the party with Webb because it was a lot closer than coming home and going back. I thought that was a good idea, so I agreed.

Morgan called about half an hour after the party was scheduled to begin to say there had been things going on that he and Webb didn't approve of so they had gone back to Webb's house. I was very proud of them. He also asked if he could spend the night, but Webb's parents weren't home so I said we would have to check with them first.

After a while, when we didn't hear from Morgan, I sent Randy to pick him up at 9:30 p.m. It was about a twenty-mile drive one way, so I figured by the time they loaded the dirt bike and drove back home it would be around 10:30.

At 11:00 I began to be concerned as to why they hadn't come home yet. By 11:30, with still no sign of them, I became more worried as all the worst-case scenarios ran through my head. Should I leave our two

26

younger children at home and go search for them? Who would be awake at this late hour whom I could call and share my concern with? My parents in Yuma? My sister in Ft. Collins? My brother in Iowa? No, the time change makes it even later there. My nearby friends, or Webb's house? I didn't know whom I could disturb at such a late hour so I could share my fear and concern. Then God entered my thoughts and I was reminded that God is available twenty-four hours a day, seven days a week. I wasn't disturbing God; I could talk to God anytime.

After I shared my prayer of concern, asking for the safe return of my family, I heard the pickup in the distance. Randy had returned to say that Webb's parents had come home and had invited Morgan to spend the night.

When will I ever learn to turn to God first?

Hymns of the Saints: No. 183, "Lord, Lead Me by Your Spirit"

Prayer Thought: Almighty God, in any anxious situation remind us to turn to you first. Teach us to rely on your power to strengthen us and to abide with our loved ones.

Monday
19
January

Abiding in Christ
By Henry Fultz
Atwater, California

"Now you are the body of Christ, and each one of you is a part of it."—I Corinthians 12:27 NIV

At the high school I attended there were strong racial tensions. For some reason, one day I ended up being part of that tension when one black student spit on me while I was standing in line during gym class. The

27

first thought that came to mind was, *What would Jesus do?* This was long before that saying became popular. I responded with a prayer to ask that I could forgive Ray and think no ill thoughts of him or react in a violent manner. With the situation at the time, this was a wise decision. Things certainly would have turned out much differently had I reacted violently. Ray was smaller than I was, and I thought later that I could have handled him. However, I didn't come in contact with Ray much after that incident.

It was interesting last year to see Ray at my twenty-five-year class reunion and speak to him. Ray now has cancer, and by the way his suit fit one could see that he had lost quite a bit of weight. In our discussions it was obvious that the incident of years past was not a part of his thoughts. We got along like old friends. I even had my picture taken in a group with my arm around him.

Ray mentioned how God had blessed him even during his experience with cancer. He stated: "I've really been blessed." I agreed and told him that in my life God had blessed me, too. Part of the great blessing of God is that we could still be friends even after our past experiences. Part of the blessing I received from Ray that night was that he could take his struggle with cancer and see that God was there in the midst of it. Isn't it amazing how God can be present even in the adversities of life? What an awesome God.

Sing for Peace: No. 43, "When on Life a Darkness Falls"

Prayer Thought: God of reconciliation, we thank you for life's years bringing us maturity, and for your Spirit granting us the grace to bear all things.

Tuesday **20** January	**An Optimistic Faith** By Bill Griffin Elkin, North Carolina	

"Nevertheless, they fasted and prayed often, and waxed stronger and stronger in their humility, and firmer and firmer in the faith of Christ, to the filling of their souls with joy and consolation."—Helaman 2:31

Twice a month I drive fifty miles to visit with a dear church friend. Some evenings there are several friends present, but often it's just the two of us sharing our concerns and prayers with each other. Over the years, my friend's health has declined. She has had to move from her townhouse to an assisted-living apartment, and then to a nursing home.

With each move she has sacrificed furnishings, possessions, privacy, independence. But when I sit down beside her, do I ever encounter a spirit of regret or despair? Never! My friend always greets me with a loving smile and a hug. She shares her stories of the Lord's blessings throughout her life. When we part she thanks me for coming, but I know that I am the one who has received ministry.

Hymns of the Saints: No. 497, "With a Steadfast Faith"

Prayer Thought: Lord, increase our awareness of your blessings in our lives, that we may freely share them with others.

Wednesday **21** January	**Lifted Up on Eagle's Wings** By Sherry Southland Temple City, California	

"...but those who wait for the Lord shall renew their strength, they shall mount up with wings like eagles, they shall run and not be weary, they shall walk and not faint."—Isaiah 40:31 NRSV

Several years ago I lived a fast-paced lifestyle that included drinking and some drug use. Both my parents had died, as well as a couple of close family friends. Even though I had gone to church regularly, I was a bitter person who did not understand the concept of God's love for me personally. I thought at the time that everyone who had loved me had died.

I became ill with pneumonia. My life was going in a downward spiral. The doctor told me I had so many toxins in my body that I could die. Hospitalization was out of the question, because I wasn't working and I didn't have insurance. Depression set in.

After facing foreclosure on my house I found myself lying on a couch in someone's living room. (I don't remember whose house it was!) I was fading in and out of reality with a 103-degree fever. The best way I can describe this experience is that my spirit was taken to a beautiful forested area with an abundance of trees and ferns (my concept of heaven). I didn't feel any pain at all. As I was walking though this forest I came upon a clearing. Before me was a meadow. I noticed some movement in the sky. I looked up and saw an eagle soaring majestically over my head. I was in awe as the Isaiah scripture was quoted to me by a gentle unseen male voice.

As I followed the eagle's path I felt a love that was beyond my comprehension. Never had I felt anything like this. It was a truly awesome experience. God, in his wisdom, used this scripture to let me know that I was a child of his and that he loved me! I am one who does not memorize scriptures well, but this scripture set me on a path to healing and wholeness.

Sing a New Song: No. 41, "On Eagle's Wings"

Prayer Thought: Gracious God, may we be reminded that your love goes beyond what we can understand. May your love bring healing and wholeness into our lives.

Thursday **22** January	**Stitches of Blessing** By Olevia Huntsman Bald Knob, Arkansas	

"Every good gift and every perfect gift is from above, and cometh down from the Father of lights."—James 1:17

Joan crochets afghans. The first day I met her she wanted to know what color afghan I wanted. She has made so many that she has lost count—large, small, lap-size. Recently she finished the last of four for my grand-children. I am amazed at how fast she works and the uniformity of her stitches. Several nursing homes have benefited from her talent, yet she doesn't feel she does anything of value.

One day I told her that I thought her crocheting talent was a gift from God. Her greatest joy is in seeing the happiness of the faces of the recipients. My afghan is beautiful to look at and keeps me warm on cold days, but when I look at it I see my friend and the many hours she worked to finish it for me—a true labor of love. Did I mention that she does this for no monetary reward? She has to be forced to take anything for her work.

God has given each of us a gift or talent. I have struggled with just what my gift might be. It is easy to see the talent in a gifted musician, speaker, or artist, but harder to recognize it in the steadfast faith of a friend, a person's optimistic outlook, or in someone's hospitality. I am thankful for my friend and for what her gift has taught me, and I am thankful to God for showing me her gift so I might better recognize what God has given me. I want to be willing to share my gifts just as my friend is sharing hers.

Hymn of the Saints: No. 400, "Source of All Gifts"

Prayer Thought: Lord, help us to recognize the gifts you have given us and to use them in service for you.

| Friday **23** January | **God's Word in** *Daily Bread* By Merna Short Melbourne, Australia | |

"Thy word is a lamp unto my feet, and a light unto my path."—Psalm 119:105

"We spent so much time in the hospital when Kristie was having chemo. With us missing church, *Daily Bread* became our church," Helen said. "Often it had just the message we needed for that day. One time between treatments Kristie was invited to stay with a relative interstate. Would she go or wouldn't she? What if she got sick?"

"She rang me at work and said, 'Mum, I've decided not to go after all.'"

"Go and have a read of *Daily Bread*. See if there is any help in today's devotional."

Kristie did this and the message gave her the strength to make the journey. She had no problems with her health and had a good time. Apart from being tired when she returned home, there were no adverse affects. It had been good for her.

Many times I have had the right message to help me through my day, or my mind has been opened to deeper insights because of the writings shared through this book. I have also used it as a witnessing tool, which has often gently led to deeper spiritual conversation.

Years ago, when I was much younger, I found a version of the scriptures that I felt put the message I wanted to deliver more plainly. I felt it would be better understood. There were also other writings I wanted to include. "What is scripture?" I asked one of our elders. He answered, "Writings that reveal God to man."

God reveals himself in many ways. I often find him in *Daily Bread*.

Hymns of the Saints: No. 299, "The Living Word of Scripture," verse 4

Prayer Thought: You lift us up, Lord, both through words of scripture and through people of our own times who share their story.

| Saturday **24** January | **The Still Small Voice**
By Dale Argotsinger
Aurora, Colorado | |

"My sheep hear my voice, and I know them, and they follow me; and I give unto them eternal life."—John 10:27–28

My daughter and I needed to acquire some special worship service bulletins for a memorial service we were having at the church. The local Christian bookstore had a limited supply. None of them seemed quite right for the service of celebration planned for the congregation member who had recently passed away. The thought occurred to us to go to another store about a twenty-five-minute drive from my home.

Neither of us had been to that particular store, although we were familiar with the area, or so we thought. We had the address and the name of the store; it would be easy to find. As we drew closer to the store's neighborhood, however, we became quite aware that there had been a lot of changes. Many new stores had been built, and a number were still under construction. There was a host of signs on both sides of the street. Since my daughter was driving, it was my job to look for the large bookstore.

I was so caught up in how the area had changed and was continuing to change, that I saw nearly every sign except the one for the selected store. We went too far and then circled back, this time looking for the cross street and the store number. Their large sign was right where it was supposed to be, and now when I drive down that street I notice it right away. They had a wonderful selection of bulletin covers, and we chose one that filled our need.

Often when seeking the peace and blessings of God, we are so caught up with various voices that we do not hear that "still small voice which giveth light, understanding, peace, and joy." This voice is available to all, and in giving attention to it we continue to expand our ability to hear its call in the midst of many voices.

Hymns of the Saints: No. 301, "O God, Our Source of Truth"

Prayer Thought: Teach us, God, to listen for your voice giving us direction.

Doorkeepers
By Phyllis Elliott
Florissant, Missouri

"Therefore, all things whatsoever ye would that men should do to you, do ye even so to them."—Matthew 7:31 IV

Several years ago I started using a walker because I had fallen so many times. Fortunately, I had not been injured. I've noticed how helpful most people are to go out of their way to open doors for me. One time at the medical center a young man in his late teens was coming out of the lab as I went to the front door. He, also, started for the door but remembered he had left something at the lab. He went back in and then came hurrying out so he could be at the door to open it for me.

Other times, people coming in or out of the building will see me getting the walker out of the car. They wait at the door to be able to open it for me.

Another time, a mother and several small children parked about four cars from mine. The boy, about five years old, ran to the door to open it for me. I thanked him and told him how helpful it was to have someone be so kind. It is always easier to go though doors and not have to maneuver the walker around the door frames while holding the door open. Often other patients in the waiting rooms will get up to help me.

On one occasion, where there were two sets of doors, a woman held both doors open and then asked if I needed help getting into the car. She said her father had used a walker and she knew how much help he had needed. I thanked her and assured her I was able to manage alone.

At the medical center there is a mailbox near the door, and I find it convenient to mail letters on my way in. Sometimes I wait to mail them on the way out because there is someone to open the door for me. These experiences have made me more watchful for situations where I might help someone else.

Hymns of the Saints: No. 443, "Jesus' Hands Were Kind Hands"

Prayer Thought: Servant of all, may our eyes always be open to the needs of others.

| Monday **26** January | **The One-Armed Man**
By Paul McCain
Oklahoma City, Oklahoma |

"Every one to whom much is given, of him will much be required."—Luke 12:48 RSV

While a student at Central High School in Tulsa, before I had my driver's license, I rode with my brother Wayne in our old '52 Dodge to a parking lot just a couple of blocks from school, where we left the car for the day. My brother didn't park the car; the lot attendant did. As we walked away I would watch this man park the cars.

The lot was small and, in an effort to get as many in as possible, the attendant would park them bumper-to-bumper and very close to each other side to side. Since several customers would arrive at about the same time, he had to do his job with great speed and accuracy, so that traffic would not be blocked on the street at the entrance. The most amazing thing was, even with most cars not having power steering, he did this with only one arm.

Sometimes when I find myself moaning about my circumstances in life I remember this man. He didn't complain; he was courteous, and he performed the job before him with great skill. He appeared to really enjoy his work. I am reminded that I should not focus on the things I don't have but do the best with what has been given me.

Hymns of the Saints: No. 381, "Hark! The Voice of Jesus Calling"

Prayer Thought: Lord, may we be found eagerly doing whatever task you place before us, using whatever skills and abilities you have given us.

| Tuesday **27** January | **God and My Mountain View** By Shirley Vallier Remmenga Fort Collins, Colorado | |

"For I am the Lord, I change not...."—Malachi 3:6

Ready or not, change happens. That's life, like it or not. My husband and I have some major changes ahead of us. After living in one place for forty years, we have decided to sell our property and move somewhere else. We don't know when it will sell or where we will move, but it will happen.

I try to think of all the changes that have occurred during all our years here, but they are too numerous. The one thing that has not changed is the view we have of the front range of the Rocky Mountains. The silhouette is the same as it was the first time I saw it. Weather conditions, the time of day, the amount of light, the reflected color, and the cloud formations give the mountains a different look each day, but the view remains unchanged. I love my view; I love those mountains. They are a part of who I am.

When I look at them I am reminded of God, who never changes, who is always there, the one who paints my world with color, clouds, sunshine, and a variety of weather. How blessed I am to have God and the mountains in my life.

Hymns of the Saints: No. 153, "Great Hills May Tremble"

Prayer Thought: God, we thank you for being the one dependable, ever-present, secure thing in our lives. We know you will be there regardless of the changes that come to us all.

Wednesday **28** January	**Look Ahead to the Future** By Joe Andrews Sr. Independence, Missouri	

"Jesus said to him, 'No one who puts a hand to the plow and looks back is fit for the kingdom of God.'"

—Luke 9:62 NRSV

While in high school, I competed in track and field and learned some valuable life lessons. Ask runners where they set their sights—they aren't focused on the one running next to them, but straight down a narrow track.

When one takes off in a race where medals are given, his or her feet are placed one foot forward, the other back slightly, in what are called "blocks," anchored to the ground by long nails or cleats. *The foot in back is the one from which the body is propelled forward.* The race master calls out, "On your mark. Get set." The runners look down their lanes as far as they can, orienting themselves down the path they will run, focusing all of their bodily energy and muscular power with a tremendous burst of physical energy to spring off the blocks and run down their assigned lane.

In my track and field events, had I looked behind, I would never have reached my goal. Once, I was anchor on the 440-yard relay. Looking behind me to see where everyone else was caused a shift in my muscular strength and forward motion. We lost! Team members got on my case—next time I didn't look back to see where *anyone* was! We won!

Too many times we are controlled by looking back to see where everyone else is, or we concentrate on our regrets about the past. Coach John Mackovic once said: "We have a tendency to place more value on failures than victories. Defeat weighs us down. When we learn to put value on victory over defeat, we will be much happier. Happy people win. Happy people have a history of doing better things."

Sing a New Song: No. 5, "Beyond the Horizon"

Prayer Thought: Keep our eyes focused on the path ahead of us, Lord, that our aim may be true as we seek to walk the path in your name.

| Thursday **29** January | **My God Is So Big!** By Cheryl Fleming Monessen, Pennsylvania | |

"[The Lord] shall feed his flock like a shepherd; he shall gather the lambs with his arms, and carry them in his bosom, and shall gently lead those that are with young."
—Isaiah 40:11

It was one of the coldest, snowiest winters in the history of western Pennsylvania. It was also my first winter alone as a single parent of two young children. One cold January day Elizabeth and Cory were fighting with each other and I had lost my patience with them. The snow continued to fall that afternoon and I was feeling quite guilty for snapping at them, and very depressed over the long winter. I sat on the couch with my head in my hands, fighting back tears.

Across the room my three-year-old son was sitting in an armchair. I could barely hear him mumbling something to himself. I asked him what he was saying and he began to belt out every word to the song: "My God is so big, so strong, and so mighty. There's nothing my God cannot do!" (He had learned the song in Sunday school a few weeks before.) I lifted my head and smiled as I realized this song was for me.

My God is so big, so strong, and so mighty, I do not have to face these burdens alone. All I need to do is place my feelings and concerns in God's hands, and I will never be alone.

Hymns of the Saints: No. 197, "Let God Be God"

Prayer Thought: Touch us in our pain, loving God, and restore us to wholeness and a bright faith in you.

| Friday
30
January | **Of God? Forgiven!**
By Hal McKain
Lamoni, Iowa | |

"Be kindly affectioned one to another with brotherly love; in honor preferring one another."—Romans 12:10 IV

My wife, Martha, and I had just finished sharing our testimonies, explaining how we felt that we had been spiritually guided to one another. We chose to share these testimonies during an 11 a.m. Sunday church service. We wanted the congregation to know of God's Spirit leading us in response to our request for divine guidance.

We wanted to bear witness to them that God shows concern, even in our lives as single, senior citizens. After the service, several members of the Pleasanton, Iowa, congregation expressed appreciation for hearing our testimonies of God's involvement in bringing us together. An older man, who is known for his quiet, laid-back demeanor, came up to me. I was really wondering what he would have to say. He said, "Hal, I want to apologize to you. I was disappointed when I heard that you had remarried."

I was surprised to hear this from this elderly friend of mine. I didn't know how to respond. I just put my hand on his shoulder and told him it was all right to feel that way and I was sorry that it had bothered him.

He went on to say, "Your wife, Rozie, who passed away eighteen months before you remarried, was a special friend of mine. I guess I felt that maybe you shouldn't remarry. However, since I heard your testimonies this morning of how God intervened in your lives to bring you together, I feel better about it now, and I'm asking you to forgive me."

Wow, was I ever glad to hear that he was able to share this with me and that this worship service had meant a lot to him in his healing process! If Martha and I had not shared this morning, I wonder how long he would have carried this hurt.

It is good that we as church people try to gain all the knowledge we can about other people's experiences before we make judgments as to whether some particular action was good or bad. We dare not share any type of harmful, hurtful feeling with anyone, let alone allow it to live in and infest our soul, for we may not know all the circumstances. We must be "soul partners" with God!

Sing for Peace: No. 38, "Christ Has Called Us to New Visions"

Prayer Thought: Forgiving God, keep us from unfair judgments of others, and may we always be ready to forgive those who judge us.

Saturday **31** January	**A Child's Gift** By Jo Ann Townsend Spokane, Washington	

"Receive the giftedness and energy of children and youth, listening to understand their questions and their wisdom."—Doctrine and Covenants 161:4a

Our congregation had just completed a year-long series of meetings to define our mission and vision statements. At a special service to present the draft, one of the committee members stood to discuss the first part, which was about inclusiveness. She read, "We commit ourselves to be a church that welcomes all people, embracing the uniqueness and giftedness of each one; a church that treasures children, acknowledging and encouraging the ministry they bring; a church that provides an opportunity for persons of all ages to belong, grow, and share."

During the continuing discussion, a one-year-old girl named Tannis came over to me from another pew and brought me a piece of paper. After a few minutes she brought me another piece. This continued several more times. I smiled, held out my hands, and motioned to her to come over and sit on my lap, never thinking she would. She walked over, put her arms up, and I placed her on my lap. We drew some pictures together. She sat there for about twenty minutes. I felt only joy as this little girl, who did not know me well, practiced the principle of inclusiveness by sharing her time with me. The scripture, "...and a little child shall lead them" came to mind, and I felt the Holy Spirit ministering to me through the presence of this one small, loving child.

Hymns of the Saints: No. 346, "Lord, Let Thy Holy Spirit Come"

Prayer Thought: Loving Father, open our hearts to the ministries small children can bring. May we embrace their giftedness.

February 2004

S	M	T	W	T	F	S
1	2	3	4	5	6	7
8	9	10	11	12	13	14
15	16	17	18	19	20	21
22	23	24	25	26	27	28
29						

<table>
<tr><td>Sunday
1
February</td><td>**Faithful in Waiting**
By Dianne Lyell Guinn
Paris, Tennessee</td><td></td></tr>
</table>

"It is of the Lord's mercies that we are not consumed, because his compassions fail not. They are new every morning; great is thy faithfulness."
—Lamentations 3:22–23 IV

I had just lost my husband of thirty-eight years and the cold February days seemed so empty. I had stumbled through another day at the office, not knowing exactly what to do next. I wasn't looking forward to going home to an empty house. It was almost dark. The traffic had backed up at the light when I saw the dog. It was a large Labrador retriever, standing in the back of a pickup truck, eyes fixed intently on the man standing inside the store conducting business. The dog's tail wagged as if to say, "I know you'll be back. I'm waiting for you." The dog trusted its master to return, and so it joyfully waited.

My mind turned to thoughts of my Master—my heavenly Father, who is faithful. He is ever aware of my situation and returns time and again to lift me up.

Several years have passed since that bleak February day and I have learned many things from my hurts and disappointments. But I will never forget God sending one of his animals to encourage me to be faithful in waiting. The "Master" had not forsaken me.

Hymns of the Saints: No. 187, "Great Is Thy Faithfulness"

Prayer Thought: Almighty God, thank you for your faithfulness to us. May we learn to trust that faithfulness and return to you our very best.

<table>
<tr><td>Monday
2
February</td><td>**Top Level Protection**
By Gerald John Kloss
Philadelphia, Pennsylvania</td><td></td></tr>
</table>

"But it is God who establishes us with you in Christ and has anointed us, by putting his seal on us and giving us his Spirit in our hearts as a first installment."
—II Corinthians 1:21–22 NRSV

The winter of 2003 was extremely harsh in the northeastern section of the United States. In the Philadelphia area we were hit with one snowstorm after another. The blizzard that hit in February left several feet of snow, which closed down the entire city for several days. After four days we were finally able to dig out and get back to work.

In addition to my teaching schedule at Philadelphia Christian Academy, I have the privilege of teaching a Dimensions of Learning course for teachers, and this is held over two weekends. The Saturday following the huge blizzard had me teaching my course for the College of New Jersey. The weather forecast that day was for downpours of rain, which would help to melt the huge mounds of snow everywhere. Concern was raised about flooding and the many roofs that still had massive amounts of snow on them.

While teaching my course, I had a phone call from a member of our congregation who told me that water was running in from the church roof and down the wall. Upon inspection the next day this was confirmed, and I immediately secured the services of a roofing contractor. The roofer inspected the main roof and told me there was a small break in the seal at the very top, which allowed a small amount of water to get in, resulting in a larger tear and major damage to the entire roof. He said that he could seal the roof and prevent further damage.

46

The seal is working effectively, and I haven't seen any more leaks.

This is much like the ministry of the Holy Spirit, whose task it is to seal us up for our work and ministry for the Lord, protecting us from the many distractions of the things of the world.

Hymns of the Saints: No. 281, "Holy Spirit, Truth Divine"

Prayer Thought: Lord God, we would ask your Spirit to keep us sealed and protected from distractions that would take us away from your work.

| Tuesday **3** February | **Celebrate Your Differences** By Merna Short Melbourne, Australia | |

"For that which ye have see me do, even that shall ye do; and therefore if ye do these things, blessed are ye, for ye shall be lifted up at the last day."—III Nephi 12:35

We arrived at church for a working bee. Lined up were sewing machines, overlockers (sergers), irons, and all the necessary extras to make curtains for the extended accommodations at our campgrounds. Each person followed instructions and was a willing worker. As the work progressed, one of the machinists said to me, "I could never do this."

I answered her. "I had five years' training to be accredited in this field. Put me into your profession and I'd lose all your money."

I looked around at the crew assembled. There were so many gifted people there, each in their own field. They were so diverse. I thought of how broad their scope of service for the Lord was because of the many different types of people they encountered in their daily lives—all such a necessary part in the weave of life.

Sing a New Song: No. 51, "Weave"

Prayer Thought: Creator of all life's variations, send us this day to serve you using our diverse gifts as we touch the lives of others.

Wednesday **4** February	**Circle of Friends** By Shirley S. Case Slater, Missouri	

"A friend loveth at all times, and a brother is born for adversity."—Proverbs 17:17

At the present time I work in a factory as an air-pollution-bag inspector. There are all sorts of wonderful people in a factory. In my area there are two young men I have come to know quite well. They make me laugh; they share their concerns, joys, and religions with me. They bring me junk food and I do the same for them. We even have nicknames for each other.

They often like to share their music with me, which can range from Kenny Chesney to Dre to Eminem or the like. They often bring their CD player over to my table so I can listen to a song they like, and the agreement is that they have to listen to what I am listening to at the time, which quite often is old rock or "Amazing Grace." We each look at the other's face to see the reaction to the music. It's not long before we bust out laughing or at least smile. I am thankful for them, and they have told me they are thankful for me, because though we are grateful for our jobs, they are boring to say the least.

I recognize that amid all the "hum-drum," God has blessed me with a wonderful gift in these two young men. I have come to cherish them as some of my dearest friends. I have told them so, and they have told me the same. Sometimes we take friends for granted, and sometimes I believe God shines a light on our path so that we might see what God has placed there as we walk along.

Hymns of the Saints: No. 86, "What a Friend We Have in Jesus"

Prayer Thought: Lord, we thank you for the blessing of friends, for in them we find a richness more precious than gold.

Thursday **5** February	**Healing of the Spirit** By Louita Clothier Lamoni, Iowa	

"The temple shall be dedicated to the pursuit of peace. It shall be for reconciliation and for healing of the spirit.... By its ministries an attitude of wholeness of body, mind, and spirit as a desirable end toward which to strive will be fostered."—Doctrine and Covenants 156:5a, c

My chaplain's pager called me to the eighth floor of the hospital. When I arrived at the nurse's station, I learned that a patient I will call "Bill" had decided he was going to die in two hours and was extremely anxious and depressed. I met first with the family in a conference room with the doctor, who told them Bill's condition was such that he could very well be right about the two hours.

So I went to Bill and sat with him, holding his hand, and encouraged him to talk freely about his death. I took his feelings seriously. (Luckily my pager remained silent, so I had plenty of time with him.) After a while, when he was calm, I began asking him about some of his memories. He reminisced about his work as a teacher. I asked him about how he met his wife. He began to speak with a strong voice as he told me about building a house for his family from lumber he had hewn himself.

After I prayed with Bill, he asked me if I would sing "Amazing Grace." I had never sung to a patient before, but sure, I could do that. After I finished he asked for "In the Garden." Because I didn't know the words, I said I would bring a hymnal and come back another day. By then Bill was at peace and had forgotten all about his two-hour deadline.

The next day, Monday, I was on duty elsewhere, but on Tuesday I took a hymnal from the chapel and headed up to Bill's room to sing "In the Garden" for him. I was caught up short to find his room empty and the bed stripped. I assumed Bill had died. Then the nurse told me he had been discharged and sent home!

About six weeks later I happened to meet Bill's son in the hall. He told me that Bill had died only the previous week, and that during those five extra weeks, they had shared many precious experiences preparing for that "big adventure." Bill may not have been cured, but by then he was healed.

What brought about the healing of Bill's spirit? First, someone listened to his feelings about dying, taking them seriously. Second, he was encouraged to talk about his memories. At the end of life there is something magic about reminiscence. It gives life meaning. It seems to bring life full circle. Third, the power of prayer brought peace and assurance in facing what was ahead. And, in this case, music was part of the experience. I only wish I could have sung "In the Garden" for Bill.

Hymns of the Saints: No. 104, "Amazing Grace"

Prayer Thought: Ever-caring God, show us how to be unafraid of death, whether facing our own or for the sake of others who need to prepare for it.

Friday **6** February	**Answered Prayers** By Lillian Bayless Kirby Blue Springs, Missouri	

"Therefore let the church take heed and pray always, lest they fall into temptations."

—Doctrine and Covenants 17:6e

My mother had a small wall hanging that said, "Prayer Changes Things." As a child, I would stand up on a chair and rub the red, fuzzy background of the picture with my fingers. This was before the modern days of "hands on" activities for children.

I often wondered why we had such a picture hanging on a wall of our home. None of my friends had one in their homes. At times, I was ashamed that it hung there in such a prominent position. Later in life, as I matured in my prayer life, I remembered that fuzzy, worn-out plaque and could verify that it was indeed true.

As my father was introduced at a series of missionary meetings he was holding in New Jersey, the presiding minister said, "I have prayed for this man for thirty years, because his daughter Lily asked the teenagers at Deer Park reunion one early morning prayer service to pray for her father." Furthermore, he added, "He now is an evangelist and I am proud to introduce him to you. His life is an answer to prayer, and this morning we both are blessed to serve in the ministry of our Lord Jesus Christ."

Most assuredly, God does hear and answer his people's prayers.

Hymns of the Saints: No. 455, "O Lord, We Come in Gratitude"

Prayer Thought: God, we praise your name for your unchangeable mercy and love. Help us to always remember that prayer can change our lives.

Saturday
7
February

Fighting Back
By Anna Davis
Harrison, Michigan

"The wolf also shall dwell with the lamb, and the leopard shall lie down with the kid; and the calf and the young lion and the fatling together; and a little child shall lead them."—Isaiah 11:6

I've been fighting depression most all of my life. But, praise God, it's now under control, and I owe it all to Jesus. I had to turn my life over to him. Sometimes I don't even know how I'll get past the problem, but God provides a way out.

I remember one time when I was so depressed, and there was no reason for it. I was in my room, sitting on my bed in tears, crying to God, "Why am I like this? There is no reason!" My granddaughter, Haley, came in. She is a treasure of God. She asked me if I was all right. I told her yes, and she went back out to her toy room. Next thing I heard was her voice singing "Victory in Jesus" over and over—those were the only words she remembered.

I called her, and she came through the door with the biggest smile of light. I told her there was more to that song. We hugged and started to sing "Victory in Jesus," and there is. I just have to learn to fight back.

Sing a New Song: No. 42, "Rock of My Salvation"

Prayer Thought: Teach us, Lord, to become as the child you want us to be, to depend on you and not ourselves.

"You have made my days a mere handbreadth; the span of my years is as nothing before you."—Psalm 39:5 NIV

Several years ago when my mother was in her nineties and living in an assisted-living facility, she would often comment, "Old age is not for sissies." I am now beginning to have some idea of what she meant, and wish I might have had more understanding of what she perhaps went through during that time. As I visited with her and others there, I came to realize that some of the residents seemed able to "bear the infirmities of age" quite well, while others really struggled.

Some time ago I spent several days in a hospital in Fort Walton Beach, Florida, hooked up to monitors and intravenous medications. I was jabbed by needles in a search for veins, and poked and prodded in more ways than I care to remember. Were it not for the concern and prayers of the small Community of Christ congregation there, where we attended church when we were in Destin, and the support of family and friends, I am sure I could not have come through it all as well as I did. I left the hospital with new heart medications, a pacemaker, and mostly fond memories of competent doctors, caring nurses and other hospital personnel, and faithful friends.

My mother was right: Old age is not for sissies. But I have discovered that with the loving support of those who care, a person can make it through a lot of grief and misery. May I be reminded of this daily as I think of those who might need my support, and be grateful when I am able to respond.

Sing a New Song: No. 35, "Make Me a Servant"

Prayer Thought: Lord, may we give active, loving support to those who are struggling, whether with physical problems or personal problems.

<table>
<tr><td>Monday
9
February</td><td>**Persistence**
By E. J. Chappelle
Rosharon, Texas</td><td></td></tr>
</table>

"He that endureth in faith and doeth my will, the same shall overcome, and shall receive an inheritance upon the earth, when the day of transfiguration shall come."
—Doctrine and Covenants 63:6b

A couple of Januarys ago we had such a long and warm false spring, the local mourning doves came out from their winter hideaways and began building nests in the usual places on the outside of our buildings. I'd thought then that the brownish-gray birds had been fooled by the weather. Soon February brought its normal rainy chill, and the half-built nests were left to dissolve in the wind.

Nesting dove pairs here are very persistent, building as soon as spring arrives and laying several eggs. One or two babies may be ready to leave the nest by mid-summer. However, nesting here has many hazzards, including cats, hawks, storms, and window washers. Any number of things can undo a dove family at any time. But the doves persist, rebuilding and laying again immediately after any such tragedy. A mid-summer egg has a good chance of success. A late summer egg's only chance is in a late fall and slow winter. Still, I've seen doves laying new eggs as late as fall, perhaps in hope that there will be no winter here at all.

The doves have no calendars as we know them, but I do not believe now that they were "fooled" by any false spring. Their only purpose for much of the year is to make more doves. Beginning at the very first opportunity and persisting until the very last chance, they will deny no possibility of bringing in their next generation, however slim the chances really might be.

I find myself envious of the persistence and faith of some simple creatures in pursuing a less than simple task. I will remember the example and faith of these mourning doves whenever I face a challenging goal or matter of faith. I will pray that I, too, can endure and persevere with the same steadfastness of purpose and faith.

Hymns of the Saints: No. 157, "My Life Flows On in Endless Song"

Prayer Thought: Eternal God, grant us the strength and endurance to continue in faith, and the wisdom to discern your purpose for us.

Tuesday **10** February	**God's Newest Promise** By Peggy Michael Cantonment, Florida

"They shall also teach their children to pray, and to walk uprightly before the Lord."
—Doctrine and Covenants 68:4c

Today I held God's newest promise in my arms. Though Matthew is but hours old, he has already touched a number of hearts. My bosom burned at the awareness of God's love expressed in this newborn baby. He has given us his most precious gift of an innocent spirit contained in a form of flesh. What a sacred trust

55

to be asked to shape this infant in the likeness of God's only begotten Son. I wondered how long I would be there for him, to read him stories and to rejoice at his discoveries.

As I felt the rhythm of life pulsating through his tiny body, the Holy Spirit quickened me with resolve. I remembered my husband's challenge to me: "My life and ministry are coming to an end, but yours must go on." I realized that it would have been so selfish to have allowed my pain rob this child.

At my husband's death, about ten years ago, the Lord beckoned me onward. He showed me an area of my future ministry and invited me to give myself to it. I saw many children gathered around me waiting for me to teach them the ways of the Lord. Then God revealed something else. I would be permitted to influence the unborn generation, and I have been able to do so for a large number of babies born since then.

I held Matthew with all the tenderness of my soul and pledged anew that I would continue to serve these children as long as I live.

Hymns of the Saints: No. 434, "When God Created Human Life"

Prayer Thought: We thank you, Lord, for renewing our lives through the gift of children.

Continuing Purpose
By Norma Holman
Wayne City, Illinois

"Let the word of Christ dwell in you richly in all wisdom; teaching and admonishing one another in psalms and hymns and spiritual songs, singing with grace in your hearts to the Lord."—Colossians 3:16

In 2002, for the first time in many years I did not send a testimony for publication in the next *Daily Bread*. I had a stroke, two surgeries, and a long period of illness and recovery before the mailing deadline. I thought that my life and the service I loved were over.

I was surprised and pleased with the number of letters and inquiries I received asking why I had failed to write, along with how much these readers had enjoyed my testimonies and how they felt they knew me.

I am thankful to God for healing and for God's presence in my life, and I pray that I might find more work to do for him in these golden years. I can witness of God's love and his hand in the Restoration movement and the Book of Mormon. Perhaps I can help keep my family close to Christ as they travel divergent pathways.

Hymns of the Saints: No. 435, "O Lord of Light and Love and Power"

Prayer Thought: God of blessing, renew our spirits with a desire to serve you and bring others into your presence.

Thursday **12** February	**God's Abiding Presence** By Penny McCurdy Independence, Missouri	

"I will give them one heart, and put a new spirit within them...so that they may follow my statutes and keep my ordinances and obey them. Then they shall be my people, and I will be their God."—Ezekiel 11:19–20

One morning in mid-February was especially delightful. The sun was shining, birds were singing, the snow had melted, and walking was easy. My small dog, Tasha, and I were out walking when suddenly she stopped and sat down. I asked what was wrong or if she was afraid. She just sat there, and I bent down, picked her up, and assured her that I was with her and that she was OK. I don't know what frightened her, but obviously something had. I started to carry her but she began to wiggle, so I put her down, and she was happy to continue our walk.

I then thought of my life and my relationship with God. God walks beside me but sometimes I am afraid and don't realize he's even there. After God has carried me spiritually and emotionally for some time, then I am brave enough to try again.

Wouldn't it be wonderful to recognize that God is with us in all that we do and therefore always face all our trials with courage? It would be much easier to witness to others of divine love and assistance. It is my prayer that I may be aware of God's love, faithfulness, and presence in my life at all times.

Sing a New Song: No. 31, "Lord, Help Me to Know Your Presence"

Prayer Thought: Abiding God, make us aware of your presence with us every day in all we do.

Friday **13** February	**Motivation for Service** By Charles Kornman Grand Junction, Colorado

"But now, by dying to what once bound us, we have been released from the law so that we serve in the new way of the Spirit, and not in the old way of the written code."
—Romans 7:6 NIV

It was World War II, the winter of 1944, and the U.S. Army in Italy slept in tents. We each had three blankets and half of a pup tent. I've forgotten how, but if we folded them a certain way we could sleep warm in the coldest of winters.

It was fairly comfortable for me to lie there with a full stomach (if I could manage to eat the C-rations) in the warmth of my "sack." But almost sixty years later I can still remember the uncomfortable feeling as I listened to the Italians going through our garbage cans. They were searching for food that we had thrown out. The cooks did the best they could, but those C-rations were always C-rations in smell and taste, which some of us could just barely tolerate.

Maybe that memory of people eating what I couldn't eat is part of the reason I give service to my church, the Red Cross, and the police department's Victim Assistance Program. In none of these areas do I give my leftovers. I give the best I have to offer. I can look at my face when I'm shaving and say, "I'm proud of you, old man." Then I bow my head in gratitude for the call to give "the fullness of the gospel" before I head out to meet the challenges of a new day.

Hymns of the Saints: No. 438, "Lord, Thy Church on Earth Is Seeking"

Prayer Thought: In gratitude, Lord, we offer ourselves in loving service to people wherever we may be.

Saturday **14** February	**Giving Our Life's Blood** By Marlene Brunner Yuma, Colorado

"And being in an agony, he prayed more earnestly; and he sweat as it were great drops of blood falling down to the ground."—Luke 22:44

Every other month my husband and I go to the blood bank and donate a pint of blood to be used by those who need it. We have no way of knowing who receives our donations, but we receive satisfaction from knowing that perhaps we have helped save someone's life. As stated in the book *In His Image* by Paul Brand and Philip Yancey, blood is what gives us life: "You lose one, you lose both."

The spilled blood and broken body of our Lord and Savior Jesus Christ is what we focus our attention on during Lent and Easter. When we partake of the emblems at each Communion service, we do so in remembrance of the gift of eternal life for which Christ sacrificed his own life.

There is little, if any, actual comparison between our small gift of just a little of our blood to Christ's giving all of his that we might be recipients of eternity. We are so thankful for his love and willingness to redeem us by this means. My true desire is to give more than just some of my blood to my fellow human beings. I want to assist in sharing Christ's deep love with my neighbors and friends.

Hymns of the Saints: No. 408, "Take My Life and Let It Be"

Prayer Thought: To you, Lord, we bring our small gifts of ministry and service for you to touch and expand to bring relief to all people.

| Sunday **15** February | **Answers on the Run** By Annabelle Taylor Locke Huntsville, Alabama | |

"Wherefore I now send upon you another Comforter, even upon you, my friends, that it may abide in your hearts, even the Holy Spirit of promise, which other Comforter is the same that I promised unto my disciples as is recorded in the testimony of John."—Doctrine and Covenants 85:1c

My seven sons are grown now, but any of you who have at least two know that what one doesn't think to do another does. I was forced to pray on the run. Among other things, my boys went in for football, surfing, racing motorcycles, flying, and jumping from planes.

It is my testimony that *God answers on the run*, not only for their protection and guidance but for my own enlightenment. I am full of questions, and theories just annoy me.

When you feel the warm, loving presence of God's Holy Spirit and receive answers, you know they are true. Not everyone you tell will believe you, but you will know for yourself.

Hymns of the Saints: No. 302, "O God, Our Source of Truth"

Prayer Thought: Holy One, may we feel the presence of your Spirit guiding us as we seek answers on the run.

<table>
<tr><td>Monday
16
February</td><td>**Jesus at Sunday Adventure**
By Ralph Holmes
Sutton in Ashfield,
Nottinghamshire, England</td><td></td></tr>
</table>

"And Jesus called a little child unto him, and set him in the midst of them, and said, Verily, I say unto you, Except ye be converted, and become as little children, ye shall not enter into the kingdom of heaven."—Matthew 18:2 IV

In our congregation Sunday Adventure meets, as you would expect, every Sunday, at 10:30 a.m. The children chose the name because they felt it aptly describes their activities at church on a Sunday morning.

It has become customary to invite the children to say the closing prayer at the end of the morning, and usually there is a host of volunteers. They stand in line at the front and one by one say their own prayer.

One Sunday morning I was impressed by what one little six or seven year old said. It went something like this: "Dear Jesus, I hope you enjoyed Sunday Adventure today"; then as she concluded she said, "Thank you, Jesus, for coming today."

It made me think about our church attendance. Do we acknowledge that Jesus can actually be present at our worship? Do we go fully expecting to meet Jesus at church in our worship experience?

Hymns of the Saints: No. 348, "We Bring Our Children, Lord, to Thee"

Prayer Thought: We thank you, Lord, for the simple insight of children. May we always acknowledge your presence in our worship.

The Doughnut Man
By Jane Henson
Fairview Heights, Illinois

"And Jesus said unto them, Come ye after me, and I will make you to become fishers of men."—Mark 1:15 IV

The Temple staff in Independence all know this man very well but I wanted my *Daily Bread* friends to know about Bob also. For quite a few years now Bob has made his rounds through the Temple offices on almost every Wednesday, distributing a tempting assortment of doughnuts and cinnamon rolls. Someone we all know well (no names please) jokingly made this comment, "Bob has done more to broaden our horizons the last few years than anyone."

Bob is a man of God (an evangelist). He also leads tours for groups at the Temple twice a week. Bob was our pastor for many years in Belleville, Illinois, before he and his wife, Jackie, moved to Independence. Bob and Jackie were very active in the youth programs and raised four children plus many other church children. Bob directed youth camps and Jackie would cook.

Bob has been a mentor for many of us through the years. Bob was on the leading edge of women in the priesthood—he was using women up front on Sundays and in many areas of responsibility some years before Section 156 was approved. Bob walks and talks with God daily, and many of us know he wears a permanent pair of "rose-colored contacts" regarding his outlook on all people and the strength and power of the Community of Christ.

Bob told us at the end of February 2003 that because of economic reasons he would be stopping his "doughnut run." But he will never stop his work for the Lord and will continue to minister for God until his dying breath.

Hymns of the Saints: No. 420, "Your Cause Be Mine, Great Lord Divine"

Prayer Thought: Creator God, thank you for all those who have dedicated their lives to you and for the work they do for you here on this earth. Give us courage to follow daily.

<table>
<tr><td>Wednesday
18
February</td><td>**Share the Good News**
By Cindy Korf
Ogallala, Nebraska</td><td></td></tr>
</table>

"Sing unto the Lord, all the earth; show forth from day to day his salvation. Declare his glory among the heathen; his marvelous works among all nations. For great is the Lord, and greatly to be praised...."—I Chronicles 16:23–25

I work at home in a basement office, and usually I don't have much opportunity to get outside to see what's happening there, especially in winter, when the days are short.

One February day, when my son Adam came home from school, he told me that I "had to" go outside. I was on the telephone with a conference call and had another one yet to make. Adam was insistent, though, that I go outside. So I finished the call and went upstairs and outside to behold a beautiful snowfall! The air was "warm" with huge white snowflakes falling gently all around, covering the ground quietly like a soft winter blanket. I felt like a child again, wanting to chase the snowflakes and let them fall on my tongue and melt like vanilla ice cream. The hills behind our house were shrouded, looking like a distant fairytale castle. It truly was beautiful!

It was one of those rare, peaceful, snowfalls that fill the heart with peace and joy. It became a moment that awoke my soul to the glory of the Lord. How fortunate I was that Adam shared the "good news" with me and insisted on me experiencing the beauty he had beheld.

I am reminded of the many moments in my life when I have felt the Spirit of God touch my soul and how I wanted to share its beauty with others. Sometimes I have not shared the joy in my heart because of fear of rejection or that someone might be too busy to listen. Yet through my son, I saw and experienced how joyful it can be to have someone share the goodness they see and experience. And how simple it is to share the good news—it's as simple as saying, "Let's go outside and see this awesome sight!"

Hymns of the Saints: No. 18, "All Things Bright and Beautiful"

Prayer Thought: Lord, thank you for those who share with us the beauty and good news that awaken our soul to you and your glory.

Thursday **19** February	**Strive for Excellence** By Paul McCain Oklahoma City, Oklahoma	

"Strive to enter through the narrow door; for many, I tell you, will try to enter and will not be able."
—Luke 13:24 NRSV

The "pattern" the aircraft were to follow to make visual landings was really two patterns: one rectangle relatively close to the runway for when there were few trying to practice landings at a time, and one larger rectangle for the times where there were more. The long leg of the rectangle parallel to the runway was called "outside downwind." In an Air Force T-37 jet trainer, since it took quite a while to get around the larger pattern, there was an uncomfortably long time for a new student to have to maintain "straight and level" flight with the instruments "pegged."

It was one of those warm Oklahoma days, with me on outside downwind, my instruments frozen in place—no variation in the required airspeed, no vertical velocity indicator needle movement, and the altimeter was locked in place. The instructor sat there for a while reading his duplicate instruments, and then, with a shake of the control stick and with considerable impatience and volume in his voice, said, "McCain, if you can hold a hundred feet low, you can hold altitude." It was good that the readings on the gauges weren't changing; in fact, everything was just as it should be except that I was one hundred feet off altitude. He saw beyond what I was doing to what I was able to do. That lesson has stuck with me and seems to come to mind when I need reminding of the need for excellence, in me or in someone else.

As a city manager I once had a clerk who worked for me who was habitually late. I tried to talk to her, wrote her a memo, and warned her that I would put a letter of reprimand in her file, but none of these things changed her behavior. Finally, after exhausting all other ideas, I called her into my office and told her that if she was late for work one more time she would be fired. She was never late again. I remember thinking of the "outside downwind" example and sharing it with her: "If you can be here consistently late, you can be here on time."

At times I have found myself consistently off the needed mark in my response to the Lord—consistently late for services, consistently procrastinating preparation for a sermon or being in charge of a service, consistently forgetting to pray or study. A remembrance of the "outside downwind" experience helps me to get back on track and strive for excellence.

Hymns of the Saints: No. 399, "A Charge to Keep I Have"

Prayer Thought: Lord, encourage us to be what we can be and not settle for less than excellence.

<table>
<tr><td>Friday
20
February</td><td>**Changing Rules**
By Jean Cottle
Alta Loma, California</td><td></td></tr>
</table>

"Jesus Christ the same yesterday, and today, and forever. Be not carried about with divers and strange doctrines; for it is a good thing that the heart be established with grace."—Hebrews 13:8–9

Growing up in one foster home after another, Georgie often felt confused. It seemed to her that as soon as she adjusted to one family's home, she would be transferred to a different family and neighborhood. Whenever she moved from one home to another, the rules changed, sometimes drastically. In one home she was required to make eye contact when spoken to. In the next home, that was considered impertinent and earned her a reprimand.

Sometimes it took her a while to learn the new rules, and she was often punished unjustly. Sometimes other children in the household would be jealous of her. Georgie would try to understand why and stay out of their way. She never felt that she was really wanted anywhere.

Georgie was exposed to a variety of lifestyles and religions. Some families were devout Christians; some were not. In one home prayer was not allowed, and the only time she could talk to the Lord was when she took out the garbage. Even then she had to be careful and not spend too much time or she would be in trouble.

Georgie grew up to be a responsible adult. She is thankful that now she can follow her own rules. She walks close to the Lord and feels secure in the knowledge that God's rules never change.

Hymns of the Saints: No. 487, "Be with Me, Lord, Where'er I Go"

Prayer Thought: We thank you, Lord, for your dependable love no matter what our circumstances are, and for always being there for us.

| Saturday **21** February | # Who Are the "Least"?
 By Denzil J. West
 Independence, Missouri | |

"Inasmuch as ye have done it unto one of the least of these my brethren, ye have done it unto me."
— Matthew 25:41 IV

When Dorothy and Cedric Evans moved to Independence from St. Louis, she introduced the Meals on Wheels program. It had been successful in St. Louis, and now through her initiation it has been a fine program for almost thirty years here, providing a hot, nutritious meal to hundreds of homebound people.

Once while delivering on a substitute route, I stopped at a home of a widow. I rang the bell and waited. After a lengthy delay, I heard a scraping noise and then the front door slowly opened. An elderly lady, using a walker, smiled at me. Holding her meal, I asked if she would like for me to put it on the kitchen table. "Oh yes," she said, as I hurried out to the kitchen. Her silverware, napkin, and drink had already been placed there in anticipation of my arrival.

Hurrying back to the front door I saw that she was just turning around to go to the kitchen. I heard her say,

"Can't you stay and talk with me a few minutes? You Meals drivers are the only people I ever see. Even the mailman is leaving the porch before I can open the front door."

I explained that I had seven more hot meals in my car and that I had to deliver them before they got cold, but in my heart I knew that she was one of the "least" of Jesus' number.

Hymns of the Saints: No. 401, "We Give Thee But Thine Own"

Prayer Thought: Forgive our insensitivity to the loneliness of others, God, and fill our hearts with the loving compassion of Jesus.

<table>
<tr><td>Sunday
22
February</td><td>**Blessings of Beauty**
By Susan Miller
North Wales, United Kingdom</td></tr>
</table>

"And I, God, said, Let the earth bring forth grass; the herb yielding seed; the fruit tree yielding fruit after his kind; and the tree yielding fruit, whose seed should be in itself upon the earth…. And I, God, saw that all things which I had made were good."—Genesis 1:15, 17 IV

As a Canadian, there is likely no season I look forward to more than spring. Months and months of winter snow and cold melt away to warm winds, dry pavement, green grass, and blossoms. Sometimes I feel like a young foal, wanting to frolic in the pastures and enjoying all that nature presents.

As children we called it "spring fever," and I'm happy to say that my spring fever faithfully returns, no matter how old I become. It has been especially prevalent since we moved to the United Kingdom two years ago.

Here in Wales spring begins in February—not April or May as in Canada. Every year I plant countless daffodils, and every spring I am rewarded with weeks of glorious color.

On Sunday afternoons we go for a drive, exploring the countryside and enjoying the ever-changing colors billowing from the gardens of our English and Welsh neighbors. When I drive to work, I never tire of passing the houses that have baskets of cascading blooms. Several of the homes here are small and are attached in a row. The "front yards," as we would call them in North America, are so small it's unbelievable. Yet young and old fill these minimal square feet with many pots of colorful flowers: pots on the ground, pots on the windowsills, pots hanging from the house, baskets at the front gate. It is simply beautiful.

In Canada I lived five minutes from work yet I hated the drive. Here, I live thirty minutes from work, and I realized one day why I love the drive: nearly everyone takes time to plant and care for their colorful gardens, and it is a welcoming sight for all to enjoy. It seems like such a small thing, but when surrounded by the beauty of nature every day, you can't help but feel good.

I encourage readers everywhere to plant flowers for all to enjoy. From the balcony, rooftop, windowsill, or garden you can make room for glorious color. And who knows, you might be brightening up the day for some anonymous traveler, as well as for yourself. Sometimes, it's the little things that count.

Hymns of the Saints: No. 194, "Earth with Her Ten Thousand Flowers"

Prayer Thought: Eternally creating God, may we always make an effort to share the beauty of your creation with others.

Miracles of Compassion

By Carol Smith Barnes
Sedalia, Missouri

"But, behold, I will show to you a God of miracles, even the God of Abraham, and the God of Isaac, and the God of Jacob; and it is that same God who created the heavens and the earth, and all things that in them are."

—Mormon 4:70

When I was a young mother I sometimes took advantage of the early morning hours to work in the yard, as I could work and pray without interruption. I was on my knees weeding an iris bed one beautiful spring morning. But to give my knees a rest, every few minutes I would stand while trimming ground cover with large clippers.

A swallowtail butterfly, flitting about from flower to flower, joined me. This delicate creature with such exquisite markings made me smile. I prayed a prayer of thanksgiving for my tiny new friend, who took my mind off my backbreaking chore. It was so quick traveling from plant to plant, unafraid of my presence.

As I worked intently with the clippers, I momentarily lost track of the butterfly; then suddenly I found myself frozen in place. In an instant my clippers had sliced halfway through one wing, and my friend lay perched before my eyes unable to fly. I was utterly heartbroken and ashamed for having been so careless. I looked closely to make sure my eyes were really seeing an injured butterfly—but it was true! I had taken its ability to fly, and unable to gather food, it would soon die.

In anxious prayer I poured my heart out to God expressing sorrow for my clumsiness. I reasoned with God that I knew he could miraculously mend the broken wing. I resumed my work while closely checking my friend's condition from time to time, but it did not change.

I bowed my head in prayer over and over again. Then, just as quickly as I had injured my friend, the wing appeared whole, truly whole, and the swallowtail took flight. I have never forgotten that early morning miracle. Why is our faith so strong for the tiny daily miracles but often shaken by the magnitude of a larger need? Over the years I have witnessed and been a recipient of such larger miracles, and I am grateful for diligent prayers.

Hymns of the Saints: No. 75, "For the Beauty of the Earth"

Prayer Thought: Great Healer, thank you for your miraculous creation, the mystery of your infinite power to answer prayer, and the depth of your compassion that heals and restores life.

| Tuesday **24** February | **Christians in Action** By Florence King Feilding, New Zealand | |

"Even though you intended to do harm to me, God intended it for good, in order to preserve a numerous people, as he is doing today. So have no fear."—Genesis 50:20–21 NRSV

The Tuesday before Easter 2003, I was walking along a street just after 11 a.m. when a young man came up silently behind me and stole my handbag out of my hand. I was devastated, as everything I have to prove who I am was in my bag, along with $90 intended for groceries. I was in shock for more than a day, and I felt like a nobody—with nothing to prove who I was, and no money.

A man saw the robber take my bag, and several other people saw him running away. Within two or three minutes the police were there, plus a police dog, but they lost him. I was taken to my granddaughter's place because she had a key to my home—my keys, of course, were in my bag. My granddaughter canceled every account and arranged to have my house locks changed.

After a while, positive things registered. First, although he had taken my bag, the robber had not hurt me. Second, as he was running through someone's property, a notebook and my checkbook fell out onto the ground. Third, I usually carry my reading glasses in my purse, but this time I had them in a bag that held my library books. Then things really started happening.

I have tried to encourage my family to come to Christ, praying that something would happen to allow them to see God in action. I contacted a woman from church who let others know where I was. First one woman and then another arrived at my granddaughter's, one bringing flowers, another a handbag to use until I could replace my own. Back home, with my locks changed, a grandson stayed with me. The next morning, after phone calls the night before and all that morning, he decided to go see his sister. He said that so many people had called, he had not had a chance to speak to me.

On Sunday I was given a large box of groceries, plus money—four times the amount of money I had lost. What an awesome God! I was completely surrounded with love from so many people. What had been meant for harm, God turned into triumph. When I phoned my daughter she couldn't believe that church people could show so much love. She was seeing Christians in action.

Hymns of the Saints: No. 484, "Make Us, O God, a Church That Shares"

Prayer Thought: May we seize opportunities to show your love in action, Lord, that others may know that Christians live what they teach. May we also turn trouble into good.

73

"If we live in the Spirit, let us also walk in the Spirit."
—Galatians 5:25

At the beginning of the Lenten season I was researching for a sermon I had been asked to give when our four-year-old, Lucy, needed my attention. She was attending a daycare in the local Catholic parish and was excited to tell me that the next day at school she was going to get "eyelashes."

Puzzled by what she had to say and the fact that I was trying to study, I responded with, "Oh, that's good, honey, now go and play." The next day being Ash Wednesday, Lucy returned from school with ashes on her forehead. Her ears had heard "lashes," not "ashes"!

How often during our busy day do we hear or overhear things incorrectly? Lucy's experience was delightfully innocent; however, may we always try to be better listeners, paying close attention to what others have to tell us. It is especially important to listen intently to God, so we don't miss that still, small voice that can offer true guidance for our lives.

Hymns of the Saints: No. 391, "Jesus Is Calling"

Prayer Thought: May we stay in tune with your Spirit, God, and become better listeners.

Courage to Trust God
By Beulah Foster
Marlette, Michigan

"O Lord, I have trusted in thee, and I will trust in thee forever."—II Nephi 3:61

I was an R.N. supervisor at an extended care facility. Things were going well, and the aides did a great job of caring for the residents and reporting any problems to me. We were an efficient, caring team. But after I had been there fourteen years the administrator asked me to do something unethical. I told him no, and he fired me. This was a very low point in my life.

After several months I found another job in a nursing home twenty miles from my home. I became assistant director of nursing. I had been there eight years when the owner asked me to do something that could have cost me my license. I refused, and he fired me. I drew unemployment, and then retired at my husband's request.

When I think back over this period, I realize I could be drawing a good-sized pension if I'd stayed at the first job and had done what the administrator wanted me to do. But I know I did the right thing. Even though I live on a strict budget, I always manage. I thank God for his guidance and courage to do the right thing.

Hymns of the Saints: No. 127, "I Am Trusting Thee, Lord Jesus"

Prayer Thought: Kind heavenly Father, help us to have the courage to live up to our principles no matter what the consequences may be.

Lessons of Life
By Janice Townsend
Spokane, Washington

"Receive the giftedness and energy of children and youth, listening to understand their questions and their wisdom.... Be reminded once again that the gifts of all are necessary in order that divine purposes may be accomplished."
—Doctrine and Covenants 161:4a, b

Getting trounced in a game of Scrabble® wasn't fun, especially when trounced by my very own daughter. But Kerry soothed the sting by explaining her strategy: "I always look for places to play where I can change a word already there and create another word at the same time. That yields the biggest scores," she said. "And Mom, you're the one who taught me to do that."

It's good to know that some of the things I've tried to teach my children have "stuck." Yet I know that their needs, desires, and priorities will never be exactly the same as mine. I respect their right to order their own lives and make decisions that they feel are right for them. So it is especially heartwarming when I see my children acting in ways that reflect the lessons I've endeavored to teach them.

And even more heartwarming are the times when I look at my own life and realize that my children have also been teaching me. I praise God for the wisdom of placing us in families where we can both teach and be taught. And I thank God for every fresh opportunity to learn, even if it means losing at Scrabble®!

Hymns of the Saints: No. 182, "Make Room Within My Heart, O God"

Prayer Thought: Inspire our thoughts, God, that we may be willing to accept and share the lessons of life.

Persuasive Love
By Elaine Linné
Tigard, Oregon

"O Lord, hear; O Lord, forgive; O Lord, hearken and do; defer not for thine own sake, O my God; for thy city and thy people are called by thy name."—Daniel 9:19

The experience was of the mystical realm and was so impressive I failed to share it, believing it to be inconceivable to listeners. Nonetheless, it happened. I know there is a God who loves me. Nebuchadnezzar's fiery furnace could never induce me to change my testimony.

A family member had made a decision that caused me to become extremely angry. I was furious and wounded. This cherished individual was going to join another church. I kept telling myself that my feelings were not justified, but I was unable to control my emotions. I vacillated between anger and "I don't want to be this kind of person."

There was only one source of help, so I went to my bedroom and knelt down to pray about my attitude. Hardly a word was spoken before a warmth invaded my whole being and even the room seemed hot. The anger vanished and was replaced by the most pervasive feeling of love. I have never felt such love! It surrounded me, and my heart was invaded. Gradually the presence subsided and I was a revitalized child of God.

Sing for Peace: No. 18, "God, When Human Bonds Are Broken"

Prayer Thought: When our emotions begin to control our behavior, call us into your presence for your calming touch, Lord.

In Winter's Depth
By Clara Covert
Ottawa, Ontario, Canada

"I know all the fowls of the mountains; and the wild beasts of the field are mine."—Psalm 50:11

The winter was long and cold, the shoveled snow piled like miniature mountains. High in the branches of a deciduous tree, a fat crow strutted, giving his raucous call to humans as they passed on the footpath below. I stood and watched him and wondered how he could be so sleek and glossy when the ground below him was covered with three feet of snow.

As he would hop along the branch and stop and peck at the bark, I realized he was finding nourishment in the soft bark of the thinner branches. The cold held no fear of starvation for him; he was undaunted by cold and snow, or that he was unable to find insects in the hidden grass below.

It was a lesson to remember. If we have a problem that we are unable to solve or a situation for which we think there is no answer, we need not give up. There is always a solution and, unlike that crow, we can turn to God to help us through.

Hymns of the Saints: No. 62, "Praise Ye the Lord"

Prayer Thought: Lord, may we remember that no situation or problem is too great for you. You are always there to guide us if we but ask.

March 2004

S	M	T	W	T	F	S
	1	2	3	4	5	6
7	8	9	10	11	12	13
14	15	16	17	18	19	20
21	22	23	24	25	26	27
28	29	30	31			

<table>
<tr><td>Monday
1
March</td><td>**Knowing God**
By Carla Long
Mound City, Kansas
(Binalonan, Pangasinan,
Philippines)</td><td></td></tr>
</table>

"Know the Lord; for all shall know me, from the least to the greatest."—Hebrews 8:11

I became a WorldService Corps volunteer in October 2002. Before I left, I wanted to know everything I could about the Philippines and what I should expect. So I did what every good college student should do: I researched and read. In all, I ended up reading five books about the Philippines. I learned a lot. I know that there are approximately 7,100 islands in this country; they were under Spanish rule for 300 years and regained their independence in July 1946. I know that the Philippine Islands have fifty species of banana and around eighty-seven dialects, and I learned a bunch of other stuff. I thought that I knew a lot and that I had prepared myself pretty well for this journey.

Then I arrived in the Philippines. All of that information didn't seem so important anymore. What the books couldn't convey were the different sounds, smells, tastes, sights, or feel of the Philippines. I didn't know about all of the wonderful people who would make me feel so welcome, or the lengths they would go to ensure my comfort. I couldn't gain that knowledge from books. I hadn't experienced it, so I didn't "know" it.

I believe we need to experience God. I don't think God just wants to be read or talked about (although those are very good things to do). I believe we need to "feel" God to really understand all of that love, joy, peace, hope, and faith everyone is always talking about. This is not "knowing" with your head; this is "knowing" with your heart. You don't need to be a genius to "know" God—just open to the possibility.

Hymns of the Saints: No. 300, "How Can Creation's Voice Be Still"

Prayer Thought: Heavenly Creator, help us to seek to really know you, not just know about you.

Tuesday **2** March	**A Friend for Life— from God** By Ruth Andrews Vreeland Albuquerque, New Mexico	

"Henceforth I call you not servants; for the servant knoweth not what his lord doeth; but I have called you friends; for all things that I have heard of my Father I have made known to you."—John 15:15

I first met Diane in 1976, at her home congregation in Salt Lake City, Utah. I was sixteen; she was seventeen. Our Central California District youth were on our annual summer "Youth Venture," and Salt Lake City was just one of our destinations. Diane and I were both young and "head over heels" for our boyfriends at the time, so we didn't have much of a chance to become friends. But we did meet, and it was just the beginning.

Then came Graceland College. I was there for only two semesters in 1979. Diane and I were in the same art history class, where we discovered we were both artists and musicians. I liked her a lot, remembering we had met before, but our paths rarely crossed, and we did not stay in touch after college. Still, I thought of her often and wondered where she was and what she was doing. I hoped I would either meet her again someday, or find friends as wonderful as she seemed to be.

In 1990, my husband and I moved to Albuquerque. We attended reunion that summer, and I made the wonderful discovery that Diane and her husband also lived in Albuquerque! She and I both felt God was saying to us, "I've put you two together *three* times; now become great friends!"

Diane and I have so much in common, and over the years we have developed the kind of friendship I wish everyone could experience. We sing together, discuss our art projects, and have reared our children together (including the adoptions of our youngest children). We pray together, cry on each other's shoulders, discuss scripture, and share the joys of our lives with one another. I could not have asked God for a better friend, and even though it took many years for just the right circumstances to bring us together, God's gift of friendship for Diane and me was perfect!

Sing a New Song: No. 7, "Companions on the Journey"

Prayer Thought: Marvelous God, we truly give thanks for bringing friends into our lives to encourage and strengthen us for life's journey.

Wednesday **3** March	**Just a Quarter** By Mary Twinn Collinsville, Illinois	

"Agree with God, and be at peace; thereby good will come to you."—Job 22:21 RSV

I was one of a large family of children during the Great Depression, and getting a weekly allowance was unheard of in those days. I don't remember the particular moment, but on one special day our father came by a little extra money and gave each of his children a quarter—to each one, that is, but me.

How I reacted to that was not what one would expect from a child, but I had such faith in my father's love and trusted him so completely that it simply didn't occur to me to question it, nor did I feel hurt or deprived in any way. I still wonder at the purity of my child heart. When my father realized what had happened, however, he was horrified, and as he gave me my quarter he explained that it was because I was so quiet and shy that I'd been overlooked.

My faith and trust in my heavenly Father have not been quite as steady but have nevertheless rescued me many times when I've been presented with painful and trying circumstances. God never has failed me and I know that he never will. I wish I could say that I'd never failed him and that I could have brought that same child's heart to my adult life's experiences.

Hymns of the Saints: No. 128, "Abide with Me"

Prayer Thought: Teach us to trust in your love for us, Lord, and to be faithful disciples no matter what our circumstances may be.

| Thursday **4** March | **Lasting Impressions**
 By Faye Williams
 Kennett, Missouri |  |

"Let the words of my mouth, and the meditation of my heart, be acceptable in thy sight, O Lord, my strength, and my redeemer."—Psalm 19:14

While my husband and I were dining in a restaurant recently, we sat across the room from some young people, both male and female. They were talking quite loudly and using foul language. When they left, they all got into a large van and went on their way. I remarked to my husband, without mentioning the language, "I wonder what group that could have been?" He replied, "I don't know, but I'm sure it wasn't a church group."

Even though my husband's remark was amusing at the time, I could only think of how rude and obnoxious those young people had acted. I found myself praying for them as we went on our way, hoping that Christ would touch their hearts and help them realize how they had represented their group to those around them.

Hymns of the Saints: No. 461, "Let the Words of My Mouth"

Prayer Thought: Lord, help us to always remember wherever we may be that our conduct and our words leave lasting impressions. May our behavior reflect the path we have chosen as your disciples.

| Friday
5
March | **Comfort Zone**
By LaVerne Cramer
Tomah, Wisconsin | |

"God did not give us a spirit of cowardice, but rather a spirit of power and of love and of self-discipline."
—II Timothy 1:7 NRSV

It sometimes takes a lot of faith to step out of our comfort zone. My son-in-law, John, is the district stewardship commissioner for the Houston area of the church. He received a call that there was a church member with AIDS who wanted to return to his home in Florida to die with his family near him. John was asked to take him $300 in cash for bus fare, food, and incidentals. He needed to deliver it to him in a parking lot at night in an area that certainly wasn't the safest place to meet.

John put his faith in God and went, and while sitting in the dark parking lot, thoughts of how unsafe it was came to mind. He was expecting to see a thin, sick-looking man, so when not only one man but two came toward him, his first impression was to leave out of fear. The first man he saw was large and didn't look sick, but John knew if he left right then, the sick man wouldn't have been able to go home.

As it turned out, it was the sick man and his large friend. John took them to the bus depot, purchased the bus ticket, gave the rest of the cash to the sick man, and left. It took a strong faith for John to step out of his comfort zone that night to carry out his mission for God. How many times does God ask us all to do likewise?

Hymns of the Saints: No. 159, "Oh, for a Faith That Will Not Shrink"

Prayer Thought: We thank you, God, for added faith to go beyond our comfort zone in life to help those in need.

Spots of Different Kinds

Saturday
6
March

By Dorene Kilburn
St. Paul's Station, Ontario, Canada

"'What do you want me to do for you?' Jesus asked him. The blind man said, 'Rabbi, I want to see.' 'Go,' said Jesus, 'your faith has healed you.'"—Mark 10:51–52 NIV

This past winter seemed unusually long because the temperature remained very low, the snow accumulation was much heavier than usual, and there wasn't even the usual January thaw. One of the first signs of spring is the bright yellow spots that begin to show on some of the many goldfinches that spend the winter with us.

In late fall, the males lose their bright yellow color and turn an olive green, the color of the females year-round. It was a joy to see one goldfinch early in March with the first bright-yellow spot, and then more and more of the finches gradually changing color. I marvel at this amazing change in a creature of God's creation.

As I was pondering this, my mind rambled on to other kinds of spots. Some cars are designed in such a way that there are blind spots that obstruct the driver's view, sometimes resulting in accidents. And people can have blind spots, too. It's easy to criticize someone who we think fails to see his or her faulty attitudes or actions.

But I need to ask myself, Where are the blind spots in my own thinking? What do I need to do to bring what I say and do more in line with Jesus' example? What personality traits might be stumbling blocks in my desire to be a true disciple of Jesus Christ? Maybe I've felt I'm too busy to sit down and try to determine the blind spots in my life. Maybe it's time I did that!

Hymns of the Saints: No. 454, "Open My Eyes, O Lord"

Prayer Thought: Creator God, help us to see with your eyes, so that we can remove whatever may hinder us from being a blessing to those whose lives we touch.

<table>
<tr><td>Sunday
7
March</td><td>**Strong, Hard Wood**
By Dorothy Cross
Paisley, Florida</td><td></td></tr>
</table>

"…till ye be left as a beacon upon the top of a mountain, and as an ensign on a hill. And therefore will the Lord wait, that he may be gracious unto you."—Isaiah 30:17–18

While taking art lessons in New Hampshire, I started buying picture frames at wholesale prices. I was able to frame my paintings inexpensively and provide inexpensive frames for classmates. I found a man in a little New Hampshire town who made frames from the pine trees growing in that area. As he was showing me the frames he had in stock, he picked up one that looked different and said, "I'll have to charge more for this one."

Most of the frames were rather plain looking, but this one had a beautiful light and dark grain running through it. He began to tell my why it was different. "This is the same kind of pine as the other frames, but this tree grew at the crest of the hill and was buffeted by every wind that blew across that hill. The stress caused the tree to grow stronger than the other trees, and while pine wood is usually soft, this one is strong, hard wood."

We also become stronger as we weather the storms of life. May the beauty of the Lord's love shine from our faces so we stand out like that tree on the crest of a hill.

Hymns of the Saints: No. 404, "I Would Be True"

Prayer Thought: Lord, help us to weather the storms of life and may your Spirit shine forth from us so we might draw others to you.

Monday **8** March	**The Gifts of All** By Geraldine Billings Greer Mesa, Arizona	

"God hath tempered the body together, having given more abundant honor to that part which lacked; that there should be no schism in the body; but that the members should have the same care one for another."—I Corinthians 12:24–25

My sister and I are very different. She is a nurse; I faint at the sight of blood. She can grow anything—her home is full of beautiful plants. All I can grow are weeds. Even though we are very different, we are best of friends. We have always been there for each other, and we tell each other things that we would never tell anyone else. But being different makes us closer.

Diversity is what makes life interesting. It would be boring if we were all the same. Even Christ recognized the need for diversity: when he was selecting his apostles, he chose men of different personalities, talents, and backgrounds. In Doctrine and Covenants Section 119 we are told that "all are called according to the gifts of God unto them." This says that everyone has a unique place and that no one person is called to provide every kind of ministry; the service of all is needed.

To serve effectively we must clarify our own thinking, acknowledge our capabilities and limitations, and recognize that there is a place for all to serve. We use our differences to work together to build the kingdom.

Hymns of the Saints: No. 414, "Beloved Community of God"

Prayer Thought: Develop in us, Lord, an appreciation for the varied gifts of all people.

Tuesday **9** March	**Futile Efforts** By Roberta Dieterman Caledonia, Michigan	

"Show me thy ways, O Lord: teach me thy paths. Lead me in thy truth, and teach me."—Psalm 25:4–5

At a certain point on my daily walk, I would hear a woodpecker tapping on a light pole. Every morning for several days I would hear the tap, tap, tap as I neared the same area.

One morning I heard the tapping but it sounded strange, metallic-like. I looked around for my feathered noisemaker and saw it on the light pole, but on this morning it was tapping on the metal band around the pole. Its feet were anchored on the wooden part, but its position caused its beak to hit the metal band. I watched for a few minutes thinking it would move to a better position but it just kept ping-pinging away.

I thought about the many times I've gotten myself into a position that afforded me no way of accomplishing what I wanted to do, no matter how hard I tried, just because I couldn't or wouldn't change my way of doing things. I know God will always help me and just wants me to be able to change direction when necessary. That woodpecker made me realize that I need to be aware when I am going about something in the wrong way—a simple attitude adjustment may be all that I need to help me change my approach.

Hymns of the Saints: No. 439, "Teach Me, My God and King"

Prayer Thought: Heavenly Teacher, show us the changes we need to make in our lives to accomplish what you would have us do.

Wednesday **10** March	**Soli Deo Gloria** By Frances Hurst Booth Prescott, Arizona

"Praise God in his sanctuary…. Praise him with the sound of the trumpet; praise him with the psaltery and harp… [P]raise him with stringed instruments and organs."
—Psalm 150:1, 3, 4

With ten years of piano lessons from age six and a series of organ lessons later, I have enjoyed playing the piano and organ for church services in various congregations throughout my life. The compliment I cherish most was given to me by a young U.S. serviceman stationed in the Washington, D.C., area who attended our Virginia congregation. He told me I played "with the Spirit."

Johann Sebastian Bach inscribed at the top of his compositions, *Soli Deo Gloria* ("To God Alone Be Glory"). I have tried to play for the glory of God and have had a strong sense of the Spirit's presence in the music over and above the limits of my ability to play the notes. May it ever be so.

Sing a New Song: No. 40, "Now Sing to Our God"

Prayer Thought: Gracious Creator, we give thanks for the many ways your name can be praised, and may we join the music of the spheres as we attempt to give glory to you.

Thursday **11** March

Why Alex Screams
By Karen Anne Smith
Ludington, Michigan

"This is how we know that we love the children of God: by loving God and carrying out his commands."
—I John 5:2 NIV

I've heard some of our own church sisters, in reference to the actions of complete strangers, say, "If that were my kid, whack!" Please, never, ever say this! You don't know what's really going on. You can't know. Yes, maybe the child is undisciplined or maybe there's a hidden disability that you know nothing about. Maybe the parents are exhausted and frustrated and at their wits' end. Instead of receiving the love and support they so desperately need from the community, they're being judged.

I attended a workshop led by a psychiatrist. The subject of discussion turned to behavioral problems and how to deal with them. The woman sitting next to me complained bitterly about a "spoiled brat" who attended the school where she taught. I couldn't stand it any longer. I stood up to speak and pointed out that it's not always behavior. I asked this woman if she was so sure the little girl was undisciplined. "There may be something else going on there," I suggested.

"Oh, no," she quickly and forcibly replied. "There's nothing wrong with that child. She's just a brat!"

"Careful," I warned her as I addressed the room. "You don't really know that for sure. My son looks like any other child his age but he's severely autistic. Things that we don't even notice often cause a sensory overload for Alex. Imagine feeling that bugs are crawling all over your body, biting you. That's why Alex screams. That's why Melonie screams. That's why Chad screams.

"If I'm standing in line at the grocery store with Alex and he suddenly begins to scream and hit and bite, I don't want anyone standing behind me smugly saying, 'What a brat! If that were my kid....'"

A couple of people came up to me after the workshop and commended me on "putting that woman in her place." That was never my intention. I only meant to defend the voiceless. We have forty-six students with autism in our own rural, two-county area. This does not include all of those children with Down's syndrome, ADD/ADHD, OCD, Asperger's syndrome, cerebral palsy, and so many other afflictions. So please, I beg all on behalf of the voiceless, judge not.... Instead, say a prayer for those strangers in need.

Hymns of the Saints: No. 389, "If Suddenly upon the Street"

Prayer Thought: Loving God, please help us see with new eyes, that we may understand the need around us.

Increase our compassion that we may truly offer the love of Jesus.

<table>
<tr><td>Friday
12
March</td><td>**Gardening Thoughts**
By Merna Short
Melbourne, Australia</td><td></td></tr>
</table>

"Teach me to do thy will; for thou art my God; thy Spirit is good; lead me into the land of uprightness."

—Psalm 143:10

I was gardening after arriving home from a holiday. We were in drought, so some things in the garden had not fared well. I had always found it difficult to prune one particular plant, because it bloomed prolifically. I was loathe to cut it back, but now it looked so sad. The only way to help it was to prune it hard. Hiding in its depths were some weeds. I hadn't known they were there, they were so well hidden. This is so much like life, I thought. Hidden in the blossoms of our lives are undiscovered weeds that we really have to be diligent in searching for and uprooting.

At the same time, flat weed had sprouted in the lawn and was sending up lots of seeds. It's amazing how the weeds thrive even in drought conditions. This can be likened to our spiritual lives, I mused. To prevent weeds with their numerous unwanted seeds from taking root in spiritual drought conditions, we need to open ourselves to the sweet rains of the Holy Spirit.

Hymns of the Saints: No. 412, "Lord, Speak to Me"

Prayer Thought: Nourish us with your life-giving Spirit, Lord, that our roots may be sturdy and our lives may bless and nourish those around us.

<table>
<tr><td>Saturday
13
March</td><td>**Redirected Efforts**
By Paul McCain
Oklahoma City, Oklahoma</td><td></td></tr>
</table>

"[T]hey shall return again to their own place, to enjoy that which they are willing to receive...."

—Doctrine and Covenants 85:6g

It will probably be easy to see why my dad wasn't the one to tell me this story. My Uncle Corky (Dad's youngest brother) told me of a time when Dad played basketball in high school. In a crucial game with the score within one point, he got the ball at mid-court and, a split second before the final buzzer, launched the ball toward the goal. It went through but, unfortunately, in the excitement of the moment, he had turned toward the opponent's goal and won the game for them.

Sometime shortly after I was born, Mom and Dad, even though they were members of the church, quit attending. But after about sixteen years of more misdirected effort, Dad had an experience with the Lord. He quit smoking and drinking literally overnight. Two of us four boys were still living at home, and he announced one Saturday, "We're going back to church." He continued his new discipline and, in time, was ordained to the office of priest. He felt compelled to set the goal of baptizing all of the family members he could. My younger brother and I had been baptized before Dad was ordained, so he focused his efforts on daughters-in-law and grandchildren.

Just recently my daughter Juli accepted a call to the office of priest; Dad would have been so proud. He passed away in 1991, but for my own immediate family's sake and the families of countless progeny down through time, I'll be forever grateful for him following the leading of the Spirit to get the family back in church.

Hymns of the Saints: No. 174, "O Christ, My Lord, Create in Me"

Prayer Thought: Almighty Redeemer, touch us with insight and power to redirect our lives, that we might be an influence for good for the generations that follow us.

Sunday **14** March	**The Red Arrow** By Gerald John Kloss Philadelphia, Pennsylvania	

"...God called to him out of the bush, 'Moses, Moses.' And he said, 'Here I am.'"—Exodus 3:4 NRSV

I am enjoying my teaching position at Philadelphia Christian Academy. Working with third and fourth graders has fanned the flame in my heart for good teaching and learning. Part of my responsibility includes training the children in spiritual and moral truths contained in the pages of scripture. One task that has presented the greatest challenge is teaching these young people to accept full responsibility for their actions instead of blaming everyone else.

As we pass through the hallway daily we walk past the kindergarten class. This class has a chart in the hall made up of a wheel with a large red arrow in the middle. The chart indicates the various locations as to where the class might be: "We are at lunch"; "We are at recess"; "We are in the library," etc.

One day as I passed by I noticed that the red arrow was slightly bent outward as a result of so many hands moving it. No matter where the arrow was turned it still appeared to point to the one standing in front of it. I then began to walk children from my class past it each time they blamed someone else for what they themselves had done. They began to realize that no matter which way they moved the arrow—trying to force it to point to someone else—it still pointed back to them. This truly helped the children realize their responsibility for themselves.

The red arrow further enhanced my ability to teach the children the importance of their response to the call of God in their lives. As they developed an understanding of this, it became easier to teach them to positively respond to the on-going ministry of the Holy Spirit and to eventually submit their whole lives to the Lord, thus enabling them to say, like Moses, "Here I am, Lord."

Sing a New Song: No. 12, "Here I Am, Lord"

Prayer Thought: Heavenly Father, as we respond to your call in our lives, may we realize we have a task to help call others to your arms of love also.

<table>
<tr><td>Monday
15
March</td><td>**Roots of Blessing**
By Sylvia Lenfestey Peabody
Beals Island, Maine</td><td></td></tr>
</table>

"The Lord is my chosen portion and my cup; thou holdest my lot. The lines have fallen for me in pleasant places; yea, I have a goodly heritage."—Psalm 16:6 RSV

The sign over our house says "Homagen." In 1995 my husband and I moved "home again" to our small island town on the coast of Maine after thirty-five years of teaching in Massachusetts and New Hampshire. I've heard it said that you can never go home again, but I did. Oh, there have been changes, of course, but the feelings of love, security, and belonging remain the same.

I'm a fourth generation member of the church now known as Community of Christ, and it's wonderful to be back in my home congregation. My dad was pastor here for thirty years. We may be few in number but we're rich in heritage and the enthusiastic energy of young adults. I'm so thankful for my heritage, both in the church and in my family. Every day I thank God he has brought us back to our roots while we can still enjoy and appreciate the blessings around us.

Hymns of the Saints: No. 433, "Faith of Our Fathers"

Prayer Thought: Lord, help us all to appreciate whatever our heritage has brought us, and may we seek to enrich whatever we leave to those who follow.

| Tuesday **16** March | **Just One Word** By Janie S. Qualls Lake City, Arkansas | |

"[R]ather the greatest among you must become like the youngest, and the leader like one who serves. For who is greater, the one who is at table or the one who serves? Is it not the one at table? But I am among you as one who serves."—Luke 22:26–27 NRSV

The six-letter personalized license plates can tell a lot about their owners. Some are clues to their name, hobby, or favorite ball team. Some are humorous, while others are a clever play on words.

I saw one recently that caught my eye. It simply said, "OTHERS." The single word was a sermon in miniature. I wondered about the driver's occupation, family, and life. Perhaps we should choose as our motto that same simple word. If everyone lived by that motto, what a difference it would make. Others were foremost to Jesus as he went about doing good. Can we do less?

Hymns of the Saints: No. 436, "Go Now Forth into the World"

Prayer Thought: Servant Lord, lead our focus away from ourselves and toward easing the burdens of others.

Wednesday 17 March

Gathered to God
By Grace Andrews
Independence, Missouri

"I [God] will unfold unto them a great mystery; for, behold, I will gather them as a hen gathereth her chickens under her wings ... "—Doctrine and Covenants 3:15e

Have you ever seen a hen gather her chickens? She elevates herself as high as possible, spreads her wings wide, and begins clucking softly, then louder. Baby chicks come running from wherever they are in the far corners of the yard or pen, to snuggle in close to her warm body. When she is satisfied that they are all accounted for, she gently lowers her body and enfolds them beneath her wings. Not knowing what just transpired, the casual observer might think she is sitting there alone—but, look again! Beneath her wings, safely hidden from all harm or danger, are her little ones, and she will protect them to the death from any and all harm.

God is like that. God calls each of us by name and asks us to "Come"! When we respond and "snuggle" against him, God covers us with his love. His arms are open wide. He invites each one personally, just as he did a group of fishermen long ago. We are his children! No one can care for you and me better than God. He sees our need for bread, our cries for knowledge, our desire for healing, our longing to be loved, to be safe and warm.

God never ignores us. Rather, God looks deep into our eyes, and offers to wash us in the clean, pure water of his word, and enfold us under his wings. We are reminded, "…if they will not harden their hearts; yea, if they will come, they may, and partake of the waters of life freely."

Hymns of the Saints: No. 188, "O Love of God, How Strong and True"

Prayer Thought: Nurturing God, you call us as a hen calls her chicks. May we find our refuge in the sureness of your love for us.

Thursday **18** March	**Symbolic Moment** By Marlene Brunner Yuma, Colorado	

"Finally, brothers and sisters, farewell. Put things in order, listen to my appeal, agree with one another, live in peace, and the God of love and peace will be with you."
—II Corinthians 13:11 NRSV

After the International Women's conference in 1993 we purchased a peace candle and put it in our front window. Since that time we have replaced the bulb in it many times. However, a most unusual thing happened on March 18, 2003. When I opened the curtain that morning, I discovered that the light in the peace candle had burned out again. This was the day President Bush issued a proclamation that the United States would be going to war against Iraq.

Perhaps this was merely a coincidence, but it touched me deeply. It helped me realize that my nation was truly entering a period of war, the extent of which we could not foresee and the outcome of which we could not predict. It opened my eyes to the fact that we were replacing any peace we may have been enjoying for a battle that would bring much devastation to many countries, perhaps even our own, and the loss of many lives.

We trust in a God who will protect us as long as we remain faithful. I truly hope there are enough strong, faithful Christians who can honestly claim to honor God and make every effort to live Jesus' teachings.

Sing for Peace: No. 21, "Behold a Broken World, We Pray"

Prayer Thought: Eternal God, we come to you on behalf of all who suffer from any form of injustice. Use us to bring peace and justice wherever we may be.

Friday **19** March	**"Over There, Over There"** By Sonia J. Studer Northglenn, Colorado	

"And be at peace among yourselves."
—I Thessalonians 5:13

Does anyone remember or has anyone heard of that song? As the war in Iraq commenced, I found myself barely able to breathe as I lived every day of my life. I spent many hours praying that all of the "hosts of heaven" (angels) and Christ were "over there," moving in peace among all peoples, whether they were our soldiers, "their" people, or anyone else who found themselves tangled up in such a situation.

How many wars does it take for people to begin behaving in the way God so lovingly intended? I realize that this planet has seldom been without war, but as weapons become more and more hi-tech, almost to the point of not needing humans to dispatch them, one would think humans would be able to see that war is absolutely unacceptable. Every generation of my husband's family has lost someone in the military in each war since World War I, and many families have lost more than that.

Our own son was involved as a naval officer in a small war with Iran. Remember that? I doubt if many do, but it was just as deadly. I hope and pray that God will help me to practice peace so that among all of us we may end such devastation. The greatest task Christ ever asked of us was to value and love each other, to forgive each other, and above all to strive to live side by side, bearing each other's burdens, while being led to abundant and joyous lives.

Now having said all that, I realize how difficult it can be. Even I become frustrated with the people around me sometimes, prompting me to say I could "kill" whomever it may be at the moment. Of course, I don't really mean it, but perhaps we all need to rethink our language and the emotions that make us talk this way.

Sing for Peace: No. 36, "Called by Christ to Love Each Other"

Prayer Thought: God of reconciliation, restore us to our sanity in moments of anger and teach us to practice peace wherever we may be.

Saturday **20** March	**Sharing the Light** By Janice Townsend Spokane, Washington	

"You are the world's light—a city on a hill, glowing in the night for all to see. Don't hide your light! Let it shine for all so that they will praise your heavenly Father...."
—Matthew 5:14–16 LB

Refrigerator humming, dishwasher running, furnace blowing warm air—secure in the comfort of our home, we sat in the glow of several lamps while we watched television. Sight and sound surrounded us as we enjoyed the usual pattern of living that fills our evenings. Then suddenly we were without power. Whether a blown transformer or a broken line, our link to electricity had been severed, and our home was plunged into darkness.

We scurried around finding candles and matches, then heard a knock at the door. Our son was there to see if we needed his help. With Kris's assistance we found our camping lantern and lit it, then carried it next door to his home to share the light. We spent the rest of the evening with grandchildren and other family, talking, reading, and enjoying one another's company. What could have been an empty and barren time turned into a rich and rewarding experience—ours because we had been willing to share the light that we had.

And besides the joy that was ours as we shared what we had, we also received the blessing of warmth. For those with whom we shared light gathered us around their hearth, where a blazing fire was burning. Share light and receive warmth—how wise is our God who calls us to share so that all can be blessed.

Sing for Peace: No. 34, "We Are Your People"

Prayer Thought: This day, Lord, in every byway of our lives, let your love flow through us to others. Let us be willing to share your light with each one.

<table>
<tr><td>Sunday
21
March</td><td>**Dot on the Map**
By Peggy Michael
Cantonment, Florida</td><td></td></tr>
</table>

"Wherefore, you must press forward with a steadfastness in Christ, having a perfect brightness of hope, and a love of God and of all men."—II Nephi 13:29

There is a town in Texas that's just a dot on the map, but its name is spoken more and more often these days. Its theme song could be, "There's a new name written down in glory. It is mine. It is mine." A Community of Christ is thriving there because God used a humble woman and her husband to plant a church some three decades ago.

The closest congregation was San Antonio or Austin, and because of distance, the couple could not participate as they desired. After asking church officials what the best plan was, they began services in their home as a study group. John was an excellent teacher, and the class grew. The group then met in a rented hall, eventually buying the house next door and converting it into a church.

Soon after moving to town, a raging flood swept into the area. They were fortunate, living on the high side of the river. Mattie met the first church member with a mop and bucket in hand. Ann and Mattie are the only charter members left in the church there. Servant ministry meant inviting neighbors in for delicious corn chowder or chicken and dumplings. People kept coming back. A deacon and an evangelist joined them, with baptisms, blessings, weddings, and priesthood calls to follow.

Mattie, a widow for twenty years and now eight-five years of age, takes no credit for the success: "All I do is love the people God sends to me." She reluctantly asked to be taken off the preaching schedule, but if there's ever been a "living sermon" it's her life. Today the members there have outgrown their building and are looking for a larger place to gather.

Hymns of the Saints: No. 392, "Go, Make of All Disciples"

Prayer Thought: God who calls us to service, may each of us be vital witnesses for Jesus Christ in our respective communities.

| Monday
22
March | **God's Guidance**
By Larry Landsdown
Midwest City, Oklahoma | |

"For this God is our God forever and ever; he will be our guide even unto death."—Psalm 48:14

I had a brother who was diagnosed with diabetes at age eight. He was three years younger than I, but we were very close. He was a good auto mechanic, and even though we lived in different states, we would often talk on the phone, and he'd give me advice on fixing my truck.

His health got worse over the years and he was often hospitalized for weeks at a time. About a week before his death, I flew down from Missouri to visit him. I felt that I should be down here close enough to help with things, and I decided to try to get moved as soon as possible. I felt God's direction in making this decision.

Although I actually moved about a month after my brother passed away, I know my move was a blessing. Our whole family is closer than ever. The church family here has welcomed me and I have become more involved in church activities than ever before. I know God directs our lives, and even out of sad times good things can come.

Hymns of the Saints: No. 311, "Guide Us, O Thou Great Jehovah"

Prayer Thought: Thank you for guiding our lives, Lord. Help us to be open to your Spirit, ready to receive and act on your direction.

| Tuesday **23** March | **Deep Roots, Strong Faith**
By Maurine Van Eaton
Yakima, Washington | |

"But he that received the seed into stony places, the same is he that heareth the word and readily with joy receiveth it, yet he hath not root in himself, and endureth but for a while; for when tribulation or persecution ariseth because of the word, by and by he is offended."—Matthew 13:19 IV

A friend gave me a tiny plant with a delicate white blossom. The container that held it had about three inches of soil. The following spring it pushed up a green sprig and showed promise for a flower to come forth. Then after a time I noticed it had become spindly and was turning yellow. The soil had plenty of water and I added food but it became more sickly each day.

One day as I was probing the plant's roots, it occurred to me that the roots could not go any farther than the depth of the soil in the pot. It could not find enough nourishment in the shallow soil of the container. Unlike this tiny, spindly plant, whose roots were in shallow soil, I realized that my roots went deep in this church, involving four generations of spiritual nourishment in the deep soil of the gospel of the Restoration.

I thought of the winter wheat that grows in the northern part of the state of Washington. In that hot, dry environment the roots go deep for moisture and nutrition as protection from the summer heat. In the harsh winters, when the green wheat can be seen under the ice, the deep soil protects the roots from freezing. The hot dry weather and sparse rainfall cause the wheat to be hard. It is tough to grind but has lots of gluten, which makes delightful bread—it's a breadmaker's delight, for it helps the bread to rise.

I compare myself to this winter wheat growing in a hostile environment. It gains protection and nutrients from its roots. My roots have been nourished by a family that shared the stories of Jesus and God's love. I was taught to pray and worship, and learned the precepts of the good news. I had church fellowship. There were challenges and lessons to learn, and blessings came through faith and prayer.

Hymns of the Saints: No. 294, "The Church's One Foundation"

Prayer Thought: Lord of love and mercy, how thankful we are that the roots of our faith go deep into the good news of the gospel. Encourage us to continue to nurture this heritage within our families.

Wednesday **24** March	**God's Wait Time** By Willa Frey Fairbanks, Alaska	

"I will praise the name of God with a song, and will magnify him with thanksgiving."—Psalm 69:30

Have you ever had spring fever? I have. It usually begins early in the spring when I glimpse a tiny hint of green in the trees in front of my home. The sky is blue with fluffy white clouds and the temperature is warm—well, at least it feels warm during the day even if the nights are still below freezing. I can almost smell the coming of spring.

My mind begins to telescope all the necessities for a lovely garden into a few minutes, and I'm eager to get going. Then I go outside where I'm faced with snow, ice, and mud. There is no way I can start even getting the ground ready! This happens every spring—I'm an eager beaver way ahead of time. It's difficult to wait, and I get very impatient.

I wonder how God feels about my impatience. I often want to rush in and get instant results from my efforts, without stopping to realize there is a lot of nurturing that needs to be done, including patient listening. My experience is that often I need to slow down and listen for God's direction and then follow it. Maybe "wait time" is needed in the nurturing process. Certainly a lot of love is, and then as I share about my personal experiences with God, the other person is ready to listen and share.

Hymns of the Saints: No. 472, "Unto God, Who Knows Our Every Weakness"

Prayer Thought: Teach us to be patient, Lord, and allow "wait time" for your Spirit to work in the lives of others.

<table>
<tr><td>Thursday
25
March</td><td>**God Can Do Anything**
By Linda French
Hastings, Michigan</td><td></td></tr>
</table>

"For to one is given by the Spirit the word of wisdom;…to another the gifts of healing by the same Spirit; to another the working of miracles…."—I Corinthians 12:8–10

Children sure have a way to make us think and bring us back to reality. My mother operated an adult foster care home for many years. My husband and I and our two little boys lived in the home while we saved money to buy our first house. I also worked various shifts at the home, taking care of the people.

During this time my family adopted an elderly lady named Marie. She and her husband moved into the home, and shortly afterward her husband died. She was alone, for they did not have any children, and her sister lived in another state. Marie was blind and afflicted with many medical problems, one being diabetes.

After Marie had lived there for five years, my mother decided to close the home. She and my step-father bought a campground, sold the home, and moved to Hastings. Marie was moved to a nursing home in Grand Rapids, Michigan. After a few years there, my mother was able to get her transferred to our hometown of Hastings. Our boys loved visiting Marie and became very close to her. We called her "Grandma Marie." After about a year in this new place, Marie's medical problems progressed, and her health went "downhill." It soon became apparent she would not get better. It was only a matter of time before she would leave this world.

I finally felt I had to tell my boys that Marie was really sick and would probably die. So they began praying for her every night. To our surprise Marie began a rollercoaster ride of getting better and deteriorating again. But after six months she began to lose the battle. She did not recognize us any longer and was not able to eat or walk, and she was barely conscious.

It was time to let my boys know she was not going to pull through. My youngest, Andy, prayed the same prayer for Marie night after night. One evening when he finished, I suggested he not pray for Marie to get better, but maybe that God would take her home so she wouldn't have to suffer any longer. Andy looked at me with tears in his eyes and said, "Mom, God can do anything! If he wanted to make Marie better he could, so I am not going to stop praying for Marie." He knew if God wanted to do a miracle he would, and he wasn't going to stop asking. Marie died a short time later, and Andy's older brother Jason played "Amazing Grace" on a small stringed instrument called the "Music Maker" at her graveside service.

Andy caused me to look at my own faith just a bit differently. I don't give up like I used to and am more fervent in asking for healing, or whatever the need may be, from God.

Hymns of the Saints: No. 489, "God Be with You Till We Meet Again"

Prayer Thought: Gracious God, may we learn to stretch our faith in your power, yet ultimately leave things in your hands, that your will might override ours.

<table>
<tr><td>Friday
26
March</td><td>**Called to Forgive**
By Barrie Fox
Kirkby in Ashfield, England</td><td></td></tr>
</table>

"Verily, I say unto you, my servants, that inasmuch as you have forgiven one another your trespasses, even so I, the Lord, forgive you."—Doctrine and Covenants 81:1a

I love reading the wayside pulpit messages that we so often see displayed outside churches of various denominations in the British Isles. If they are ones that particularly appeal to me, I jot them down in my diary for future reference. Recently, I read in the newspaper of one such message that simply said, "Love thy neighbour," but someone had, apparently, written with a black marker underneath it, "I can't! I know him too well."

The Holy Spirit seeks to help and encourage us to be forgiving. In this day and age it is still reminding us of both the need we have to be forgiven and the need we have to be forgiving. We do tend to think at times, I suggest, of forgiveness and tolerance as options that Jesus Christ gives to us, rather than as commands. The real truth of the matter for Christians is that when we fail to forgive, we are letting ourselves down as would-be followers of Jesus, our Lord.

Hymns of the Saints: No. 171, "Help Us Accept Each Other"

Prayer Thought: Help us, Lord, to learn to forgive as you forgive us. Let us not dwell on what has happened in the past but look with joy to the hopes of the future.

"And the glory which thou gavest me I have given them; that they may be one, even as we are one; I in them, and thou in me, that they may be made perfect in one; and that the world may know that thou hast sent me, and hast loved them, as thou hast loved me."—John 17:22–23

The TV news had reported a fatality on the freeway I was planning to take. The accident was in the opposite direction, just before an on-ramp where I would enter. The traffic in my direction looked like it was flowing along, but on the opposite side it was virtually still for quite a distance. I started thinking about the people in those cars. When they got in their cars that morning, most did not know the person who would die in the crash, yet their lives were affected by him.

Later I learned he was the driver of a speeding car that had crashed so hard it had split in two. Not only did this driver's death affect the people waiting in the cars behind the accident, but it affected the people and events at the destinations of the other travelers. We can only speculate about how far into the day this delay would have an effect.

This event made me think of how connected we all are and how influenced by others, even when we have never known them, or have never even known *of* them. God has placed us in a world where our lives touch many others, connecting us as one with each other and eventually with God.

English writer and poet John Donne, in meditating on a bell tolling a man's death, stated this so eloquently: "No man is an island....Any man's death diminishes me, because I am involved in mankind."

Hymns of the Saints: No. 466, "We Are One in the Spirit"

Prayer Thought: Lord, help us to so live that our influence in our relationship with others brings your Spirit into the interaction, and ultimately leads us to be one with you.

Sunday **28** March	**Labor of Love** By Ferryl Cash Troy, Kansas	

"I will praise you, O Lord, with all my heart."

—Psalm 138:1

Mom did many nice things for us while we were growing up. She spent many hours making things for my four sisters and me. One Easter stands out vividly in my mind.

At that time it was much cheaper to make our clothes, so she sewed much of our wardrobe. She was always particular about the way we looked, and she had very little money to work with. One spring, Mom decided to make new Easter dresses for each of us, and spent many hours at her sewing machine. Each dress was a different pastel color. I remember that mine was yellow. The dresses were two layers, the top a see-through material that matched the color underneath with flocked flowers on it. It took many weeks for her to accomplish this task, but it was a labor of love.

Easter morning we were all dressed up in our new dresses. We were very proud of them. Even though I was happy and thankful for the dress at the time, my thoughts were mostly of the new dress and being able to wear it to church. But as the years have gone by I have thought less of the dress and more of Mom's labor of love for her family. She loved us so much and expected nothing in return for having made the dresses. It was a gift she gave freely simply because she loved us.

God has given us a free gift in his Son, also given out of love. Aren't we blessed that God loves us so much?

Hymns of the Saints: No. 205, "My Children, 'Hear Ye Him,' My Word"

Prayer Thought: God, we thank you for loving us so abundantly. May our love for you show in what we do for others.

<table>
<tr><td>Monday
29
March</td><td>**Reaching Out**
By Florence Ourth
Nauvoo, Illinois</td><td></td></tr>
</table>

"For [God] has said, I will never leave thee, nor forsake thee."—Hebrews 13:5

Jesus reached out to those in need with love and compassion. As I thought about this I remembered an experience of how God had used me to reach out to someone who needed to know of divine compassion.

A woman from Elgin, Illinois, visited our branch. As she and I talked after church she told me how her husband of four years, a diabetic from his youth, was soon to have surgery for his eyes. She feared he would lose his sight. She was discouraged, wondering if they had been forgotten by God. She had been searching the scriptures for a message of reassurance. She thought there was a scripture about not being forsaken but had not been able to find it.

It so happened I had that very scripture from Hebrews 13 on a ballpoint pen in my purse. I showed it to her, and she asked if she could copy it on a piece of paper.

I said, "You may have the pen." I could tell by her face that this was a testimony to her that God had indeed not forsaken her.

Hymns of the Saints: No. 213, "I Sought the Lord"

Prayer Thought: Our Creator, how comforting it is to know that no matter what happens, you are with us.

| Tuesday
30
March | **Confirmation of a Call**
By Deb Luce
Camanche, Iowa | |

"Listen to the voice of the Lord your God, even Alpha and Omega, the beginning and the end, whose course is one eternal round, the same today as yesterday and forever."
—Doctrine and Covenants 34:1a

Sometimes the Lord needs to speak in more than a still small voice in order to gain my attention. Such was the case one Friday when I felt prompted to travel five hours to visit a friend who had recently experienced a medical crisis. Having a family and a busy schedule kept telling me I couldn't make the trip, so I listened to that busyness and waited. Finally on Monday, which happened to be a holiday, I could refuse the nagging feeling no longer, and I started my journey.

I put on my watch, which I had broken several days before, because my wrist felt bare, so I wore it anyway. I tapped it a few times in an effort to make it go but to no avail. As I drove along and talked with God it occurred to me that God had the power to make my watch work and confirm to me that I was correct in making the trip. At 12:15 I turned my watch and my need for confirmation over to God, and immediately the watch began to work. That was many months ago and it is still ticking.

Perhaps it was just coincidence, but it was a message I needed at that time, showing me that God does indeed hear us and that we need to listen to him.

Hymns of the Saints: No. 371, "Jesus Calls Us O'er the Tumult"

Prayer Thought: May we be tuned to hear your voice, Lord, as you call us to bring ministry to others.

Wednesday **31** March	**Gifts of Many Colors** By Shirley S. Case Slater, Missouri

"A gift is as precious stone in the eyes of him that hath it; whithersoever it turneth, it prospereth."—Proverbs 17:8

My sis Lou has a gift for crocheting. Her evangelist's blessing states that she will be guided as to whom to share this with, as well as the colors to use. This is part of her ministry, woven into the fabric of her being, as much as the pattern of an afghan.

Lou is a priest in the Community of Christ and shares the afghans she makes as gifts to others. Just before my surgery she presented me with one and said, "Little sister, this is for you, so that every time you wrap up in it, you'll feel my love wrap around you and keep you warm." Sounds like something Jesus would have said.

She's donated her beautiful afghans to school and church raffles, and quite a few tickets have been sold because of her outreach and care. She's also given them to brothers and kids for their birthdays, to friends she loves, and to mere acquaintances. When shopping she's always on the prowl for new colors, bigger skeins, and different textures.

I can only smile as I wonder who the next lucky person will be to end up with an afghan. Lou shows God's love by sharing it through the ability God has given her.

Sing a New Song: No. 32, "Lord, I Give You"

Prayer Thought: Let us discover and refine our gifts, Lord, that we may use them to bless others wherever we may be.

April 2004

S	M	T	W	T	F	S
				1	2	3
4	5	6	7	8	9	10
11	12	13	14	15	16	17
18	19	20	21	22	23	24
25	26	27	28	29	30	

"Thou sendest forth thy Spirit, they are created; and thou renewest the face of the earth."—Psalm 104:30

Each year I eagerly look forward to the arrival of spring and the opportunity to begin working outside in my garden. I truly love the outdoors and spend many hours of pleasure taking care of my lawn and planting flowers and a nice vegetable garden. But the past few years I have found it difficult to grow flowers along the back of my garden because it is shaded most of the time by the back wall of a church.

My neighbors also have beautiful gardens, and many spend quality time taking care of this treasure from the Lord. I often admired a tall purple flower that grew in a neighbor's garden two houses up from me. No one was quite sure what kind of flower it was; my neighbors called it a "nice-looking weed."

The fall of 2001 was warm with many windy days, allowing for more opportunity to work outdoors. I cleared the back of my yard and wondered what I might plant there the next spring. To my amazement, when spring arrived I noticed small shoots springing up along that back garden wall. I decided to just let them grow since I didn't know what they were. I was delighted to discover that these plants were the same beautiful purple flowers that were in my neighbor's yard. The seed had blown over from their yard to mine. And I am excited that the same plants are springing up in April 2003.

As I thought about this, I realized that this is exactly like our testimony of the Lord Jesus Christ through the actions of our lives. Seeds of witness blow over into the lives of others and are used by the Holy Spirit to renew them and draw them to the source of the beauty—the Lord Jesus Christ himself.

Hymns of the Saints: No. 255, "Lo, How a Rose E'er Blooming"

Prayer Thought: Lord God, gracious Redeemer, use the actions of our lives to plant seeds of beauty in the hearts of others that will lead them to you.

| Friday **2** April | **What Is "Poor"?** By Olevia Huntsman Bald Knob, Arkansas | |

"Those who despise their neighbors are sinners, but happy are those who are kind to the poor."

—Proverbs 14:21 NRSV

I grew up in a family of nine children. We all worked to help support the family. Many times I felt that life was unfair when I saw my friends playing while I had to work. At Christmas, I wondered just who "Santa" could be to leave bicycles, jewelry, and toys for the neighbor kids when all I received was a plastic tea set or a small doll with homemade clothing. There were many times I thought we were poor because of all the things we didn't have. When I was just reaching my teenage years I met a girl at school who answered the question of what "poor" really can be.

It was my second year in junior high school and I had made a new girlfriend. I gave her a birthday party at my house, which was not something I usually did. Some of the boys began to make fun of her looks and called her names, though I don't think she heard them. Ordinarily I am a passive-type person but I lit into them verbally, telling them just what I thought. I don't think they meant any harm but I was really mad. I think I was identifying with my friend on some level.

Later on this girlfriend got into some kind of trouble and was going to be sent to a home. She asked me to go with her to get her things because she didn't want to face her parents alone, and my dad was the one who would be taking her to the home. The place she lived was sort of a run-down shed-type building. We went inside and I followed her up a ladder into a loft area where she slept on a ragged old quilt. The only possessions she had fit into a paper bag. When we left, there were no hugs or tearful good-byes. I think it was then that I began to realize just how well-off I was, and not only in a material sense. This friend made an impression on me that will be with me forever. I have often wondered what became of her, and it is then that I pray for her and her well being.

I have had so many blessings in my life, and I am so thankful to be aware of them. I have always had food to eat, clothes to wear, wonderful relationships with family and friends, and, most important, I have been exposed to God and his love all along the way. Today I am thankful anew as I relive these memories.

Hymns of the Saints: No. 60, "Now Thank We All Our God"

Prayer Thought: Lord, help us to be aware of the blessings we have been given. May we be instruments in bringing your blessings into the lives of others.

<table>
<tr><td>Saturday
3
April</td><td>**Little Blessings**
By Jo Ann Townsend
Spokane, Washington</td><td></td></tr>
</table>

"And all thy children shall be taught of the Lord; and great shall be the peace of thy children."—III Nephi 10:21

It was my turn to do the church cleaning. I had many other things to do that day, yet I set my sights on the task ahead. As I entered the sanctuary, the quiet of the moment set my mind to thinking of the services that had taken place there recently and of the people, my church family, who filled this place. As I moved to the back pews to dust, I saw where crumbs had been left by the little ones I knew sat there on Sunday mornings. My first thought was of how messy children can be. But then their faces, actions, and sounds came to mind and I remembered what a blessing they were, and I was humbled by what I was doing. It was no longer a boring, tedious task. I felt honored to be there to provide a clean, comfortable place for them to return to on the next Sunday.

Children are so essential to the life of the church. In the sacrament of the blessing of little children we are often charged, as a congregation, to uphold and support them as they grow and become part of our larger church community. Before I left that day I thanked God for the opportunity to be of service and the reminder of how beautiful and precious our children are.

Hymns of the Saints: No. 349, "The Vision of a Life to Be"

Prayer Thought: God, we thank you for each precious life. Help us to be more aware of our children, your treasures.

A Time for Everything
By Paul McCain
Oklahoma City, Oklahoma

"To every thing there is a season, and a time to every purpose under heaven."—Ecclesiastes 3:1

The phrase "God's time" has always seemed a mystery to me. But then, God *is* mysterious. Some things have crisper boundaries than others: something awful or harsh will happen if the timing is off. It was such a simple directive from the instructor: "Do not put the gear down until the air speed is below that for 'gear down' or the gear doors will break off." I don't remember it being said, but it certainly was in my mind that if the gear doors broke off, I would lose control and "crash and burn." Needless to say, I never tested that directive.

Life is like the "overhead" pattern we used to fly when coming in to the training base in an Air Force T-38 plane, in that there is a "time" for everything. The approach was in the same direction that the landing would be a few minutes later, at pattern altitude, and at 280 knots (nautical miles per hour). We did a "pitch out" like most have seen the Thunderbirds or Blue Angels do in their shows, the purpose of which was to turn 180 degrees and, at the same time, slow the aircraft to a speed below which the gear could be lowered for landing. That acceptable envelope (time) was between when the airspeed was low enough for the gear and before reaching the "perch."

Like in life, our skill and technique determined how much of an envelope we had to accomplish the task. Upon reaching the "perch" (the point across from where we would touch down) we were to lower the flaps and start the descent for landing, but, of course, the flaps could not be lowered until the gear was down.

My impatience can only partly be blamed on the world I live in, where "fast" describes the food, the cars, and the pace of life. It's easier when the boundaries are "crisp"—that is, something awful will obviously happen if they are exceeded. The soft boundaries are the difficult ones: sensing the right time to call a friend, knowing when words of encouragement are needed by my granddaughter, being aware of when listening to my wife is really important.

I find that constant practice is needed to identify the right envelope and lovingly act in it; "crash and burn" is perhaps just another way of saying that the opportunity may not come again.

Hymns of the Saints: No. 387, "O My People, Saith the Spirit"

Prayer Thought: Divine Instructor, you know the best time for everything. Help us figure it out, too, for those things we need to do for you.

| Monday **5** April | **Annual Resurrection**
 By Helen M. Green
 Toledo, Ohio | |

"Then spake the Jews and said unto him, What sign showest thou unto us? ...Jesus answered and said unto them, Destroy this temple, and in three days I will raise it up."
—John 2:18–19

On the first day of spring, Toledo was covered with heavy snow, which closed schools, canceled meetings, disrupted community services, and generally made things uncomfortable for about three days. Just before the snow fell we experienced severe winds and heavy rain. In combination, residents were inconvenienced by flooding and downed power lines. It was *not* a nice introduction to spring at all!

Still, after three days the sun came out in all its glory. Our spirits lifted, the snow melted, and sure enough, tulips were pushing their tips skyward and trees were heavy with swollen buds, giving a clear message: *Spring will come! Indeed, spring is on its way.* But why are we amazed?

After three days the sun came out. Jesus promised, "After three days I will rise again." True to his word, after three days the Son came out. After the gloom and sorrow, after the tears of mourning, the world was renewed, and life continued. The angels asked the grieving women who came to his tomb on that first Easter morning, "Why seek ye the living among the dead?"

The older I grow the more I realize that Easter is not a one-time happening. Every year we review it again while all around us resurrection takes place once more.

Hymns of the Saints: No. 272, "Christ Is Alive"

Prayer Thought: Eternal Creator of life, we thank you for the risen Christ, who overcame death and opened the way to eternal life.

"Journey in Trust"
By Anne Loughran
Melbourne, Australia

"But neither be captive to time-bound formulas and procedures. Remember that instruction given in former years is applicable in principle and must be measured against the needs of a growing church, in accordance with the prayerful direction of the spiritual authorities and the consent of the people."—Doctrine and Covenants 161:5

I recently called on a close relative who no longer attends church. "It is not the same church I joined," she said. This is true. But she is not the same person she was when she was baptized many years ago either. None of us is; we have all changed—some in mind, some in our beliefs, some in stature.

It is the same with the church. The principles of the church have not changed, but the times have, dramatically. New insights have been gained; new technology has opened up avenues that we never thought possible not so long ago.

God is opening up opportunities of service in ways that did not exist years ago. We have been admonished to "journey in trust, assured that the great and marvelous work is for this time and for all time," for our God is a creator and continues to create, and so must we.

Sing a New Song: No. 44, "Seek Ye First"

Prayer Thought: Creator God, may we learn to never quit seeking, asking, or knocking at your door for what the church needs to be in our day. Grant us courage to trust as you lead us forward.

<table>
<tr><td>Wednesday
7
April</td><td>**A Grateful Heart**
By Melba Jean Dixon
Farwell, Michigan</td><td></td></tr>
</table>

"Oh, give thanks to the Lord, for he is good; his love and his kindness go on forever."—I Chronicles 16:34 LB

I had gone to the dentist for a routine cleaning. During the cleaning, a tooth was broken. I was not happy with the prospect of going through an expensive procedure to restore the tooth. On my way home, I was lamenting about the perplexities of aging: teeth falling out, body falling apart, expensive health maintenance. By the time I drove into the village I was already fifteen minutes late for Wednesday evening prayer and fellowship service. I almost passed the church and continued on home, but somehow I didn't.

I entered the door and walked quietly into the church. Then I received the reality check I deserved. Pearl, age ninety-six, was on her feet, offering a prayer of praise and gratitude for all of the blessings God had bestowed on her. She was not complaining that her husband had died many years ago as the result of an auto accident. Nor was she grieving because five of her children had already passed away, victims of cancer, and several other family members were no longer living.

As I listened to Pearl's prayer, my attitude changed. Now, my problems seemed insignificant. That experience helped me to recognize that God had truly blessed me with family, friends, faith, and hope for the future. Pearl's life bears the mark of a true disciple: a grateful heart.

Hymns of the Saints: No. 362, "A Diligent and Grateful Heart"

Prayer Thought: Generous Lord, remind us in our times of self-pity that you have bestowed on us a multitude of gifts.

| Thursday **8** April | **Lift High the Cross**
By Dorene Kilburn
St. Paul's Station, Ontario, Canada | |

"And just as Moses lifted up the serpent in the wilderness, so must the Son of Man be lifted up, that whoever believes in him may have eternal life."—John 3:14–15 NRSV

It's the day before Good Friday as I write this and I've been thinking about what the people of Jesus' time, who did not know that he would live again, thought as they saw him hanging on the cross. We have the advantage of knowing that Christ was resurrected.

I've been trying to imagine what I might have thought and felt if I had been there on that fateful day. This gentle Jew, who wanted so much for everyone to understand God's plan of redemption, was dying a horrible death. If I had lived back then, I probably wouldn't have understood Jesus' message either, but I would have understood the love that radiated from him and the compassion in his eyes. Perhaps he would have talked with me and assured me that I was a child of God, a person of inestimable worth. If I were among those who witnessed Jesus' anguish on the cross, I know I would have felt a profound loss. This man who brought good news, healed the sick, and touched the lowliest of souls was being crucified for contrived wrongs he did not do. Thinking that he was gone forever must have been almost unbearable for his followers that day.

And then Mary came running to the disciples with the wonderful news that Jesus was alive! The excitement would soon have spread. How I would love to have been there! Gradually the people would come to understand that Jesus sacrificed his own life that they might have eternal life. They were given an important commission: to go into all the world and make disciples of all nations. Christ issues the same commission to us today!

Hymns of the Saints: No. 263, "Lift High the Cross"

Prayer Thought: May we stand daily before the cross, Lord Jesus, so that we will be reminded of the enormous sacrifice you made for humankind. Empower us by your Holy Spirit to share your message of love and redemption with those who do not know you.

| Friday
9
April | **Resurrection**
By Janice Townsend
Spokane, Washington | |

"I am crucified with Christ; nevertheless I live; yet not I, but Christ liveth in me; and the life which I now live in the flesh I live by the faith of the Son of God, who loved me, and gave himself for me."—Galatians 2:20

How precious to me are my childhood memories of Easter: new clothes in bright springtime hues; special treats lovingly prepared by Sunday school teachers; dyed eggs mirroring the colors of the rainbow; daffodils and tulips creating polka dot lawns; wild Easter lilies lifting their blossoms in mossy forest settings; an extended family gathering around an extended table for feast and celebration.

My childish heart delighted in the traditions that graced the day, and my adult heart still knows joy and delight as I join in the outward observances of the holiday. For now I understand that the traditions that fill our Easter celebrations are all significant symbols of resurrection and rebirth. New clothes, the reappearance of flowers and green leaves, the gathering of young and old, and yes, even those wonderful eggs and bunnies—each of these speaks of new life and the hope that can be ours because of Christ's resurrection.

New life can be mine; resurrection can be mine. I ponder the imponderable. I seek to know the unknowable. And I conclude that the only choice I can make is that of believing the unbelievable. I can do nothing else but choose to accept in faith the unbelievable miracle of God granting forgiveness and mercy to me, a sinner. Humbly I ask, "God, how can I possibly thank you for all you have done for me?"

Then comes an inner voice, speaking gently and lovingly, "My child," it tells me, "become the one I created you to be. Follow my Son and be resurrected into new life."

Hymns of the Saints: No. 199, "He Lives in Us! Immortal King!"

Prayer Thought: Let our praise ascend to you, O God, as a sweet savor. Jesus lives, and so too shall we. Alleluia!

| Saturday **10** April | **The Spirit's Prompting** By Ethel Knackstedt Kansas City, Kansas | |

"For unto such hath God promised his Spirit. And they who worship him must worship in spirit and in truth."
—John 4:26 IV

More than twenty years ago, while attending a weekend seminar, I became aware of the need to leave my job and get on with some work the Lord wanted me to do. My experience at that time was that the needs of the people were so great I almost had to run to keep up.

I liked my job, and I had been there fifteen years and had no intention of quitting, but the feeling I was having wouldn't go away. So I asked to be administered to. I told the elders I had a need but was not specific in what the need was, so they proceeded to anoint and pray for me. In the confirming prayer every feeling I was having was verbally spoken.

I had my answer, but I still hadn't discussed leaving my job with my husband, Lloyd. He was agreeable, and so on Monday morning I submitted my resignation. My boss was a Christian woman, and when I explained why I was leaving, she was understanding and didn't try to talk me out of my decision.

Little did I know that in a very short time I would need to travel to Michigan to help my ailing sister, who was in the early stages of Alzheimer's disease. It had progressed to the point that I had to take her car away and remove her from her home. I lived 700 miles away and so the decisions on her behalf became grievous.

I placed her in an assisted living facility in Michigan, hoping she would get better with extra care. But that wasn't to be, so I moved her to an extended care facility near me. I would be her advocate for the next fifteen years, a very real privilege I would not have had if I had stayed with my job.

In those ensuing years, there have been countless opportunities to assist with the needs of others, including my family, my church family, and others along the way. My needs have been abundantly supplied, and the Lord's prompting that day at the seminar has been reaffirmed countless times.

Sing for Peace: No. 13, "God of the Sparrow"

Prayer Thought: Lord God, may we be ever sensitive to the promptings of your Holy Spirit.

129

<table>
<tr><td>Sunday
11
April</td><td>**Called to Reconciliation**
By Alma J. V. Leeder
Wiarton, Ontario, Canada</td><td></td></tr>
</table>

"…first be reconciled to thy brother, and then come and offer thy gift."—Matthew 5:24 IV

In January 1996 I was a member of a twelve-person World Accord team in Honduras. Our mission was to build a school and the necessary desks for it. The locale was El Carreto, a mountain village near La Buena Fe. The actual building site was down the valley from El Carreto at Tontola.

The team was divided into two groups: one worked at laying the cement blocks and the other at fabricating the desks. An amazing amount of progress took place, so much so that within the two-week period the school was constructed and the desks were ready to be installed. A dedication service was planned, and I was asked to give the prayer. I wanted to be sure that everyone could understand what was happening, so I asked the interpreter to repeat each sentence of the prayer in Spanish to the large crowd of villagers, who turned out in their finest clothes to be a part of the celebration.

When the prayer was completed, Felix, the village president, rose to his feet and gave an impassioned speech to the audience. He seemed truly inspired as he exhorted the people, and after his remarks, I asked the interpreter about the content. I was told that he counseled the people to have love for one another, and to leave behind the friction and jealousy that had divided the villages previously. The Good Spirit had once again entered our midst to bring peace, reassurance, gratitude, and reconciliation.

Hymns of the Saints: No. 284, "Gracious Spirit, Dwell with Me"

Prayer Thought: God of reconciliation, with your help may we let go of past grievances and extend the hand of forgiveness, even as we are blessed by being forgiven.

| Monday **12** April | **Pilgrimage Home**
By Carol Smith Barnes
Sedalia, Missouri | |

"These all died in faith, not having received the promises, but having seen them afar off, and were persuaded of them, and embraced them, and confessed that they were strangers and pilgrims on the earth."—Hebrews 11:13

Some years ago a group from the Sedalia congregation of the Community of Christ traveled to Independence, Missouri, on a weekend trip to the newly completed Temple. Built as an ensign of peace, it is a place where people can go to learn the ways of peacemaking. We took a Temple School course; traveled the worshiper's path, leading to the sanctuary for meditation; and participated in providing the daily Prayer for Peace. It was a wonderful experience. I love to go to the Temple when we're in Independence, for quiet reflection and prayer from time to time.

Why do we humans need places we can call holy, and why do we yearn for sacred space? Are we yearning for home? Why did one of our biblical fathers, Jacob, insist his body be taken from Egypt and returned to the country of his lifelong pilgrimage for burial? I believe something in us says we need to go home, not only spiritually, but also physically.

I am drawn to places where the Spirit of Christ embraces me, and where I have been made to feel I belong to him. Perhaps this is what makes the dream of Zion so enticing to me. Yes, I believe Zion is an intangible condition of the heart that makes me feel at home in many places, but while I am on this earth in a body of clay, I will always understand it through what I see, touch, smell, and feel.

Before my earthly father passed away not long ago, Dad, my sister, and I traveled to the place of his birth. We walked the church grounds where our ancestors were buried, visited living relatives, and had a nurturing experience together. The most outstanding part was visiting the home of Dad's grandfather. A cousin and her family live there. Shortly after we made ourselves comfortable in the living room, Dad began to open up with a flood of memories surrounding the old place. We smiled as he began telling stories unfamiliar to us about those he loved from his youth. I believe with all my heart that Dad was impacted by the good spirit of those relatives who currently live in the old homestead, but I also believe he felt the familiar when he touched the entry door and once again remembered the sights and sounds of his youth.

These places where we have found peace are places where we have felt the love of God fill us. We yearn and long for them until we return. These places are different for each of us. I want to witness about where I have found the sacred to others struggling to find meaning in life.

Sing for Peace: No. 2, "What Is This Place"

Prayer Thought: God who embraces all generations, from time to time, draw us to those places that are sacred to us, that we may be renewed and lifted up in your presence.

A Well-Marked Path
By Bill Griffin
Elkin, North Carolina

"He restoreth my soul; he leadeth me in the paths of righteousness for his name's sake."—Psalm 23:3

Our High Adventure Camp spends a week each summer backpacking the Appalachian Trail. One afternoon we had taken a long side trail to refill our water bottles at a spring. As we rested in the serenity of the forest, a frantic young woman came hiking toward us. She had become separated from her companions and couldn't find their trail. I accompanied her back along the steep ridge until we came to a meadow. By tracing its perimeter, we discovered a tree blazed with the familiar white rectangle of the AT. Now she was back on the right path that would lead to her friends.

How often do we overlook the signs that might guide us in the path of joy and peace? Perhaps if we lift our eyes from the dusty trail, we will see the way that leads to our best friend, the Lord Jesus.

Sing for Peace: No. 31, "Lord Jesus, of You I Will Sing"

Prayer Thought: Lord, open our eyes to see your way. Lead us in paths of righteousness, joy, and peace.

"This one thing I do, forgetting those things which are behind, and reaching forth unto those things which are before, I press toward the mark for the prize of the high calling of God in Christ Jesus."—Philippians 3:13–14

Years ago I was going through pilot training in the U.S. Navy. In the navigation phase of our training, we were instructed in planning overseas flights. An important part of such a flight plan is to determine the point of no return. Up to that point, it was possible to turn around and fly back to the place we had departed. After passing the point of no return, there was no turning back. In the event of an emergency, we were committed to continuing to the destination.

I have often thought of the point of no return as a metaphor for my spiritual journey toward the kingdom of God. As I reflect on that journey, my point of no return was undoubtedly the day I stepped into the waters of baptism. Although I am sure that I was not fully aware at the time of the significance of such a decision, there was no turning back.

As I have continued on the journey, my life has been filled with periods of learning and encouragement by my brothers and sisters in Christ from several congregations. I have responded to various priesthood calls, experienced God's loving presence on occasions too numerous to recall, and attempted to provide ministry and blessing to God's children within and outside the Community of Christ. God has been my constant companion on the journey.

A particular experience some thirty-five years ago represented another point of no return for me. As I was preparing a Communion message for our congregation, I was completely immersed in the presence of God's sweet Spirit. I mentally asked what God would have me tell the people. The response that was burned within my bosom, "Tell them that I love them, especially those who are not members of the Reorganized Church of Jesus Christ of Latter Day Saints [now Community of Christ]." Under the impact of the presence of that Spirit, three friends presented themselves for baptism. But I came to realize that the message was for my benefit as much as it was for those in the congregation who responded.

I did not know at the time that my call to the office of seventy was in process. From that point on, I could never return to any lesser understanding. My ministry has been shaped ever since by my conviction of God's love for people, all people, and God's desire to gather them in love. Through subsequent calls as a high priest and an evangelist, my ministry has been undergirded by that simple yet powerful invitation, "Tell them that I love them."

Hymns of the Saints: No. 107, "The Love of God"

Prayer Thought: Surround us, God, with an overwhelming assurance of your love for us and for your children everywhere.

Amish Friends
By Enid Stubbart DeBarthe
Lamoni, Iowa

"Zionic conditions are no further away nor any closer than the spiritual condition of my people justifies."
—Doctrine and Covenants 140:5c

Our Lamoni community offers us a diversity of challenges for witnessing Christlike love. Many Amish families have moved to this area in recent years because of southern Iowa's "cheaper land." Joe and I have come to truly love our Amish neighbors, and they reciprocate with home-produced products: food, woven baskets, and woodcrafts. And we have, by invitation, shared some of their worship services and multi-family meals.

Joe and I were recently visiting family in Kansas, when one of our long-time friends died. Because his wife, Jackie, was one of the Community of Christ "angels" who had provided transportation for the Amish to hospitals and bus or airline depots, she requested a section be reserved immediately behind the pews reserved for her family. Seven Amish families were represented. Our neighbor, Menno Swartzendruber, had recently suffered a broken leg and was on crutches. Jackie specified that a chair with a cushion on it was to be placed in front of Menno, in the aisle of the Lamoni Community of Christ church, so he could rest his broken leg on it.

Since our Amish friends use horse-drawn buggies, Jackie invited them to park them at her place not far northwest of the church. They walked to the church and, after the service at the cemetery, shared lunch with all those who chose to stay. Special Amish dishes were part of the menu. What an expression of Zionic community!

The Lamoni area was a specially designated "Latter Day Saint" gathering place (1881–1901) and celebrated its centennial as a "stake of Zion" in 2001. A few "old timers" have questioned, "Is God letting the Amish move in as punishment for our failure to establish a Zionic community?" Surely, this diverse gathering in 2003 was a triumphal response to our call to be a community of joy, hope, love, and peace.

Hymns of the Saints: No. 386, "Come Now, Sound the Call of Zion"

Prayer Thought: God of all peoples, help us to serve, accept, and share with all who seek community through servanthood.

| Friday **16** April | **Lessons on the Road**
By Hal McKain
Lamoni, Iowa | |

"And walk in love, as Christ also hath loved us, and hath given himself for us an offering and a sacrifice to God for a sweet smelling savor."—Ephesians 5:2

Martha and I were privileged to go from Iowa to Colorado in January 2003. Both of us have family there as well as friends. I lived in Greeley with my family for twenty-four years, so it was good to be there and renew church family and friend relationships.

One of the side trips was a drive down the Poudre Canyon. Martha had never taken this trip, so it was especially exciting for her. As we started down from the uppermost point, snow was our companion. It was beautiful, as it gently fell and made a picturesque scene of winter in the mountains. As we traveled, the snow turned to rain and then gradually dissipated as we drove into the sunlight. Martha was driving and was enthralled at the beauty of the canyon. I had traveled this highway many times and was well aware of its beauty as well as its many curves.

On the journey, a couple of times, as we enjoyed the scenery a bit too much, Martha ran onto the center line, which was made of bumps as a warning to stay in one's own lane. This reminded the two of us of the spiritual journey we are on. Many times we have hit those "bumps" through careless behavior, which told us that we must keep our eye on our own life and stay in the Lord's lane of traffic. Being aware of this will surely help us to more closely reach our potential and develop the gifts and talents with which we have been blessed.

We have learned in our married life of three months that the Lord will open many doors for us, but it is our choice to walk through them. Our testimony is that when we enter those doors blessings abound, and yes, there are fewer "bumps" there.

Hymns of the Saints: No. 183, "Lord, Lead Me by Your Spirit"

Prayer Thought: Lord, may we keep our focus on the opportunities of service that await us. Guide us in our decision making, that we might make *great* plans with you.

Filled with Joy
By Charlotte Jones
Sherman Oaks, California

"Although you have not seen [Christ], you love him, and even though you do not see him now, you believe in him and rejoice with an indescribably and glorious joy, for you are receiving the outcome of your faith, the salvation of your souls."—I Peter 1:8–9 NRSV

Truly my heart had been filled with joy. My stay at World Conference was with a dear friend who had moved to Independence. It was good to visit with Opal like old times. The mutuality of common values in the gospel brought rich experiences like no others. We attended Conference sessions as we were able. The Daily Prayer for Peace and recital afterward were so rewarding. I wish all could have attended. The Spirit of Christ was evident in the planned sessions we were able to attend or watch on television. It made me feel the church is active in carrying the message of Christ into all the world. I was fed spiritually.

Like frosting on the cake, Opal's daughter, Pam, picked us up for a stay at her house with seven dogs, three cats, and two ferrets. As an animal lover with congenial company, I came away refreshed, having experienced the love of Christ in both humans and other creatures. There are no words to completely relay the joy I experienced. The memories will be a reservoir to draw on in down times. They were based on sharing love with the Divine, humans, and nature in general. They remind me that it is with Christ that love is kept alive in all situations, and that builds a community of joy.

Sing for Peace: No. 14, "For Beauty of Meadows"

Prayer Thought: We offer our praise and thanksgiving to you, Lord, for the many blessings of love shown in friends and creatures. May we be instrumental so that others may share in this joy.

<table>
<tr><td>Sunday
18
April</td><td>**Led by the Spirit**
By Merna Short
Melbourne, Australia</td><td></td></tr>
</table>

"But grow in the grace and knowledge of our Lord and Savior Jesus Christ. To him be glory both now and forever! Amen."—II Peter 3:18 NIV

We had been corresponding with Ans and her son Sander for four years after touring up the center of Australia. Now they were again in our country and we could renew our friendship. They had just come from a tour of New Zealand. It had been enjoyable except for one incident—a thief had stolen some of their possessions.

Ans said, "I had this strange feeling during dinner that I should go to our room. I dismissed it momentarily but it persisted. I spoke to Sander about it. He said he felt the same. 'Let's go,' we said and immediately left the company. Only a camera and a small sum of money were taken. We had disturbed the intruder."

From our correspondence, I knew she was strong in her faith. Deciding I had nothing to lose and that the Lord had an opportunity here, I said, "I believe that was a prompting because of your faith."

"Yes. I believe it was, too. I only wish I had been quicker to respond. I should have known."

Talking later, she said that when her husband died she had asked many questions in her heart facing the short length of our mortality. She said, "I asked myself, *Where is he? What do I believe about God and his creation?*

I realized in my search we can never know all there is to know or understand everything about God. I am more of a Christian now than I would have been without this experience. I am more mature in my faith."

During our conversation we talked about our minute spot in the galaxy and the wonder of God. I shared that we believe in God revealing himself and that part of our modern-day revelation says, "and there is no end to my works, neither to my words."

Ans stood from the table and came around to me with her arms outstretched. "I must embrace you," she said. "It was not by chance we met." I felt so happy for the opportunity given to me to witness on that day.

Hymns of the Saints: No. 301, "O God, Our Source of Truth"

Prayer Thought: Lord, we thank you for the prompting of your Spirit, which gives us the opportunity to share with others.

| Monday **19** April | **A Lovely Surprise** By Shirley Vallier Remmenga Fort Collins, Colorado | |

"He sends out his word, and melts them; he makes his wind blow, and the waters flow."—Psalm 147:18 NRSV

Tiny flowers, white and perfect, seemingly jumped out at me from among the hundreds of dried leaves lying there on the forest floor. I could have crushed them under my shoes had I not looked down at just the right moment.

I knelt down and looked at them more closely, marveling at their presence and their beauty. The life force within the mother plant had awakened from its winter nap and had, with determination and strength, pushed the rusty old leaves aside as it reached for the sun. Then with the joy of new growth, it had produced these lovely little flowers.

What a nice surprise. What a beautiful living picture it made for the world to see, and I happened to be one of the lucky ones to see it. I got up with sunshine in my heart and practically ran out of the forest. I knew I had received a little "I love you" reminder from God.

Hymns of the Saints: No. 29, "With Happy Voices Ringing"

Prayer Thought: Loving God, our hearts overflow in those special moments when we are profoundly aware of your love as revealed in the wonders of your creation. May we be so touched by your Spirit that we can't help but reach out in joy to others.

<table>
<tr><td>Tuesday
20
April</td><td>**Attaining New Heights**
By Denzil J. West
Independence, Missouri</td><td></td></tr>
</table>

"Wherefore, seeing we are compassed about with so great a cloud of witnesses, let us lay aside every weight, and the sin which doth so easily beset us, and let us run with patience the race that is set before us."—Hebrews 12:1

When our children were small, we took them for an afternoon outing to a nearby park. It was a beautiful, warm fall day, and we thought that this might be the last warm day before a cold winter.

The children bolted from one activity to another, and we watched as our youngest looked longingly at the steps of the slide and down its long, slippery surface. Eric must have been wondering if he also could climb that long ladder before him. At age eighteen months, this must have been an awesome challenge. His mom and I said, "You can do it, son. Climb on up and slide down." Gingerly he started up. Holding tightly to the handrails, he placed one foot on the next step and pulled himself up. "You can do it, Eric," we called. He continued on, one step at a time until he had only four more steps to go, and then he froze.

By now his older sisters were at the bottom of the slide saying, "Come on, Eric." Again one more step and then another, until finally he sat down at the top. He took a deep breath and then slid down into our waiting arms. We scooped him up, and a big smile came across his face. He had done something that had seemed impossible, but with a great cloud of (family) witnesses supporting him, he had succeeded.

How many times has Jesus been rooting for us to try harder? And his voice calls out to us, "You can do it. Lo, I am with you always." He is the one in whom we can always place our trust.

Hymns of the Saints: No. 376, "We Are Living, We Are Dwelling"

Prayer Thought: We are grateful, Lord Jesus, for your promise that you will always be with us. May we trust you to help us achieve our goals.

"There is no fear in love; but perfect love casteth out fear."
—I John 4:18

Love can overcome fear, distrust, and misunderstanding, but it takes courage. The best illustration I know of this is a little book I used to read to my children. Jesus used simple stories or parables in his teaching, and I find many parables in the children's library. The book is titled *There's a Nightmare in My Closet* by Mercer Mayer. The little boy who is the subject of this book learned how to best solve problems and face fears.

Every night there was an ugly monster in the little boy's bedroom closet. First he tried barricading the closet door. Then he put on an army helmet and surrounded himself with toy guns and cannons. When the monster came out, the boy threatened to shoot him. The monster began to cry, and the little boy realized that he was really a lonely, frightened creature who needed to be comforted. Finally he decided to invite the monster to get in bed with him. The illustration on the last page of the book is precious. It shows the other monsters in the closet looking longingly through the door at the two of them sleeping peacefully, tucked in the same bed.

As that wise little boy showed compassion to his imagined enemy, he discovered some profound truths. He learned that love is better than violence in making an enemy into a friend. He learned that understanding can tear down walls of fear and hate. He learned that others don't have to change before we accept them. And most of all, he learned that it sometimes takes courage to reach out in love, especially to what frightens you.

Sing for Peace: No. 46, "Peace for Everyone"

Prayer Thought: Lord, as we look at those who are less than lovely, reveal to us their fear and insecurity and show us how to accept what they have to offer.

Thursday **22** April	**Devoted Example** By Russell Grinnell Cookeville, Tennessee	

"...and all should consecrate of their talents, abilities, and substance for the prosecution of the great work intrusted to us."—Doctrine and Covenants 133:3b

My father and my grandmother were baptized together when he was eight years old. My grandfather was a good, honorable man, but he never joined the church.

When World War I came along, my father and four other young men from the church he attended went into the army. One Wednesday night, the pastor, under the influence of the Spirit, told the congregation that each of the boys would return home safely after the war, and each of them did. Shortly after my father returned home, he saw an ad in the newspaper from U.S. Rubber Co. in Detroit, saying they needed workers, so my father went to Detroit to work in the rubber plant.

After he got settled he decided to look up the church, and there he saw a young woman he had seen at the plant. She became my mother. Priest Arthur Peer performed the wedding ceremony for my parents. Arthur and his wife were leading the church in Juniata, Michigan. When the Peers moved to Independence, Missouri, my father, who had been called to elder, took Arthur's place. My mother's parents were caring for their two younger boys. When my mother's parents died, my parents moved to care for the boys.

For many years, my father served as pastor. It was a struggle, and he did most of the preaching. He held meetings for the youth and would walk the young girls home by the light of a kerosene lantern so they wouldn't be bothered by the neighborhood boys. We had moved to Juniata on an eighty-acre farm east of the church. The neighborhood boys would throw green apples at the cows while my father was milking. But when the boys grew up, several of them asked my father to perform their wedding ceremonies. One time my father came in from the field in the middle of the afternoon to marry a young couple in his overalls and then went back to the field and continued his work. And he would drop whatever he was doing to go and administer to someone.

He and my mother were always helping the less fortunate. The railroad ran through our backyard, and sometimes hobos would stop to get a meal. One even stayed all night.

During World War II, my dad worked at the Buick plant on tanks. He worked there for twenty years. He rode back and forth with several men who worked there. When the conversation wasn't very desirable, he would turn it to something more uplifting. He taught them the capitals of each state and from time to time would quiz them. By the time he retired, the men couldn't be fooled on the capitals.

Only once when I was growing up did my parents take a vacation. They ministered to many people during their lifetimes.

Hymns of the Saints: No. 425, "God Send Us Saints"

Prayer Thought: God who calls us to serve, help each of us to minister to the needs of others as others have ministered to our needs. May we do so without any thought of what we will receive in return.

"So if anyone is in Christ, there is a new creation: every-thing old has passed away; see, everything has become new! All this is from God, who reconciled us to himself through Christ, and has given us the ministry of reconciliation."
—II Corinthians 5:17–18 NRSV

The leaves of pin oaks cling to the trees all winter, as though they must hang on and stay just as long as pos-sible. In fact they do stay until the new leaves come out and force the old ones to let go. By May, the oaks have brand-new leaves; they have shed the old ones and look refreshed and clean.

Are we this way with our sins? Can we have Christ in our lives and still cling to sin? No, to have new life we must let go of the old and allow Christ to cleanse us. We then become new and completely refreshed.

Hymns of the Saints: No. 108, "Forgive Our Sins as We Forgive"

Prayer Thought: Lord, we praise you for your transform-ing power. Make our hearts new and ever in tune with you.

<table>
<tr><td>Saturday
24
April</td><td>**Coming Home**
By Shirley S. Case
Slater, Missouri</td><td></td></tr>
</table>

"For this my son was dead, and is alive again; he was lost, and is found. And they began to be merry."—Luke 15:24

Our family has been blessed twofold this summer. A niece had moved to Kentucky to live despite all our objections. We tried to reason with her, but her mind was made up. She just wouldn't listen, as teens are wont to do when they are determined to try their wings.

One evening three months later, I received a phone call at work from a crying niece saying, "Aunt Shirley, I want to come home. You are my only hope." I vowed we'd get her here somehow. My sister and her husband and Carl and I got her a ticket to come home by bus. We anxiously awaited her at the bus stop, and we squealed, hugged, kissed, and lovingly looked each other over. There were no "I told you so's." She shared stories with Carl and me. And as she did, I thought to myself, "This must be what the father of the prodigal son felt like."

Then a few days ago, we got a call from an aunt telling us her son had come home. Our aunt is of Cherokee lineage, and a month before, when he had called her, she said she had had a vision that her son was sick or dying. In fact she thought him to be dead. She was sick with worry, hadn't seen this son in two years, and didn't know where he was. As she told us this, I gazed on her beautiful face and saw worry lines where trails of tears had traveled. And I prayed God would ease this little mother's heart.

Two weeks later, she received a phone call from a treatment center in Minnesota telling her that her son was there and very sick. She brought him home to care for him. He is still very sick but theirs is a haven of love and tenderness for him.

This is just a small bit of news in a big world of prodigal sons and daughters. But as we each experience it in our own lives, we realize how God must feel when we finally return.

Sing a New Song: No. 41, "On Eagle's Wings"

Prayer Thought: Merciful God, thank you for the wisdom and tenderness it takes to recognize the weary traveler, the bruised and the brokenhearted. May our arms be open wide to our brothers and sisters, just as if our arms were indeed your arms.

| Sunday **25** April | **The Child Inside**
By Ardith Lancaster
Paisley, Florida | |

"Be a joyful people. Laugh and play and sing, embodying the hope and freedom of the gospel."
—Doctrine and Covenants 161:1b

Visible from the dining hall at Deerhaven Campground in Florida is the children's play area. During a quiet time, the sight of the tall slide brought back pleasant memories. We were having a deck added to the back of our house in Tennessee. I asked the builder one morning if he could include a slide from the side of the deck with a six-foot drop. "Of course," he assured me. On my arrival home from work that afternoon, the slide was in place. Thinking I would be the first to try it out, to my disappointment, the builder and his helper had already gone down. My reason for wanting the slide was for my grandchildren, of course.

At another church reunion grounds, in Foundry Hill, Tennessee, there was a playground with a tall slide, also. There is a treasured picture on my wall of our granddaughter, Chelsea, then only about two and a half, as she was about to step on the top platform of that slide before going down. She has a very determined look on her face, and standing immediately behind her is her grandfather, Arnold. He had encouraged her to not give up. She had climbed partway up several times, only to go back down. As I remember, her father, Arnold Jr., had stationed himself at the side to ensure her safe ride. The look of pride of achievement and pleasure on her grandfather's face depicts the joy God must feel to watch all of us when we have successes in which we have been encouraged.

When we enjoy the gift of life, when we find joy in this earthly experience, one way we can show our appreciation is to never let go of the child inside.

Hymns of the Saints: No. 44, "Come, Rejoice Before Your Maker"

Prayer Thought: Thank you, God, for the joy you give us when we find the treasure of laughter and play. Help us to be a joy to those we meet today.

Monday **26** April	**Prayer Power** By Ken Hall Renton, Washington	

"The prayer of the righteous is powerful and effective."
—James 5:16 NRSV

For twenty-five years, I was a police officer in the city where I lived. Sometimes friends would call me for advice or help concerning law enforcement issues.

One day, a good friend from our congregation, Ruth Porter, called me. She said she had inadvertently locked her keys inside her car. She wanted to know if I could possibly help in getting the car door open. I told her I would be right down to see what I could do. I have my own "Slim Jim" tool for just this sort of occasion. The only problem was that at best my success rate was only about 50 percent in getting cars unlocked.

I arrived at her home and worked very hard for about twenty minutes or so. I was about to tell Ruth that I just could not get the car unlocked. When I turned to Ruth, I could see that her head was bowed and her eyes were closed; she was obviously praying. I thought, *Well, I cannot tell her just yet.* I turned to the car door to make yet another attempt to open it. Immediately on trying, the door opened. There were grateful smiles and a show of relief from both of us. A faithful prayer is indeed powerful.

Hymns of the Saints: No. 312, "Let Us Pray for One Another"

Prayer Thought: Lord, may we always seek your help through prayer when we have problems that we cannot solve. Teach us to trust in your Spirit to guide and bless us.

Love—God's Panacea
By Elaine Olson
Porcupine Plain,
Saskatchewan, Canada

"Love is patient, love is kind. It does not envy, it does not boast, it is not proud. It is not rude, it is not self-seeking, it is not easily angered, it keeps no record of wrongs. Love does not delight in evil but rejoices with the truth. It always protects, always trusts, always hopes, always perseveres."
—I Corinthians 13:4–7 NIV

We were on our way home from Moose Jaw. We had gone there to pick up Gary, our three-month-old son, the very day (July 7, 1953) that was also our fifth wedding anniversary. We stopped over at Govan and were visiting at Ev and Lloyd Hamilton's home. I sat with Gary on my lap, holding him so he was facing me.

He looked at me so intently, his brown eyes sparkling, and Grandma Olson said, "Look at him—you'd almost think he already knew she is his mother." We never can read the mind of a child, especially when they are so young, but if after less than twenty-four hours, our little son could comprehend our relationship, he was no more clever than we were. He was already so much a part of us, it was as if he'd always been with us. From the day we knew he was our promised child, months before, we'd prayed for him and loved him.

So much for babyhood response. Fourteen years later, the same brown eyes looked straight through me. By then, the body, stretched to a healthy five-foot eight-inch boy, towered above me. We had just had an ordinary parent–child altercation of some sort, and he voiced his opinion this time. "Mom, you don't know anything!" But he must have measured the remark on some scale of civility, and he modified it by adding, "about horses." I was glad to know I wasn't completely ignorant, and we survived the crisis.

About thirty years later, the same young man, by then married and the father of two teenagers of his own, came to our house. On entering, the first thing he said was, "Mom, do you remember when you didn't know anything?" We both had a hearty laugh, and I said, "It's all coming back to you now, is it?"

Life is such a wonderful learning process! Usually every life makes the complete cycle or as my daughter-in-law says, "What goes around, comes around!" Every generation owes the following one enrichment as it gleans from experience, learning, and the legacy of testimony.

Sing for Peace: No. 17, "To Live at Peace with Others"

Prayer Thought: When we face moments of anger and doubt in our families, let love surface, Lord, to keep us close. Assist us as we try to share what we have learned with those who follow us.

Wednesday **28** April	**A Way to Remember God** By Elaine Linné Tigard, Oregon	

"The wind blows where it wills, and you hear the sound of it, but you do not know whence it comes or whither it goes; so it is with every one who is born of the Spirit."
—John 3:8 RSV

Nailed to the doorframe of my kitchen door is a mezuzah. It is a small plaque containing a very small scroll that one nails on the main doorframe of one's house. It is used by some Jewish families as a reminder of their faith. It is on my kitchen doorframe because that is where I enter my house from the attached garage.

It is a way of remembering the words in Deuteronomy 6:4–7, 9, which command the people of Israel to put God above all else:

> Hear, O Israel: The Lord our God is one Lord; and you shall love the Lord your God with all your heart, with all your soul, and with all your strength. And these words which I command you this day shall be in your heart; you shall teach them diligently to your children, and shall talk of them when you sit in your house, and when you walk by the way, and when you lie down, and when you rise. And you shall write them on the doorposts of your house and on your gates.

On entering the house, one kisses the hand and touches the mezuzah, saying, "Peace to those who enter. Peace to those within." The peace found within a dwelling starts in the hearts of those living there, with a desire to work toward peaceful ends. Basically it is a challenge of surrendering oneself to the will of God and seeking tranquility and harmony as we open our hearts to the "breath" of God's Holy Spirit.

Hymns of the Saints: No. 179, "Breathe on Me, Breath of God"

Prayer Thought: God of all generations, teach us to find ways of remembering you daily, that your Spirit may dwell with us wherever we live and guide us in your ways.

Thursday **29** April	**Time Choices** By Beulah Foster Marlette, Michigan	

"Thou shalt not idle away thy time; neither shalt thou bury thy talent that it may not be known."

—Doctrine and Covenants 60:3e

Sometimes I get so stressed out from so many demands on my time. It causes me headaches, muscle tension, and apprehension. When I'm asked to do something, it is difficult for me to say no. I think about my sister, Ruth. She had five children and always took time out to go on picnics at a minute's notice, made them unique Halloween costumes, and made birthday cakes that were beautiful and different. She made their pancakes in shapes or put up a canvas and painted a mural. She always took time to do the really important things in life. It didn't matter whether she had all her household chores done or not; her children always came first. She passed away at fifty and is sorely missed.

The things that her children remember are the great times they had with their mother. It doesn't matter now whether she had all her work done. I will never be as talented as she was, but I can learn from her example. I am trying to set priorities and not become overloaded. When I feel better, I am more relaxed and accomplish much more. God deserves the best service I can give, and I have learned not to become involved in more than I can handle.

Hymns of the Saints: No. 115, "Dear Lord and God of Humankind," verses 1 and 4

Prayer Thought: Tender heavenly Parent, guide us to wisely seek a balance in spending the time you have given us. May our choices of how to spend our time leave a legacy of beautiful memories for others.

| Friday
30
April | **Trust in God's Call**
By Ellen L. Wang
Colville, Washington | |

"For therefore we both labor and suffer reproach, because we trust in the living God, who is the Savior of all men, specially of those that believe."—I Timothy 4:10

After being told repeatedly to get her hands out of a kitchen drawer, the two year old was asked why she didn't listen to her mom and mind her. The little girl frowned as she looked at her mom and very sternly replied, "'Cause I don't want to!"

How many times do we make this comment to God in words or by our actions when we are prompted to follow the Spirit's urging? Learning to accept God's will in our lives, and not insist on having our own way, is a maturing process that takes time and work on our part.

May we learn to trust that the Spirit's urging is the voice we must listen to, for God calls us to serve in his name.

Hymns of the Saints: No. 141, "Father, in Thy Mysterious Presence"

Prayer Thought: Loving Parent, help us learn to trust you with our lives and those of our loved ones. When we hear your call, may we respond positively.

May 2004

S	M	T	W	T	F	S
						1
2	3	4	5	6	7	8
9	10	11	12	13	14	15
16	17	18	19	20	21	22
23	24	25	26	27	28	29
30	31					

<table>
<tr><td>Saturday
1
May</td><td>**Pray Always**
By Martha Harrison
Tucson, Arizona</td><td></td></tr>
</table>

"Rejoice always, pray without ceasing, give thanks in all circumstances; for this is the will of God in Christ Jesus for you. Do not quench the Spirit."
—I Thessalonians 5:16–19 NRSV

It had always seemed a blessing to be in good health and independent as I grew older, free to come and go whenever or wherever I chose. My family lived some distance away, but we maintained a closeness through the use of the telephone and e-mail. We shared the good things about our everyday lives during our conversations but never did I divulge any problems I might be having, for it wasn't my wish to cause them worry.

The time came, however, when I needed some surgery. I confided in a friend, who offered to drive me to and from my appointments. Asserting my independence, as usual, I assured her that I didn't need help, but she insisted, and I reluctantly accepted her offer.

It was during our conversation that she asked if I would be telling my family. "Of course not," I replied, "I don't want to worry them." Being a wise friend, she resisted suggesting that I really should let them know.

It was during the next conversation with my family, however, that I felt guilty in not sharing my medical problems with them. Everything wasn't all right. I was worried. So I reluctantly described the situation to my daughter-in-law. Her reply made me ashamed of my independence and lack of consideration for my family.

"I have just been reading an article about the healing that prayer can bring," she surprised me by saying.

"How can you deny your family the opportunity to pray for you if you don't let us know what is happening?"

Never have I felt so selfish, and then so at peace, knowing that their prayers would be with me, that my distant family could have that wonderful faith-building experience that comes through the use of intercessory prayer.

Sing for Peace: No. 33, "Heal Me, Hands of Jesus"

Prayer Thought: Subdue our fierce, independent spirit, Lord, when we truly need assistance from others. May we learn to welcome the healing support of prayer offered on our behalf.

Sunday **2** May	**Behind Prison Walls** By Florence King Feilding, New Zealand	

"If you forgive anyone, I also forgive him. And what I have forgiven—if there was anything to forgive—I have forgiven in the sight of Christ for your sake."—II Corinthians 2:10

The Sunday evening after Easter weekend 2003, I went with a team of people for outreach at a prison. We were each asked to give a testimony of God's love in our lives. The men we met with in prison had given their lives to Christ. Different groups come in to hold worship and praise services with them in the prison chapel.

When it came my turn to speak, I told them how I had felt as a victim when my handbag was snatched. I told them how it happened, how I felt like a nobody, and then how God had turned it into something positive. You could have heard a pin drop, as each man watched me. I was not frightened, for I felt God's Holy Spirit supporting me.

When I had finished, they all clapped; then when they were leaving to go back to their cells, each one gave me a big hug. I learned that there is a standard of conduct in prisons. The lowest of the low are people who attack children or older people. Afterward, I found I was praying for the young man who had attacked me. He must have been really desperate to do this in broad daylight.

God tells us to forgive those who sin against us. I found I have not only forgiven my attacker, but pray that the time will come when I can meet him face to face to let him know how much Christ loves him. He is the one who needs help. So my prayer is that I will be given the opportunity to witness to him of God's love. At the prison I again was surrounded with love by people who wanted to show how much they really cared.

Sing for Peace: No. 43, "When on Life a Darkness Falls"

Prayer Thought: Lord, lead people to cross our paths so that we may be able to witness about your great love for everyone.

Monday 3 May	**Daily Exercise** By Larry Carroll Glen Easton, West Virginia	

"Bodily exercise is all right, but spiritual exercise is much more important and is a tonic for all you do. So exercise yourself spiritually and practice being a better Christian, because that will help you not only now in this life, but in the next life too."—I Timothy 4:8 LB

For the past several years, I have been riding an exercise cycle in my room. I often pedal twenty miles a day. As a result, I have pedaled more than 19,000 miles since I got the bike!

I balance my physical exercise with spiritual fitness. For example, I read *Daily Bread* every day, attend church regularly, say grace before meals, attend reunions at Camp Bountiful, and do many other things to be spiritually fit.

Each one of us can be more physically and spiritually fit. Let us each do daily whatever we can to stay fit.

Hymns of the Saints: No. 403, "Brothers, Sisters, Let Us Gladly"

Prayer Thought: Our Creator, help us seek to be physically and spiritually stronger every day, that you may use us to bless others.

<table>
<tr><td>Tuesday
4
May</td><td>Seizing the Moment
By Dorothy Premoe
Mesa, Arizona</td><td></td></tr>
</table>

"Whosoever shall not receive the kingdom of God as a little child, shall in no wise enter therein."—Luke 18:17 KJV

My husband, Pete, and I were parked at an auto repair shop in Wells, Nevada, after losing a vital bolt that was anchoring the van on our trailer. The temperature was in the thirties, and it was sleeting. There were puddles everywhere. It wasn't long before a husky repairman, who was wearing rain gear and big boots, came by to help. One of those puddles was directly in his path, so, as most big people do, he tiptoed through it, and I asked myself, *Don't all of us "big" people do that?* Adults see a puddle and assess how far it is around it, how deep it might be in case we have to go through it, and knowing we can't go over it.

Our puddles of life seem to get deeper and wider as our lives move on. We carefully approach and go through on tiptoe, afraid of what will happen next, but not so with children. If you have ever watched children go through puddles, you know that they do it with the exuberance of marathon runners. There is no measured caution but a movement with a purpose. Getting their shoes wet is not a problem but a joy. Their sole purpose in life is to seize the moment.

My prayer is that we, as adults, will be as little children and seize the opportunities of our lives.

Sing for Peace: No. 3, "Gather Your Children"

Prayer Thought: Call us forth, Lord, to lose our fear of "getting our feet wet" as we seize opportunities to savor all of life.

| Wednesday
5
May | **Practicing God's Word**
By Shirley Mallas
Corning, Iowa | |

"Therefore owe no man any thing, but to love one another; for he that loveth another hath fulfilled the law."

—Romans 13:8

My daughter and I took our first trip to Las Vegas, Nevada, in April 2003 for the wedding of my great-niece, Hilery. We spent three full days there and stayed at the Treasure Island hotel, where the wedding was held in the wedding chapel.

Being a stranger in a big city, I discovered, is like being a stranger in a foreign land. We had to ask questions of those we didn't know. We had to trust that those around us were trustworthy. In turn, we had to practice kindness and truthfulness to other strangers by being helpful if we had already discovered a way or place that someone else was now seeking. The distance from one place to another on the Vegas Strip was deceiving. We learned that the city transit system was reasonably priced but correct change was a rule; those who did not have the correct change had to trust a friend or stranger to quickly exchange currency for the correct amount, or be left behind at the bus stop.

My sister, Virginia, who works at the Excalibur hotel, took us sightseeing on her day off. Through the eyes of a Vegas resident, I discovered that one of the most upsetting things to a driver was pedestrians who crossed the street at crosswalks after the "Walk" sign turned red. Many of the Vegas guests seemed not to realize or care that they were putting their safety at risk and causing stress in the life of the drivers.

Having come from a small town to a city of over half a million was a learning experience. What I learned was that God's word, put into practice, works anyplace. Being loving, caring, kind, gentle, patient, and trustworthy to all those around you no matter who they are, their age, or whatever their reason for being in that particular place, be it as a visitor, vacationer, resident, or employee, is honoring God's love.

Hymns of the Saints: No. 284, "Gracious Spirit, Dwell with Me"

Prayer Thought: May our hearts always acknowledge your presence in our lives, God, wherever we may be in the world.

| Thursday **6** May | **Born of Goodly Parents** By Dianne Lyell Guinn Paris, Tennessee | |

"I Nephi, having been born of goodly parents, therefore I was taught somewhat in all the learning of my father."
—I Nephi 1:1

As I write this, my nation is engaged in military action in Iraq. While listening to the daily reports, I went back in my mind to my childhood. The day that World War II ended, I remember my father listening to the news on the Philco radio in our living room. He turned the radio off, turned to the family and said, "Let's have prayer." One of my earliest memories of my childhood was kneeling beside a straight-back chair and thanking our heavenly Father for the end to the war.

This was the first memory I have of our family prayers together, because it was a special time in our nation. There were countless other times we prayed together as a family, as my parents taught me to trust in God and to give God praise and thanksgiving. For this reason I can identify with Nephi in the Book of Mormon when he mentions that he was born of "goodly parents." I trust that my own sons can say the same for their childhood. At least, we gave it our best.

We are all the family of God. May we each reach out to our brothers and sisters to share with them the love that has been shared with us.

Hymns of the Saints: No. 447, "Would You Bless Our Homes"

Prayer Thought: Heavenly Father, thank you for all those who have shared your love with us. May we share that goodness wherever we find your children in need and hurting.

<table>
<tr><td>Friday
7
May</td><td>**Gifts from the Heart**
By Helen M. Green
Toledo, Ohio</td><td></td></tr>
</table>

"Who can find a virtuous woman? for her price is far above rubies.... She looketh well to the ways of her household, and eateth not the bread of idleness. Her children arise up, and call her blessed; her husband also, and he praiseth her."
—Proverbs 31:10, 27–28

Three weeks before Mother's Day, my "other" daughter's mother fell and broke her hip. She was eighty-six years old, blind, and suffered from diabetes and congestive heart failure. Patti's days and nights were spent at her mother's bedside. Mother's Day was put on hold until a more opportune time for celebration.

When I talked with her the next day to get an update on her mother's condition, she told me she had received the best Mother's Day gift of her life. When she came home from the hospital late in the afternoon, her three daughters had prepared a spaghetti dinner, cleaned her house, and folded the laundry. The one daughter who still lived at home proudly displayed that she had cleaned her bedroom. Patti said that no gift-wrapped package she had ever received was as precious as her daughters giving of themselves and the awareness that their mother needed a rest.

The best gifts are free; they require effort from the giver; they touch the heart of the receiver; and their value cannot be measured in monetary terms. And usually, they are given through the example of others.

Hymns of the Saints: No. 415, "Help Us Express Your Love"

Prayer Thought: We thank you, heavenly Parent, for the gift of mothers who give so freely of their love and service. We are grateful for the life they gave us and for the example of faith that brings us into a worshipful relationship with you. Help us to pass it on.

| Saturday
8
May | **Kindnesses Are Always Remembered**
By Dorene Kilburn
St. Paul's Station, Ontario, Canada | |

"As God's chosen ones, holy and beloved, clothe yourselves with compassion, kindness, humility, meekness, and patience.... And whatever you do, in word or deed, do everything in the name of the Lord Jesus, giving thanks to God the Father through him."

—Colossians 3:12, 17 NRSV

My husband and I recently decided to go for breakfast to a restaurant we hadn't been to for many years. It's Madeline's, named after the woman who opened it almost twenty years ago. I wasn't even sure she'd be there, but as we were eating, I saw her sitting in a booth at the far end of the restaurant. I felt compelled to go to her and tell her of a kindness I have never forgotten.

My parents had moved into a smaller apartment and my father died just eleven days later. Shortly after that, Madeline's Restaurant opened just a block away, and one day Mom and I went there for lunch. As we paid our bill at the cash register, we were telling Madeline that Dad had just died and Mom was now alone in her little apartment. Madeline immediately reached to a stack of brown bags, used for take-out muffins and doughnuts. She wrote her phone number on one, handed it to my mother, and said to her, "If you ever need someone, here's my phone number—call me." My mother was a total stranger to Madeline, but she was willing to make

166

herself available to Mom, if she was needed. This simple offer was true Christian kindness.

How often in our lives have we been the recipient of someone's small act of caring that we have never forgotten? How often have we spontaneously responded to another's need, and created a memory for that person that will never be forgotten?

Hymns of the Saints: No. 443, "Jesus' Hands Were Kind Hands"

Prayer Thought: Compassionate Lord, we know that the smallest act of kindness can bring affirmation and healing to another's life, and we would not miss an opportunity to be a blessing to one of your creation.

Sunday **9** May	**Mothers and Daughters** By Janice Townsend Spokane, Washington

"Love does not delight in evil but rejoices with the truth. It always protects, always trusts, always hopes, always perseveres. Love never fails."—I Corinthians 13:6–8 NIV

Receiving mail can be a highlight of the day, especially when we open an envelope and find treasure such as my daughter sent me last year after Mother's Day. Kerry had enclosed two clippings from the newsletter published by her congregation. I smiled as I read the first short article: "A few months ago," Kerry had written, "I was brushing my hair and looked in the mirror and saw my mom looking back at me. I realized that as I am getting older I am beginning to look more and more like my mom." Kerry finished the selection by saying, "My mom is a beautiful person and I'm so thankful that when I look in the mirror I see her looking back at me because that means she has given me the best gift possible—herself."

Any mother would appreciate such a loving compliment, but I knew even more joy when I read the second article, written by Kerry's daughter. "What do I think about my mom?" wrote Michele. "Goofy jokes. Escapes to the beach. Gardening. Smiles. Long phone conversations—I talk for hours, Mom listens. Quiet patience. Chinese food and 'chick flicks.' Lover of hugs. Fun-loving. Determined. Comforting. For all these things and more—love you, Mom!"

I am grateful for the thread of love that binds the generations of our family together, and I pray that I will never neglect my calling as a mother and grandmother. I will safeguard the sacred things I have seen, keep them in my heart, and share them continually with my children and with every child of God.

Hymns of the Saints: No. 434, "When God Created Human Life"

Prayer Thought: Divine Parent, thank you for the love that binds us to you and to each other. May we faithfully fulfill our family roles in ways that honor you and help bring your purposes to fruition.

<table>
<tr><td>Monday
10
May</td><td>**Loaves and Fishes**
By Shirley E. Phillips
Independence, Missouri</td><td></td></tr>
</table>

"And when he had taken the five loaves and two fishes, he looked up to heaven, and blessed, and broke the loaves, and gave to his disciples to set before the multitude; and the two fishes divided he among them all. And they did all eat and were filled."—Mark 6:43–44 IV

The walls and ceilings of our house needed repainting. This task was impossible for me to do, since I have lived from a wheelchair for the past ten years.

One day two friends visited me. "We want to do something nice for you. You enjoy doing volunteer work at the Temple and the school. May we have the joy of volunteering for you and paint your house? You buy the paint, and we'll furnish the labor."

I couldn't believe it.

They painted my bedroom walls lavender and the ceiling white. They picked out a wall trim of purple grapes with lavender flowers surrounded by green leaves on a white background. They asked a very close friend (a professional paperhanger) to assist them. He agreed and donated his labor.

The three of them worked hard. When they were preparing to cover the last foot of the wall, they ran out of paper. Only small scraps remained. They were trying to decide what to do.

I rolled into the room to see how it looked. "It's so beautiful," I said excitedly. Glancing down, I pointed and asked, "What is that on the floor under my computer table?" The paperhanger checked and exclaimed, "Where did that come from? It matches the pattern where we stopped. It's the exact length. Forty-five feet

169

of border has just covered forty-six feet of wall. It's the loaves and fishes parable."

God had supplied our need. We were grateful.

Hymns of the Saints: No. 125, "My Shepherd Will Supply My Need"

Prayer Thought: Lord, may we appreciate more deeply those times of special blessing in our daily living.

| Tuesday **11** May | **Hold On in Hope**
 By Barrie Fox
 Kirkby in Ashfield, England | |

"Be steadfast and trust in the instructions which have been given for your guidance. I will be with you and strengthen you for the tasks that lie ahead if you will continue to be faithful and commit yourselves without reservation to the building of my kingdom."
—Doctrine and Covenants 153:9c

Illustrations appropriately used in sermons and addresses have always fascinated me and often given me food for thought. One I heard used recently fit so well into the ideas that were being presented and triggered for me some useful and challenging thoughts.

We were told of an electrical power circuit failure in a hospital wing, which, among other things, stopped the main elevator mid-floors. One of the male occupants in the elevator started to become agitated, and one of the other occupants trapped in that small space with him sought to calm him down. "All will be sorted out shortly," he said, "once the maintenance man restores the power." The anxious one quickly retorted, "But I am the maintenance man!"

How often in life do we find ourselves "trapped" in places where we just do not want to be at that particular time? Such is life, but there is food for thought!

The occupants of that elevator didn't know when they would be freed from their plight. Similarly, in many of the things that we come up against in life, we just don't know how soon that health problem will disappear, that relationship problem will be resolved, or that financial difficulty will be put right. However, if we are true to our Christian beliefs, this we do know, we will be willing to hold on in hope and faith.

Hymns of the Saints: No. 160, "God Is My Strong Salvation"

Prayer Thought: Sustaining God, when all seems bleak, frightening, or profoundly trying, renew our faith in your knowledge of our difficulties and your presence with us in the midst of it all.

Wednesday
12
May

That We Might Not Forget
By Charles Kornman
Grand Junction, Colorado

"For the Lord hears the needy, and does not despise his own that are in bonds. Let heaven and earth praise him...."
—Psalm 69:33–34 NRSV

Lately I've discovered that when I find things I've lost (my checkbook was in the car), hard on the heels of "Ahha!" it is so natural to say, "Thank you." God's use of our memory is an interesting phenomenon. He did promise that "I will bring all things to your mind."

Often during visits to Denmark I would go to a restaurant to get a sandwich tray. Usually there are two levels. One has several kinds of Danish bread. The other level

171

has what in Danish is called, "that which is laid on the bread." Often on these trays (perhaps only in Denmark) is a small jar of plain lard. I once asked a Danish friend why this jar of lard. His answer: "Danes who lived during the Nazi occupation of their homeland often finish their sandwich feast with a taste of lard. It reminds us of a time when that was all we had to put on our bread. This is our way of reminding us of how good we've got it now."

So as I write and remember, I bow my head in gratitude in awareness of God's presence in my life and how good I've got it. I try not to ask God to be present, but I do ask for awareness of that eternal presence.

Now back to my lost pocketknife, which I just found: *Thank you, God, for all the things that so mysteriously appear such as memories of how you have blessed us.*

Hymns of the Saints: No. 74, "Thank You for Giving Me the Morning"

Prayer Thought: Almighty Creator, we thank you for every time you have helped us remember the blessings of our lives. Make us keenly aware of your presence.

| Thursday **13** May | **Lessons in a Shell** By Carol Hyden Lamoni, Iowa | |

"Train up a child in the way he should go; and when he is old, he will not depart from it."—Proverbs 22:6

It never ceases to amaze me how God teaches lessons about life through nature.

Brian brought a few of the seashells he had collected into the office. He was telling me the story about how he found them. Occasionally he even has a sermon that he shares about them. When he asked me if I wanted one, I had a hard time choosing. Finally, I decided on a small perfectly shaped one with no flaws that my eyes could see. Then I noticed one that was far from the prettiest in the collection, but I could see it had weathered many storms. It had barnacles of all sizes inside and out.

As I held this shell, I thought of how beautiful it looked and about the habits in our lives, good and bad, that take years to form. Just as barnacles are hard to pry loose, habits are difficult to remove because they have been attached for a long time. They start out small. We don't even notice that a habit is forming because it is just a comfortable way of doing something.

But as we perform a behavior routinely, it attaches itself to us more firmly and begins to grow, soon becoming a part of who we are. Habits can either distort our thinking and dim our inner light, or they can disciple and reshape us in positive ways.

Christian concepts are like those barnacles. The more completely we incorporate them into our lives, the better protected we are against the storms of life. In those tender years when we start to learn about Christ, it is important to learn the basics well so they will stick to us and multiply. When the storms of life hit, we have something to cushion and protect us.

Hymns of the Saints: No. 52, "This Is My Father's World"

Prayer Thought: We thank you for the gospel, living Lord, which illuminates our understanding of life.

<table>
<tr><td>Friday
14
May</td><td>**Weekend of Renewal**
By Mark E. Megee
East Windsor, New Jersey</td><td></td></tr>
</table>

"Heed the urgent call to become a global family united in the name of the Christ, committed in love to one another, seeking the kingdom for which you yearn and to which you have always been summoned."
—Doctrine and Covenants 161:6b

Have you ever looked into the eyes of a child and seen excitement and enthusiasm? For one weekend out of the year, the men of my congregation take the kids camping. The timing seems perfect—the third weekend of May—the weekend after Mother's Day and just before Memorial Day. I've always seen that excitement and enthusiasm in the families as they prepare for the camping trip.

The men are excited as they return to nature—no fax machines, no Internet, not a lot of luxury, but some good food, sometimes good fishing, and a lot of laughter and fellowship. The women are excited to have time to themselves. The children are excited as they fellowship and are able to be little children without concern for getting their Sunday-best clothes messed up, or for making too much noise during the service. It's a win-win situation for everybody.

Chores are divided among the men without any squabble—each according to his ability and health. The children are supervised by everyone. In that one weekend, Zion is realized and shared. No harsh words, no complaining. And each year it keeps getting bigger and bigger. More and more people wanted to be included. One of the simplest "kingdom" principles is shown through the simplest method: by doing it and living it.

Sing for Peace: No. 9, "Bring Forth the Kingdom"

Prayer Thought: God of joy, call us to renewed, creative living that ministers to the needs of all. Lead us to embrace the call to Zionic principles and thereby discover joy.

| Saturday **15** May | **The Lord Has Blessed Me Indeed** By Jacqueline Crawford Independence, Missouri | |

"But, behold, verily, verily I say unto you, that mine eyes are upon you: I am in your midst and ye cannot see me...."
—Doctrine and Covenants 38:2a–b

My eyes hurt and reading was very difficult. The ophthalmologist had diagnosed my condition as *blepharites meibomitis.* The oil glands under my eyes had developed scar tissue, and my eyes were not getting the protection afforded by healthy, functioning glands. My doctor advised me to apply warm compresses to my eyes several times a day for relief from the pain. He also prescribed drops for dry eyes. He said that nothing else could be done.

I decided that I could live with this and used the time applying compresses as a special prayer time. Sitting quietly with eyes closed actually proved to be a blessing to me and with this extra quiet time of sweet meditation, I seemed rejuvenated. During this period, I started repeating the Prayer of Jabez. It is a powerful prayer. It begins, "Lord, bless me indeed..." This prayer does not limit God. Often we are blessed in ways we could never anticipate.

Months passed and my mind was preoccupied with surgeries scheduled to remove a basal cell cancer growing on the side of my nose. I requested administration. The gift of laying on of hands brought me peace. The surgery went well; however, a second biopsy found a second cancer. This time it was a squamous cell at the base of my lower right eyelid. So again, I requested the ministry of laying on of hands. God blessed me, and again everything went well.

My attention had been diverted by my surgeries, and I realized one day that I had no longer been using warm compresses on my eyes. I also realized that I was nearly pain free. This to me was a miracle. Even though I had not asked for a healing of the oil glands, the Lord had blessed me according to my needs. Nearly a year later now, my eyes are normal and pain free. In faith, we all should praise the Lord and ask for God's blessing and healing.

Sing a New Song: No. 27, "Lay Your Hands"

Prayer Thought: Lord whose touch healed so many, lead us to seek you out through the laying on of hands. As we leave our condition with you, may we find peace and blessing.

| Sunday **16** May | **Shaping the Stone** By Eileen Turner Portland, Oregon | |

"The heavens are telling the glory of God; and the firmament proclaims his handiwork."—Psalm 19:1 RSV

During a Sunday service, the special music was presented by a young man in our congregation. The theme of his rendition was, "Every drop of water shapes the stone." The image that brought to my mind was of a time when my family and I traveled to a cave at Akiyoshi-do,

Japan, in the inland area of Yamaguchi Prefecture with our Japanese friends. There, we were able to behold the wonder and beauty of creation. Over hundreds, perhaps thousands of years, the stalactites and stalagmites that had evolved from the perpetual dripping of moisture created a virtual forest of icicle-shaped formations of gigantic proportions. The beauty was awesome.

Don Michael Hudson, a founding member of CAST (Center for Arts, Social Justice, and Theology) believes that scripture tells us there is no difference between the sacred and secular. At any moment, that which is secular can become sacred, and anything sacred can become secular. When the beauty of a landscape, or the caves I've described, moves me, I see the sacred in it. It is a memory that stays with me. I know I have been touched by the finger of God.

How we live our lives should represent "God within us." Every small act of kindness shapes who we are, just as every drop of water shapes the stone.

Hymns of the Saints: No. 14, "O God, Whose Presence Glows in All"

Prayer Thought: Lord, let the beauty and kindness we share this day shape the lives of those we encounter.

Dancing for Joy
By Lillian Bayless Kirby
Blue Springs, Missouri

"Praise him with the timbrel and dance; praise him with stringed instruments and organs…. Let everything that hath breath praise the Lord. Praise ye the Lord."

—Psalm 150:4, 6

For six years, I have provided daycare for three of my grandchildren three days a week in my home. There have been days of joy as we followed a relaxed schedule of meals, outdoor play time, indoor games, puzzles, crafts, and very little television time. They especially enjoy my piano playing as they sing along with me. I even took a children's CPR course at a local hospital in case an unexpected emergency should arise. Thanks to the good Lord, I have not had to use that information.

An e-mail friend sent a "SMILE" letter to me over my computer. A catchy tune of "Rockin' Robin" accompanied the reminder of our friendship. The children watched it and listened intently. They suddenly started jumping up and down and joyfully broke into dancing around the computer room. Such joy and movement in their little bodies I had not seen before. They twirled and twisted with happiness and youthful glee. Laughter filled the room as they swung round and round in time to the music.

Filled with the Holy Spirit, I then knew that the kingdom of God would be like that moment in time, filled with the holy dance of innocent children.

Sing a New Song: No. 23, "Jesus Gives Me Joy"

Prayer Thought: Bless innocent children, Lord, as they dance for joy and bring happiness to our lives.

A Clear Lens
By Charlotte Jones
Sherman Oaks, California

*"God is our refuge and strength, a present help in trouble....
Be still, and know that I am God."*—Psalm 46:1, 10

It was amazing to me how much better I could see.
I had cleaned the lenses of my glasses with a special
cleaning liquid and wiped them with a special cloth.
Things looked sharper, only because the cloudy lenses
were cleaned. It occurred to me how sometimes our
spiritual sight gets clouded with "things" like the rush
of time and all the potential choices based on diverse
factors that confuse and influence us. Sometimes our
spiritual lenses need cleaning so we can see more clearly
the choices God would have us make.

Spending some time apart to meet with God allows his
Spirit to touch us so that we can develop clearer vision.
Things come into focus and choices become clearer with
God in the equation. The frantic pace of daily living is
tempered. A peace comes bringing the blessed assurance
that God's love is always a ready resource. All we need
to do is to seek God's help, and it will be given.

Hymns of the Saints: No. 410, "Master, Speak! Thy Servant Heareth"

Prayer Thought: Thank you, God, for the love you express for us by keeping your promise to be with us always in our need.

Refreshed by Hope
By Lois Bourgonje
Porcupine Plain,
Saskatchewan, Canada

"In everything give thanks; for this is the will of God in Christ Jesus concerning you."—I Thessalonians 5:18

As I gaze out across the yard this morning, I look in awe at the beauty around me—the green grass, the leaves sparkling in the breeze, and the small puddles of water on the driveway. Even the dandelions poking up their yellow heads on the lawn are pretty. A doe just pranced across the yard, adding more of God's creation to the scene.

We just received one and a quarter inches of rain after a very dry spring. The crops weren't coming along properly and everything looked so colorless and grubby after all the wind and dust. People were losing hope. Everyone is calling this a million-dollar rain, even if we do need much more.

Perhaps our lives are like my yard. They get into a hopeless state of becoming rundown and colorless. They need that "watering" of the Holy Spirit that can come through listening to a good, inspiring sermon and lots of study. When all seems so hopeless, life can change so fast. Great and marvelous are God's works!

Hymns of the Saints: No. 21, "Declare, O Heavens, the Lord of Space"

Prayer Thought: Gracious God, help us to be more aware of you daily and how you are forever meeting our needs.

Making a Good Day
By Frances Hurst Booth
Prescott, Arizona

"This is the day which the Lord has made; let us rejoice and be glad in it."—Psalm 118:24 RSV

"Have a good day," is a common phrase these days. Some time ago I heard someone say, "Make a good day." I have repeated it. I have found that a positive attitude produces positive results, and we can make a difference in even the simplest of daily activities.

A saying goes: There are three kinds of people—those who let it happen, those who make it happen, and those who ask, "What happened?"

It reminds me of the words of Napoleon Bonaparte, "Circumstances—what are circumstances? I make circumstances." A favorite scripture of mine is Philippians 4:3, "I can do all things through Christ which strengtheneth me." I like this older version, which to me has always meant that I am *strengthened through the doing* of what needs to be done, with the help of Christ.

Hymns of the Saints: No. 378, "Rise Up, O Saints of God"

Prayer Thought: As we strive to bring about the kingdom wherever we may be, Lord, strengthen us with a positive attitude and a loving spirit.

Godly Grandparents
By Larry Landsdown
Midwest City, Oklahoma

"Honor thy father and thy mother; that thy days may be long upon the land which the Lord thy God giveth thee."
—Exodus 20:12

When I was growing up, we lived in the same small town as my grandma and grandpa, my father's parents. They had been farmers all their lives, then retired and moved to town. Although they had attended church quite regularly when they were young, health problems now prevented them from going very much. Grandma was a good cook, and she loved to fix dinners for us. Almost every Sunday, after we returned from church, she would have a nice dinner ready, with peach cobbler and pumpkin pie. She loved doing things for people and family.

Grandpa had a big garden and sometimes I would help him there, tilling it and picking the ripe vegetables and ripping off the ears of corn. Grandpa had a great sense of humor and plenty of good old-fashioned horse sense. He used to fix the neatest things for us kids to play with, like a gunny sack punching bag that he hung from a rafter in the garage and a rope-and-pulley swing that allowed us to rappel from one big tree to another.

My grandparents did not know of our church until very late in life but had always lived as Christians, setting good examples and doing good for others. When my dad was a boy, Grandma even played the piano at the little Baptist church they attended in rural Oklahoma. After my father was converted to the Community of Christ, they began to attend occasionally and learn of our doctrines.

About a year before Grandma passed away, she and Grandpa were both baptized. What a joy to know that they had accepted the gospel and we were all united in the same faith. What a blessing it was to have had such good and godly grandparents. Their influence on my life will always give me guidance and strength.

Hymns of the Saints: No. 485, "Blest Be the Tie That Binds"

Prayer Thought: We thank you, Lord, for the blessing of good people in our lives. May we also strive to set good examples for those who come after us.

<table>
<tr><td>Saturday
22
May</td><td>**One Brave Lad**
By Peggy Michael
Cantonment, Florida</td><td></td></tr>
</table>

"O God, be merciful unto me, for my soul trusteth in thee; yea, in the shadow of thy wings will I make my refuge, until these calamities be overpast."—Psalm 57:1

One night on a deserted road, six-year-old Sammy saved his mother's life. As she drove her compact car toward home, a jackrabbit jumped out in front of her. The car skidded, tumbled over a steep embankment, and landed in a dry creek bed. They were hidden from view. The mother was slipping in and out of consciousness. In her waking moments, she pleaded with her son to stay with her. She was afraid he would wander off and be lost.

However, Sammy was concerned about his mother and knew she must have help. He climbed the rough embankment and walked down the road. No cars passed. Eventually he saw a light in the distance. When he reached the house, a woman saw his condition, and she invited him in. His mother's rescue began.

This brave lad was honored by his community. The school declared "Sammy's Day." And, of course, his family was proud of him. His mother still has some residual effects from the accident, but gave Sammy a brother and sister. His mother and father both became registered nurses and have served many people with skill and compassion. And yes, Sammy remains a hero to many people, especially to his grateful mother.

Hymns of the Saints: No. 499, "Who Will Go Forth and Serve?"

Prayer Thought: God, grant us courage when we are the only ones who can give someone else a future.

| Sunday **23** May | **One of the "Family"**
By Russell Grinnell
Cookeville, Tennessee | |

"Behold, I say unto you that your heavenly Father knoweth that ye have need of all these things."—Matthew 6:37 IV

On July 1, 2002, we moved to Tennessee from Murphysboro, Illinois. My son, Jim, his wife, Heather, and their daughter Sydney, had moved here in June, as Jim had been hired by Barnes and Noble to become the manager of their bookstore at Tennessee Tech University. We came here to help care for Sydney and now her brother, who is to be born in May 2003.

The apartment complex that we moved into has 198 apartments, with plans to build sixty-two more. The people who work at the office—the staff and the management—have always treated us well. We don't have a church in Cookeville, and it is too far to go to Nashville or Manchester. Being retired, I don't have enough to do.

When I went to the office to pay our October rent, Brenda asked me to come to the October meeting of Neighborhood Watch. They had other activities scheduled that the group would be involved in. This interested me and I went to the meeting. The people there made me feel welcome. It wasn't long and we were like one big family. We prepared chili and hot dogs to be served to the residents, a Halloween party for the kids, and in December, had crafts for the kids to make and take home. It not only helped me feel useful, but I made a lot of new friends and got to meet many people whom I probably would never have gotten to know otherwise.

Because we don't have a church here, I have been going to a small Presbyterian church in the country. It's not like I am used to, but the people are nice and they help the less fortunate in the area. It is better than not attending church at all.

Hymns of the Saints: No. 369, "Bear Each Other's Burdens"

Prayer Thought: Help us to be ever alert, God, to the needs of our fellow beings and to do our best to improve their lives.

Monday **24** May	**Finding My Way** By Anne Loughran Melbourne, Australia	

"Forget the former things; do not dwell on the past. See, I am doing a new thing! Now it springs up; do you not perceive it? I am making a way in the desert and streams in the wasteland."—Isaiah 43:18–19 NIV

Not long ago I needed to go to a place I had not been before, so I got out my street directory to find the best way to get there. I started out but unfortunately could not locate some of the places marked on my map. In desperation, I pulled off the road, parked by a nearby embankment, and called to a home along the road to ask directions. With their help, I eventually located my destination.

My dilemma was caused because my street directory was twelve years old. New roads had been constructed plus a freeway. My destination was still in the same place, but the route to arrive there had changed.

Our service to God is sometimes retarded if we fail to try new ways that will better achieve our objective.

Sing for Peace: No. 38, "Christ Has Called Us to New Visions"

Prayer Thought: Loving Lord, inspire us as we try new ways to bring the gospel to a needy world.

| Tuesday **25** May | **Special to God** By Denzil J. West Independence, Missouri | |

"The Lord thy God hath chosen thee to be a special people unto himself."—Deuteronomy 7:6

Zachary had completed a prebaptismal class and at age eight was eagerly looking forward to his baptism and confirmation. One morning I took this fine grandson to school, and before the other children arrived, he and I sat on a bench by the flagpole. Pointing to the flag overhead, waving in the breeze, I asked Zachary why the flag was moving. He replied, "The wind is blowing it." While we could not see the wind, it was evident that the flag responded to its power. I told Zachary that when he received the gift of the Holy Spirit at his confirmation, that as he listened for the still, small voice and responded to the gift of the Holy Spirit, he could feel God's guiding presence all during his life.

A day or two later Zachary told his mother that he felt God wanted him to do something special. His mother assured him that he is a special boy. Zachary answered, "Yes, I am!" A few minutes later he returned to where his mother was working and stated, "It's not that I am special. Everyone is special. It is just that they all have to understand it!"

Zachary is a boy who is filled with God's love, and his deep understanding has challenged me to listen more closely for the still, small voice and to be motivated by the gift of the Holy Spirit. I also must understand that all of us are special to God and need to respond to God's love for everyone.

Sing a New Song: No. 35, "Make Me a Servant"

Prayer Thought: God who calls us special, help us to convey to everyone that they, too, are special in your sight.

| Wednesday **26** May | **Trust and Wait**
 By L. Joyce Wilcox
 La Mesa, California | |

"And the elders of the church, two or more, shall be called, and shall pray for, and lay their hands upon them in my name; and if they die, they shall die unto me, and if they live, they shall live unto me."
—Doctrine and Covenants 42:12d

Ryan Wilcox was three years old when he was diagnosed with a tumor on the back of his brain. We have been so grateful for friends in the United States and even other countries. What would we do without the love of so many and their faith and prayers? We thank you one and all. When I wrote this, not knowing the outcome, I kept it until yesterday. A good sister of the Claremont, California, church attending Bridge Builders, mentioned she missed my articles this year in *Daily Bread*. She inspired me to try again.

Ryan is our great-grandson and the only one to carry on the family name. When he was four years old and working on his computer, his folks walked in and asked, "How did you figure this out?" They couldn't do it. He said, "Taa." They asked, "What did you say?" "Talent." He was four then and kept right on working on his computer.

Ryan just turned five and has finished with chemotherapy and blood transfusions. In 2002, Ryan ran a marathon for children with cancer; he came in first. He and his family were given tickets for the Padres game that evening at the stadium in San Diego. Ryan was thrilled. They brought him down onto the field before the game. Ryan watched the game for a while, but then his little body was too tired and they went home.

Ryan attends school and holds his own, and his mind is sharp. I'm happy to say the tumor hasn't grown, but they cannot operate to remove it until he is around twelve. So until that time comes, we trust and wait.

Hymns of the Saints: No. 126, "I Know Not What the Future Hath"

Prayer Thought: Lord, we place our faith and trust in your love for us. Carry us in the palm of your hand no matter where our journey takes us.

Created for a Purpose
By Shirley Vallier Remmenga
Fort Collins, Colorado

"In this is love, not that we loved God but that he loved us and sent his Son to be the atoning sacrifice for our sins. Beloved since God loved us so much, we also ought to love one another."—I John 4:10–11 NRSV

As the soil was turned over by the plow, the field became a sea of white motion. The gulls came from everywhere it seemed and hungrily, greedily snatched up the exposed earthworms. The earthworms had been busily doing their thing under the crust of the earth and were now furnishing a spring meal for the gulls. The gulls, in turn, would someday furnish a meal for some carnivores—the coyotes, perhaps. Coyotes become food for mountain lions, and on and on it goes.

It seems somewhat cruel unless we realize that the earthworms, gulls, coyotes, and mountain lions are only doing what they were created to do, and each of them is equally important in the food chain and in the ecological balance of the earth. Such a complicated set-up mystifies and amazes me. Who but God could put such a system in place? We have seen throughout the world instances where this delicate balance has been upset and the disastrous outcomes that have resulted from this imbalance.

Where do we fit in this ecological balance? What were we created to do, and are we doing it? God has commanded us to love God with all our heart, mind, and strength, and to love our neighbor as ourselves. I believe that is what we were created to do. If love is the driving force in our lives, then we will care for ourselves, each other, and for the earth. We will take care that we do not upset the ecological balance of the earth and we will live in harmony with all of God's creation.

Hymns of the Saints: No. 398, "Let Us Give Praise to the God of Creation"

Prayer Thought: Great God, may we live in harmony with all you have created and fulfill your purpose in us.

| Friday
28
May | **My Precise Time**
By Judy Oetting
Levasy, Missouri | |

"I Jesus have sent mine angel to testify unto you these things in the churches. I am the root and the offspring of David, and the bright and morning star."—Revelation 22:16

My thirty-three years in the classroom were rewarding and fulfilling but left little time for anything else. I looked forward to retirement and the opportunity to spend more time studying scriptures instead of textbooks. But after a few months of retirement, I began to feel like the "Push-me-pull-you," the fanciful creature in the original *Dr. Doolittle* movie.

This creature had a head on each end and no tail. It was either being pushed or pulled. Like it, I was frustrated when everyone wanted me to go a different direction, and I found my time disappearing like water down the drain.

I was sleeping so restlessly one night, I finally just gave up at three a.m. and slipped downstairs in the dark. I curled up with a blanket on the porch and began to pray. I don't know if there is a special window to heaven at this time of morning, but I began to feel a wonderful sense of God's presence, a closeness I hadn't felt in a long time.

The Romans called this time between three and six a.m. the fourth watch. It was during this time of morning Christ walked on the water. I've also heard this time called "monk's time." I've come to call it "my precious time."

I don't always get up at three a.m., but I'm usually up before five. No one calls. No one visits. My husband sleeps until much later. I finally have time to pray and study every day. I no longer mind being pulled in different directions during the day, because I've already had my precious time with the Lord.

Hymns of the Saints: No. 22, "Morning Has Broken"

Prayer Thought: Lord, lead us to set aside a time daily that can become our "precious time" with you, thereby nourishing our spirits.

| Saturday **29** May | **Jesus, the Only True Friend** By Susan L. Berg Gladstone, Michigan | |

"Comfort ye, comfort ye my people, saith your God."
—Isaiah 40:1

When my son was a small boy, he asked me, "Mom, who's your best friend?" Sometimes I would answer, "Your dad," or this person or that. But as the years have rolled by, and friendships have changed, I have come to realize I have but one best friend—Jesus Christ.

He is the only one who has always been there for me, always listened to me, was always honest with me, and never ever deceived me. He has lifted me up when I was down and laughed with me when I was having fun. He has cried with me in sorrow and smiled when I've pleased him. He has held my hand when I've been frightened and comforted me when I was nervous. But most important, he has always, always loved me, no matter what.

Oh, what a great friend he is to me. I hope and pray I can be just as good a friend to him.

Hymns of the Saints: No. 86, "What a Friend We Have in Jesus"

Prayer Thought: God, lead us to cultivate a relationship with Jesus Christ that we may know the meaning of true friendship.

| Sunday
30
May | **The Least of These**
By Myrna Landsdown
Midwest City, Oklahoma | |

"Open your hearts and feel the yearnings of your brothers and sisters who are lonely, despised, fearful, neglected, unloved. Reach out in understanding, clasp their hands, and invite all to share in the blessings of community created in the name of the One who suffered on behalf of all."
—Doctrine and Covenants 161:3a

Two young women, Tammy and Sheila, started attending our congregation about two years ago. They are sisters and are both quite handicapped, both physically and mentally. They don't have a car because neither of them can drive, but their apartment is only about five blocks from the church, so they walk in good weather. I'm sure that our being in the neighborhood was the main reason they chose to worship with us. To be totally honest, I think it was a little hard for some of us to welcome them as openly and lovingly as we should have. Perhaps I am only speaking for myself.

They are quite hard to visit with, as their interests and conversational skills are minimal, their personal hygiene leaves a lot to be desired, and they always interrupt the service by arriving when it's about half over. When they first started attending, we had a food pantry at our congregation, and they were always so needy. We freely gave to them whatever we could, month after month. At times it seemed as if they only came to church to get free food.

Having said all this, however, let me assure you that we have grown to love them, and we do try to make them feel welcome and loved in our church family. They bring a unique ministry to us, too, in their happy faces as they walk in, as they diligently try to look up the scriptures during the sermon, and in their childlike faith.

I was so humbled and greatly ministered to one evening during prayer service. Tammy told of their apartment being broken into and their television set stolen. Someone had just kicked in the door and taken what they wanted. She said that they were pretty scared and afraid to stay in the apartment. It filled me with such anger to hear what had happened to them, that cruel people just run roughshod over the weak and helpless.

We were all concerned for them and prayed that they would be protected and have peace of mind about it. Tammy also said a prayer and prayed for safety, and then she said, "And please forgive the one who broke in and took our things, that he will learn a better way to live." What a beautiful example of a forgiving heart! Here was this "child" of God reminding me about true forgiveness!

Everyone has a gift to give and a work to do for the Lord, even "the least of these."

Hymns of the Saints: No. 377, "Let Your Heart Be Broken"

Prayer Thought: Forgive us, God, when we are judgmental in our attitudes toward people. Let us reach out to all your children, even the neglected and unloved, and share your gospel with them.

<table>
<tr><td>Monday
31
May</td><td>**Silver and Gold**
By Roberta Dieterman
Caledonia, Michigan</td><td></td></tr>
</table>

"Silver and gold have I none; but such as I have give I thee...."—Acts 3:6

It was a good day to sit and reflect on things. The sky was dark and storm clouds were fast approaching, and I felt very safe and comfortable in my chair by the big window.

I began to remember all the friends who have come and gone in my life. While I was growing up we moved a lot, and when I was seven, my parents divorced. My mother and I moved from place to place frequently, but I always found a friend every place we lived. Many times I lived with my grandparents, and I know my grandmother prayed for me whenever I was to make another move.

I know her prayers on my behalf were heard by God. So many times in my life I've thanked God for those people who came into my life as strangers and left as friends. I know, too, that God wants me to be a friend. Some friends are for a lifetime; some come into our lives at a point of need.

We naturally are drawn to some people and develop closer relationships, but the old saying "One is silver and the other, gold" is so true. Both are precious, but the best friend of all is Jesus Christ. He is the friend who is always there. Surely, God must love all creation to give us the precious gift of Jesus, our Lord and friend.

Sing a New Song: No. 7, "Companions on the Journey"

Prayer Thought: Gracious God, we are so thankful for the joys of friendship in this life. Show us how to nurture our friendships, that they may sustain us always.

June 2004

S	M	T	W	T	F	S
		1	2	3	4	5
6	7	8	9	10	11	12
13	14	15	16	17	18	19
20	21	22	23	24	25	26
27	28	29	30			

Tuesday **1** June	**Nevertheless, Follow Him** By Grace Andrews Independence, Missouri	

"In all this I have given you an example that by such work we must support the weak, remembering the words of the Lord Jesus, for he himself said, 'It is more blessed to give than receive.'"—Acts 20:35 NRSV

I learned from early childhood that Jesus was my best friend—I *wanted* to be near him. But following his path has not always been an easy road for me. My life began to crumble as a series of personal crises occurred. I was confused. I wondered about a God who would allow my father to live out his life with Parkinson's disease; a God who could see my precious mother struggling to keep our family fed and clothed; a God who would allow my brother to go to Korea wearing this country's uniform, only to be brought home in a closed casket. Nevertheless, I tried to walk God's path and trust his word. I projected my life as far as I could see, but then I had to rely on the Holy Spirit for whatever lay "beyond the horizon." And, oh my, have I been blessed!

I finally realized that problems happen in life to all of us—tragedies, illness, death. We get tired and perhaps depressed; we're worn out from overwork, stress, family situations, high costs of living, war, and rumors of war. But through it all, if we just reach out, we will find that God is there, ever ready to comfort us and cradle us in his loving arms. God understands. If we would just trust in God and continue to follow, no matter what—with all our might, mind, and strength—how blessed we would be. Not only that, someone, somewhere, perhaps today, maybe tomorrow or next year, will need us to be their strength when they go through similar problems. And we can do that—because we've "been there."

Hymns of the Saints: No. 457, "My Lord, I Know That All My Life"

Prayer Thought: Ever-loving God, in our times of tragedy and pain may we yet realize that you love us. May every life experience enable us to help someone else.

| Wednesday |
| **2** |
| June |

Many Chances
By Jane Henson
Fairview Heights, Illinois

"Who gave himself for us, that he might redeem us from all iniquity, and purify unto himself a peculiar people, zealous of good works."—Titus 2:14

I like cable television channels because they repeat many of their programs two, three, or many more times during the week or month. Regular networks air a program once, and if you miss it, if it is preempted by important world news, or your VCR malfunctions, you may never see that program. You just might be able to catch it in the rerun season several months later. Having many cable channels affords a person many chances.

God is truly a loving, caring, and patient God. Have you noticed in your life how patient God can be? Sometimes he gives me two, three, or maybe more chances to get a life lesson or task right. God is so patient it makes me truly ashamed of the impatience I sometimes displayed as a mother, and now as a grandmother.

Many of us tend to be "slow learners" with regard to our spiritual lives. I am grateful to God for giving me so many chances.

Hymns of the Saints: No. 178, "Lord, I Was Blind, I Could Not See"

Prayer Thought: Ever-patient God, we are so appreciative of your patience with us. May we learn from your example as we minister to our family, friends, and humanity.

Thursday **3** June	**Golden Years** By Jeannine Blasick Monongahela, Pennsylvania	

"He hath shown thee, O man, what is good; and what doth the Lord require of thee, but to do justly, and to love mercy, and to walk humbly with thy God?"—Micah 6:8

Are the golden years really as golden as they say they are? Yes! In my corner of the world they are as precious as gold.

As I sat one day reflecting on my life's experiences, I felt impressed to write about my childhood and how I would go about singing a song we were taught at church school. It went like this: "I want to be like Jesus in all I do and say, I want his loving kindness to shine through me each day." The more it came to mind, the more I realized what it was saying to me. As I sang in my moments alone, I really began to take it seriously, not realizing until much later in my life how much my heavenly Father had blessed my life.

I was recently reading my evangelist's blessing, which states: "God loves you because of your good desires." It's all coming together for me now in the twilight of my life; it has been a blessing throughout my journey here on earth.

What a wonderful Savior is Jesus, our Lord.

Sing for Peace: No. 12, "Of All the Spirit's Gifts to Me"

Prayer Thought: Lord of life's journey, continue to guide

us with your loving hand, that we may be a source of blessing for those who have not met you.

| Friday **4** June | **Learning New Ways** By Ferryl Cash Troy, Kansas |

"Trust in the Lord with all your heart, and do not rely on your own insight. In all your ways acknowledge him, and he will make straight your paths."—Proverbs 3:5–6 RSV

One year, due to scheduling conflicts at school, my daughter had to dance in a more advanced-level dance class. She wanted back in an easier class, but it couldn't be arranged. At first this was difficult for her, and she wanted to give up and quit, but she still loved dance and had already invested many years in it, so she decided to just keep going. As the year went on, she improved, and it got much easier for her, but it took a lot of hard work and determination on her part. Her teacher was proud of her tenacity and improvement and told her so.

Following the Lord's way also takes a lot of hard work and determination. Going against what everyone else does is not always easy. Sometimes we want to give up, too, and go back to our old bad habits or to a less demanding lifestyle. It is not always easy to learn new ways, do what is right, and break away from old habits. It takes practice, prayer, study, and commitment, but it can be done. If our hearts are truly committed, with God's help, we can also grow and learn to be the kind of person that is pleasing to God.

Hymns of the Saints: No. 112, "Heavenly Father, We Adore Thee"

Prayer Thought: Lord, we ask you to help us keep going when the road is difficult, to not give up when doing right isn't the easy way. Help us develop new habits that bring us closer to you.

| Saturday **5** June | **This Old Rocking Chair** By Karen Anne Smith Ludington, Michigan | |

"Salvation is not a reward for the good we have done, so none of us can take credit for it. It is God himself who has made us what we are and given us new lives from Christ Jesus...."—Ephesians 2:9–10 TLB

My old rocking chair had been repaired with squares of paneling, pieces of burlap, and particleboard. It had a broken leg that had been glued and nailed. In fact, there were nails everywhere. Its cushions were long gone and had been replaced with pillows that had, themselves, faded through the years. The poor old thing seemed ready for the scrap heap but I needed a rocking chair. I thought about it, prayed about it, and began to see new possibilities.

Carefully, I sanded the old finish away and pounded in all protruding nails. I then painted it with mahogany polyurethane, all the time picturing the new and beautiful chair that was slowly emerging. Finally, I made old-fashioned tapestry slipcovers for the pillows—pillowcases if you will. The old, ugly chair is now gone, and a lovely new rocker will serve its purpose for many years to come.

I was once like that old chair, patched together and rough. God has stripped away the old finish and replaced it with a coat of pure light. God has transformed my life into something new and beautiful, as he can do for anyone who opens up to his guidance and care. Like my old rocking chair, I hope to be able to serve God's purposes for many years to come.

Hymns of the Saints: No. 143, "My Faith Looks Up to Thee"

Prayer Thought: Father, you have granted us new life in Jesus Christ. Help us to use this gift wisely, for the benefit of those still in need of your transforming grace.

Sunday **6** June	**Bringing Us Closer** By Betty Yeager St. Louis, Missouri

"Wherefore, seeing we also are compassed about with so great a cloud of witnesses, let us lay aside every weight, and the sin which doth so easily beset us, and let us run with patience the race that is set before us, looking unto Jesus the author and finisher of our faith."—Hebrews 12:1–2

We are on our way to church for the baptism of two of our grandchildren. This is a happy time for us all, especially to see the enthusiasm in the children and to feel that this is what they need in their lives.

I sense the great responsibility we have as adults to guide them through the hard times and enjoy the good that comes to them. May we too learn from them as they show their love to Jesus and to us. We must teach them that love, not hate, is what they need.

As I sit here this beautiful Sunday morning, waiting for my ride to church, and as I read my *Daily Bread* message for the day, I think about the many writers, some whom I know, and others whom I don't. Yet their writings bring us closer to our brothers and sisters in the Community of Christ faith.

I am brought closer through prayer to those I read about, and I sense their faith. Our Lord has blessed us as a church and has guided our leaders through the years. May we all sense our Lord's closeness to us.

Hymns of the Saints: No. 482, "Let Us Breathe One Fervent Prayer"

Prayer Thought: Ever-present God, we give thanks for all that draws us close to one another and to you.

| Monday **7** June | **Opportunity to Witness** By Eva Mildred Kuppart Harrisburg, Illinois | |

"If we receive the witness of men, the witness of God is greater; for this is the witness of God which he hath testified of his Son."—I John 5:9

On a beautiful spring morning, my husband, Edward, was in the backyard when a new neighbor and family came over to get acquainted. They were building a new house on property that adjoins ours. Edward brought them to the front door to meet me. We all visited for a brief time. Mr. Williams said, "When the house is finished, we plan to have a housewarming. We'll invite you." I told Ed later that because our health was so poor, maybe we should give them a gift now. I wondered what we could give, because we didn't know what they might need. Suddenly a picture of Jesus came to mind. We went shopping and found a nice one of Jesus knocking at the door. We bought a "Welcome to our Community" card. I wanted to write some loving words, so I prayed and meditated. These are the words I wrote.

Jesus the greatest Guest of all,
    While he hangs so silent on your wall,

He is the Master of joy, hope, love, and peace.
His loving care will never cease.

If you accept him in your life,
He will be with you both day and night.
He is your Savior, Redeemer, and Friend.

May your journey of life be filled with love,
To share this house, with thanks from above.
Not just a house, but a home of praise,
Give God the glory, for all things he gave.

His Son, who died and went away,
That we might live in a new home up above.
No sin or sorrow, sickness or pain,
With Jesus, our Savior, who will come again.
—Eva Mildred Kuppart and Edward

We took the gift and visited a brief time. Mrs. Williams opened the gift and the card. She read the card and said, "I will hang it with the picture. I won't wait until the house is finished."

I invited them to come worship with us at Community of Christ. They have no church home, as they do not attend church. We fell in love with their youngest daughter, Alyse, age five. She is like a little angel. She has gone to church with us twice. Her mother has attended twice, bringing Alyse and her other daughter, Nacole, twelve. Edward built a small bridge across the ditch between our houses to make it easier to visit. We plan to keep in touch as loving, caring neighbors and friends, remembering the church goal: "Each one, win one."

Hymns of the Saints: No. 399, "A Charge to Keep I Have"

Prayer Thought: Heavenly Parent, help us to be willing and prepared at all times to witness of your love.

Lost, but Not Alone

By Carla Long
Mound City, Kansas
(Binalonan Pangasinan,
Philippines)

"Behold, God is my salvation; I will trust, and not be afraid; for the Lord Jehovah is my strength and my song; He also is become my salvation."—Isaiah 12:2

I had only been in the Philippines for ten days, and in Baguio City for two. I hardly knew where anything was, but I felt prepared and ready to ride public transportation (a jeepney) to my language tutor. I got off at the right stop and started my ten-block hike. After a while, I knew I must be close, but nothing looked familiar anymore. I backtracked. Nope. I went another direction. No, that was the way I came in. I didn't know anyone to ask where the building was, and at that moment, I couldn't even remember the name of my school.

I was in a foreign country, half a world away from everyone who loved me. I didn't know what to do, and I started to panic. Finally, I forced myself to stop. I stopped everything—my feet, my clenching hands, and my jumbled thoughts. Only one prayer came to mind: "God, please help me find what I'm looking for. Please." After only a second, complete calm overtook my senses and my feet started moving—not with panic as in the moment before, but with assuredness. Suddenly, there it was, visible from a spot I had passed at least three times.

How many times have we been lost? How many times, in our fright, have we overlooked just the thing we were seeking? How long have we stood somewhere, scared for no reason? God loves to be depended on. There is no reason for us to carry all of the responsibility when there is another who wants to be our protector and will happily guide us through the scary parts of life.

Hymns of the Saints: No. 131 (verse 1), "Unmoved by Fear, My Praise Is Due"

Prayer Thought: Lord, help us to remember to turn to you, not only in times of panic, but always.

| Wednesday **9** June | **God's Child** By Ruth Andrews Vreeland Albuquerque, New Mexico | |

"Jesus straightened up and said to her, 'Woman, where are they? Has no one condemned you?' She said, 'No one, sir.' And Jesus said, 'Neither do I condemn you. Go your way, and from now on do not sin again.'"
—John 8:10–11 NRSV

While I was running errands one day, driving down the busy streets of our city, a young man impatiently cut around me with his car, causing me to slam on my breaks to avoid hitting him. My first impulse was to angrily lay on the horn, but I noticed that from the back, he looked a great deal like my oldest son. I know it sounds silly, but I just couldn't direct such an angry act at someone who so closely resembled my own beloved child, who also seems to have the "need for speed." My anger melted away and I laughed instead!

When I look into the face of this son of mine (who is now nearly an adult) I still see the sweet, angelic face he possessed at the age of two, and my heart melts all over again. I believe this is what allows mothers everywhere to unconditionally love and forgive their children. We mothers remember the sweet innocence that was once our child's. We see all the potential there too, sometimes buried deep inside, and it gives us renewed hope.

God looks on and loves *all* of the children he created, too. Max Lucado once wrote a beautiful, touching story about Jesus' encounter with Mary Magdalene. Jesus, the co-Creator, was able to see in Mary's eyes the sweet innocent child she had once been and love her with a parent's love. He also saw the great potential in this child of his, though she had traveled down the "wrong road" for many years. When God himself sees us through eyes of hope, believing we can and will do better, we are assured of his great love for us.

I am learning to view all people everywhere as children of God. I know God loves them as only a parent can, but he wants me to love them, too. And not just the ones who resemble my own children, but the ones who resemble their Creator, made in his beautiful image.

Sing a New Song: No. 51, "Weave"

Prayer Thought: Loving God, teach us to see others through your eyes, that we may see their great potential.

| Thursday **10** June | **Blessed by Resourcefulness** By Eileen Turner Portland, Oregon | |

"For the measure you give will be the measure you get back."—Luke 6:38 RSV

As I was attending patients with my nursing students in the hospital, one student was preparing her patient for discharge. Days before, he had been riding his bicycle and was hit by a car. He sustained a few broken bones and a large gash that required suturing. The physician had obviously not considered the patient's personal situation when he wrote, "Discharge home. Return to my office in three days for suture removal."

My student nurse knew he was homeless and lived under one of the bridges in our county, a location he was unwilling to share with us. Getting him ready for discharge required teaching him how to care for his wound, providing him with packets of sterile gauze dressing material, some cleansing solution, and tape. We discovered his clothing had been cut off in the emergency room as we tried to get him dressed to leave, and found only bloody cut-up jeans and shirt. We dressed him in a pair of surgical scrubs, and then he asked about his bicycle. Realizing that this was probably his only possession, I went off to find out what had become of it.

I tracked it down in the maintenance department and found it to be a mangled mess. I explained the patient's plight to the men and that despite the bike's condition, it would have to go with him when we called for it.

I went back upstairs to attend to the final details of the discharge with my student nurse, and to place a call to the one friend the patient thought could transport him and his bicycle. To our utter amazement and delight, when the maintenance man met us at the exit, the bicycle had been miraculously transformed into an almost ride-able vehicle. This maintenance team had rallied all their resources and ingenuity and provided a labor of love for a perfect stranger, one who probably had not been on the receiving end of an act of kindness for a very long time.

We need only to look around us to see "Godlike" behaviors in others.

Sing for Peace: No. 36, "Called by Christ to Love Each Other"

Prayer Thought: Inspire us, Lord, to use what we have available to bring blessings to the lives of others.

Persistent Love
By Diane F. Schwartz
Las Vegas, Nevada

"But from the beginning of creation, God made them male and female."—Mark 10:6

Last summer, my daughter, her two children, and I went to California for the weekend. While at Sea World, we visited the manatee exhibit. As we first walked in, we saw what we thought was a tragedy. On the bottom of the tank lay a baby manatee. It was lying so still, there were no signs of life. We watched for several minutes, but the baby did not move.

By then there were lots of people staring at this scene, wondering why they would leave a dead baby in the tank with all these little kids around. Suddenly one of the larger animals began to nudge it and try to lift it off the bottom. Another adult joined in on its other side. These huge animals ever so gently raised the smaller one to the top of the water so it could get a breath of air. It quickly started to sink again, but they were right there to buoy it back to the surface. This time it took a big breath and set right off to eat the water lettuce in the tank. Due to the watchfulness of its parents, it was now fine.

The love and tenderness shown by these huge animals for their young made me so conscious of the love that God has placed not only in us but in animals also as they care for their young. The adults didn't fuss over the baby as we humans do; they let it go off on its own—a lesson I've not yet learned. God, our heavenly parent, loves us more than we can comprehend, yet has given each of us our agency, gently guiding and letting us grow. God doesn't smother us, but is always there when we have need.

209

Sing for Peace: No. 13, "God of the Sparrow"

Prayer Thought: Creator of all creatures, teach us how to let our young go, even as we are always available to help them.

Saturday **12** June	**Hands Raised in Thanksgiving** By Gerald John Kloss Philadelphia, Pennsylvania	

"Thanks be unto God for his unspeakable gift."
—II Corinthians 9:15

My neighbors next door are Arab. The family consists of the father, mother, son, and grandmother who came from Palestine and four daughters who were born in the United States. This wonderful family shares many things with me including food, language, and various components of their culture. The family practices the Islamic faith, and we often share many of our beliefs with each other.

In September 2001 I was told that I needed heart surgery, which delayed needed surgery for a double hernia. When the date was set for the surgery, I shared this with my neighbors, who planned to keep an eye on my house while I was in the hospital. On the day before the surgery, my mother was in my living room and noticed the grandmother from next door walking by the house and stopping in front of the door. Mom said that she did this several times. I thought nothing about it, as I was concerned about the next day's surgery in Einstein Hospital.

The surgery was successful and I recovered well. My neighbors were in my house when I returned from the hospital, and when I told them how well I was doing, the grandmother, who speaks no English, raised her hands toward the sky and with tears in her eyes said some words. The mother told me that she was thanking Allah for blessing and healing me. She also explained how she had walked past my door at least seven times the day before the surgery, praying for me to be well. These words of unspeakable love, concern, prayer, and thanksgiving have deeply touched my soul and will never be forgotten. Truly this is the same when we consider the unspeakable gift of Jesus and his impact on our lives.

Hymns of the Saints: No. 440, "Teach Us, O Lord, True Thankfulness"

Prayer Thought: Lord God, may we truly appreciate the love and devotion of people whose faith has blessed our lives.

| Sunday **13** June | **The Back Row Gang** By Melba Jean Dixon Farwell, Michigan | |

"Receive the giftedness and energy of children and youth, listening to understand their questions and their wisdom. Respond to their need to be loved and nurtured as they grow."—Doctrine and Covenants 161:4a

Several years ago the back rows of the church in Farwell were filled with teenage boys. I'm sure friendship was one good reason they came. Leftover bulletins revealed the notes, drawings, and games they would play. The fellowship extended throughout the week also. If a new boy came, he was welcomed into the group. They attended youth camps together, where they were strengthened by their experiences there, and their faith in God increased.

The "Back Row Gang" grew up. A few of them who moved away continue to attend church in the areas where they now live. Many of the young men remain in the congregation and are now bringing their own children to church. Several of those who moved away, as well as those who stayed, serve in priesthood and leadership roles.

As I notice young men hanging around after a worship service, visiting with one another, much the same as they did in years gone by, I thank God for the gift of friendship, and for the young boys of the "Back Row Gang" who have graced our congregation.

Hymns of the Saints: No. 158, "There's an Old, Old Path"

Prayer Thought: May we nurture our children and youth, Lord, encouraging them to grow in their understanding and faith in Christ.

Monday **14** June	**Needs Met through Faith** By Sherry Southland Temple City, California

"Now faith is the assurance of things hoped for, the conviction of things not seen…. By faith we understand that the worlds were prepared by the word of God, so that what is seen was made from things that are not visible."
—Hebrews 11:1, 3 NRSV

Shari, who is one of the neighborhood kids, knocked on my door recently. She was so excited and was talking as fast as she could while pointing to the ground right next to my front door. I wondered why she was so excited. Then I looked to where she was pointing, and I had to smile.

There was a four-foot-long iguana sunning himself there. He looked peaceful and happy. Once I realized why my young friend was so excited, I let her know that this animal was someone's pet. It was used to human contact. It seemed to know that it would be cared for.

Doesn't faith work the same way? There are times when we have new challenges or new opportunities for growth. We need to see beyond the horizon and take risks if we are to grow into the people God wants us to be. Isn't it wonderful that God is present, and will take care of our needs when we are moving into new territory?

Hymns of the Saints: No. 185, "Lord of All Hopefulness"

Prayer Thought: Eternal Guide, may we be open to new opportunities and be willing to risk through faith in you.

Tuesday
15
June

Gathering
By Louita Clothier
Lamoni, Iowa

"Behold, it is my will, that all they who call on my name, and worship me according to mine everlasting gospel, should gather together and stand in holy places...."
—Doctrine and Covenants 98:5a

A compelling image has remained with me all my life from many years ago when I was a camper at Nauvoo youth camp. At the final campfire on the bank of the Mississippi River, we were each given a candle on a paper plate, which we lighted and set afloat on the river. At first, when the fifty or so candles were together, the river and bank were lit up in a blaze of light. Gradually, however, the candles drifted apart, and soon each one was only an insignificant speck of light in the darkness.

To a young girl who was soon to go off to college, the lesson was a persuasive one. The "gathering" is an important principle of seeking out relationships with those of like faith and purpose. This principle has influenced my choice of friends, my choice of college, certainly my choice of husband, and where we as a family have made our home. I am gratefully aware how favorably my life has been shaped by the friendship, support, and loving care of living among other church members.

Now, a half-century later, we are known in the world as a community. The early day Latter Day Saint tradition of intentional togetherness has evolved into Zionic ideals of mutuality, relationship, and caring for one another. The church is a worldwide family held together by an unmistakable bond, made up of individual congregations that share heritage, worship, joy, and service.

In our gathering, we combine the individual lights into one great beacon that "the places where they occupy may shine as Zion."

Sing for Peace: No. 4, "Gather Us In"

Prayer Thought: Great God who calls us to be in community, may we seek often to gather together with those of like faith, that we may be strengthened for further service.

Beneath the Cover
By Helen M. Green
Toledo, Ohio

"Ye blind guides, who strain at a gnat and swallow a camel; who make yourselves appear unto men that ye would not commit the least sin, and yet ye yourselves, transgress the whole law."—Matthew 23:21 IV

A young mother who had been deserted by her husband was left to care for three children by herself. When the youngest was eight years old, the mother enrolled her in a prebaptismal class. Sometimes they were accompanied by a young man and his daughter. Although some wondered about the long ponytail the man wore, he was made to feel welcome. He was neat and tidy, and the congregation found him pleasant and companionable. Still there was the occasional remark: "Doesn't he know he would look better without that ponytail?"

After several weeks, one Sunday he came to church with a short haircut. We had grown so accustomed to his long hair that the new look was almost shocking. But either way, the length of his hair had no effect on a pleasant relationship between him and the congregation.

It wasn't until later when the young couple was married in the pastor's home, that the bride's mother explained what had happened. Don, the young man, had learned of an organization that collected human hair to be made into wigs for children who had lost their hair during chemotherapy for cancer. A donor's hair had to be a certain length before it would be accepted. Don's hair grew fairly fast, and he made a pledge to himself that he would make such a donation. He did not announce his goal to others. Friendships did not depend on the length of one's hair.

Such a gift has caused more than one person in our congregation to rethink their position on the length of hair a man chooses to wear. More likely than not Jesus' hair was down to his shoulders or longer when he walked on earth as a young man.

Hymns of the Saints: No. 226, "Fairest Lord Jesus"

Prayer Thought: Forgive us, Lord, for being too quick to judge others based on how they appear. May we look for your image within the people we meet.

Thursday **17** June	**Sharing Offertory Thoughts** By Jean Cottle Alta Loma, California

"I would exhort you, my beloved brethren, that you remember that every good gift comes of Christ."—Moroni 10:13

When I am assigned to do the Sunday morning offertory, I consider that a solemn privilege. It is my responsibility to choose whatever thoughts I want to read to share with the congregation. In preparation, I prayerfully consider the theme for the morning worship service. While pondering and searching for the right material, I am often led to read a certain article. I don't always know why but I am impressed that someone needs that particular message. Sometimes, after the service, a member of the congregation will ask me for a copy of what I have read, telling me why the message was special to him or her.

Through the years, I have gathered a variety of inspirational resources. Some even date back to 1947 when I attended Graceland College. My inspirational library also includes copies of eighteen years of *Daily Bread*. Articles from *Daily Bread* have often helped me through a difficult situation in my own life. Many of the authors are known to me personally or through the testimonies they have shared through the years. I have shared some of those testimonies with my congregation during the offertory. I am thankful for this helpful resource.

The offertory is such an important part of a worship service. It is one way that each one present can participate. The giving of our offering can represent our appreciation for the love of Christ in our lives.

Hymns of the Saints: No. 401, "We Give Thee But Thine Own"

Prayer Thought: Generous God, may we budget our resources so that we can support the needs of both our congregation and the wider World Church.

| Friday **18** June | **Bear Witness** By Janie S. Qualls Lake City, Arkansas | |

"And whatsoever ye do in word or deed, do all in the name of the Lord Jesus, giving thanks to God and the Father by him…. And whatsoever ye do, do it heartily, as to the Lord, and not unto men."—Colossians 3:17, 23

Prayer and testimony service on Wednesday night gives me a needed boost in the middle of the week. Some share new testimonies, good news of things that have just happened. Sometimes someone shares a testimony of something that has had a great impact on their life, and they have shared the story often over the years. Even though I may know such testimonies by heart, there is something comforting and strengthening about them as they are retold.

217

Early disciples told stories of Jesus over and over. No doubt they benefited from the telling, for the experiences remained fresh in their hearts and minds. Those who heard also benefited as the stories became a familiar strength in their lives. We should always be willing to share our testimonies for the same reason.

Hymns of the Saints: No. 83, "'Tis the Blessed Hour of Prayer"

Prayer Thought: Lord who walks each day with us, free us from whatever holds us back from sharing of your goodness in our lives.

Saturday **19** June	**Are We Ready?** By Neta Minthorn Nelsen Beaverton, Oregon	

"Indeed, I am longing to pour out greater blessings than you have ever known if you, my people, will open yourselves through preparation, study, and prayer."
—Doctrine and Covenants 158:11b

While attending a leadership conference in Lamoni, Iowa, on the Graceland University campus, a rainy day came unexpectedly, and we were all caught in a deluge. Those of us who were inexperienced with the area, found that being prepared was essential. I was one who waded the puddles, trying to keep from becoming soaked as I fled to my next class. It was all pointless. I arrived with wet shoes and socks, and my attire drenched. I realized how unpresentable I had become as I surveyed myself in the bathroom. My coat did not pass the waterproof test, and I looked like a drowned rat.

Are we like this with the Lord's work? Do we "dress" ourselves without thinking or praying? Do we walk into the world without God's armor? Have we become "soaked" with sinful ways? Are we wading in puddles of despair or waiting for someone to hand us a towel?

Let's study and meditate on God's word. We have Jesus as our example of grace. We have the promises of God's love. If we are God's people, we follow in Jesus' footsteps. Let us prepare ourselves and make ready for the "feast" so that we will be presentable and our "garments" will be clean and dry.

Sing a New Song: No. 12, "Here I Am, Lord"

Prayer Thought: Lord of love, thank you for your holy scriptures, for your servants who help to guide us, and most of all for loving us, even in our weakness.

Sunday **20** June	**Living in Rural Iowa** By Don Richardson Osceola, Iowa	

"And, behold, I tell you these things that you may learn wisdom, that you may learn that when you are in the service of your fellow beings you are only in the service of your God."—Mosiah 1:49

On my way to school, I had stopped at a parent's home to get some papers signed. This parent lived on a secluded gravel road several miles from the nearest village. Later, at school, one of the students asked what I had been doing at his neighbor's that morning.

A few days later, again on my way to school and again several miles from the nearest village, I picked up a hitchhiker. At school a different student asked me if I had picked up the hitchhiker.

Even though I did not expect anyone to see either of these events, someone did. These incidents remind me that people do see what I am doing. I need to ask myself, Am I in service to my fellow beings or only out for myself? I want others to see that I am a follower of Christ. He has asked us to be in service to our fellow beings. That is my goal, for then I will be serving my God.

Hymns of the Saints: No. 432, "If by Your Grace I Choose to Be"

Prayer Thought: God, in our daily activities may we always remember to put you first. May our lives demonstrate servanthood.

| Monday **21** June | **Called to Respond** By Janie Fehrenbacher Broken Arrow, Oklahoma | |

"And I will bring the blind by a way that they knew not; I will lead them in paths that they have not known; I will make darkness light before them, and crooked things straight. These things I will do unto them, and not forsake them."—Isaiah 42:16

A *Daily Bread* article that I recently read quoted, "Ways have grown short that seemed once to be long," from the hymn, "Tenderly, Tenderly" by Joseph Smith III. As I read the words, I began to see that in my own life this quotation has been such a remarkable reality.

The other side of the coin is that often we make the short ways unbelievably long! As human beings, we often talk the positive talk, but live in negative ways. We sometimes feel we are not worthy of all the blessings that are bestowed on us in often minute and sometimes spectacular ways. We tend to forget that a loving God, being the loving parent that God is, really wants to bestow wonderful blessings. But God wants us to respond with not only a casual "thanks," but with non-casual living.

We simply do not have the challenges that we used to have in technological ways. We are able to arrive anywhere we want in minutes and hours instead of days. We immediately see the results of great joy and basic tragedy on our television screen as they unfold. We may visit with anyone either on the Internet or telephone at a moment's notice, and yet we still agonize over things not being like they used to be.

Personally, I do not want to "go back"! I want to sing a new song. The words of the hymns in the praise and peace hymnals speak to me every time I hear them. I want to be a responsive disciple to a loving, personal Savior. I want to respond to the good news. I want to recognize that the paths that have seemed so long have been really replaced by a Savior who has always carried me, even when I thought I was walking alone.

Sing for Peace: No. 38, "Christ Has Called Us to New Visions"

Prayer Thought: Lead us to look ahead to paths of service and possibility, Lord, and not spend our time longing for old ways. May we know that you will be with us.

Drooping Spirits
By Ina G. Beggs
Goodwood, Ontario, Canada

"But whosoever drinketh of the water which I shall give him shall never thirst; but the water that I shall give him shall be in him a well of water springing up into everlasting life."—John 4:16 IV

We have plants in our church sanctuary that occasionally have sadly drooping leaves by Sunday morning. Someone may notice and water them, and it is interesting to observe how they revive during the hour of worship and are no longer wilted and sick looking. Their roots have received what they required.

Similarly, it is often that way with each of us also. Perhaps we enter God's house bowed down with discouragement and concerns, saddened, or perplexed in some way. If we are rooted in faith we will absorb the "spiritual water" received in this hour, which will revive our whole being, leaving us less burdened and noticeably uplifted.

Hymns of the Saints: No. 134, "I Heard the Voice of Jesus Say"

Prayer Thought: God of living water, may we be found in your house seeking the spiritual refreshment that will heal our drooping spirits.

| Wednesday **23** June | **Three Special Examples** By Ilean M. Williams Sarnia, Ontario, Canada |

"Suffer the little children to come unto me, and forbid them not; for of such is the kingdom of God."—Mark 10:12 IV

There are three special people I often remember with gratitude, for each one made a significant impact on my life. Ella Carrington is one of them. I always called her "Aunt Ella." She was in charge of the junior Sunday school for many years. I always felt that all of us kids were her family. She treated every one of us the same.

When Aunt Ella quit teaching junior Sunday school, Marguerite Green took the job of directing it. She was another special person. She gave me a few small jobs to do and explained many things to me. With little training and at only fourteen, I became her assistant. Before long, I was the one in charge of junior Sunday school. I was blessed to have had the best teachers in whose footsteps I was able to follow. I tried my best to be a good example of Aunt Ella and Sister Marguerite. These two women were "chosen vessels."

One Sunday as we started our opening exercises, Lois came in with her son, Jeff, a mentally challenged boy. When I saw him, I felt upset and wondered "why" she would bring him to Sunday school. As I was saying the opening prayer, I opened my eyes to see what Jeff was doing. There he stood, his eyes closed, his hands folded in prayer. I felt so ashamed. He was setting the example for me and all the children.

Jeff became my special friend. We had a large stand to hold the hand-printed words to the hymns. When I would start to play the piano, Jeff would come up and stand beside the music stand. I would nod my head if he needed to turn the cardboard over for a second verse. He helped fold Sunday school papers, and then took them to the teachers.

During the eleven o'clock service, Jeff always sat at the back with his dad. One Sunday morning as I stood up to sing a solo, he leaped up, got away from his dad, and came up beside me to hold the corner of the book (his job). When I had finished singing, Jeff looked up at me, smiled, and then returned to sit with his father. I'll never forget his participation and commitment to responsibility.

Hymns of the Saints: No. 171, "Help Us Accept Each Other"

Prayer Thought: Heavenly Parent, we are all your children: of every color, whether sharp of mind, average, or mentally challenged. We know that every human being is precious in your sight.

 Thursday **24** June

Lioness Club Blessings
By LaVerne Cramer
Tomah, Wisconsin

"Let love be genuine; hate what is evil, hold fast to what is good; love one another with mutual affection, outdo one another in showing honor."—Romans 12:9–10 NRSV

Today I went with the Tomah Health Care Center residents for dining out at the Badger Café. I wish everyone could have seen their smiles as they tried to decide what they wanted to eat; it was great watching them.

My mind went back to the first time that the Lioness Club donated money for healthcare residents to dine out. We went to Jermo's in Oakdale. I can't remember the name of the particular woman who happened to sit by me. When I handed her the menu, she looked at me and asked, "What do I do? I have never eaten out before." She shared that she had lived on a farm and had been too poor to ever eat out. I told her to look over the menu and choose what she would like to eat. I wish you could have seen her as she read the menu—she read it like a book, and when she got the food, her eyes sparkled like diamonds. There are no words to describe or capture the smile on her face.

A couple of weeks later, this woman died. But thanks to the Lioness Club of Tomah, she had one special day that brought her great joy. May God bless the people in such good organizations for the joy they bring to others.

Hymns of the Saints: No. 484, "Make Us, O God, a Church That Shares"

Prayer Thought: We thank you, God, for those people who, through their united efforts, bring joy to others.

| Friday **25** June | **Flawed** By Roberta Dieterman Caledonia, Michigan | |

"And we will go on unto perfection if God permit."
—Hebrews 6:3

While on vacation, we visited a shop that featured blown-glass dishes, vases, and other items. The glass blower was working there that day. We saw a beautiful dish and noticed that the price was quite a bit lower than other dishes the same size. On closer inspection, we saw a tiny dark speck in the glass. When we asked about it we were told it was the pigment in the color that caused the piece to be flawed. The beauty of the dish, at least to us, would make it a wonderful addition to our home. We noticed that the artist's other works were signed, so we asked him if he would sign the dish for us. He declined, saying he didn't want his name connected to a flawed piece of art.

I'm so glad the Master Artist does not hesitate to acknowledge me with all my flaws. Sometimes we let those small imperfections hide the real beauty around us and in those we love. Every time I look at that beautiful dish, I see that tiny flaw and thank my heavenly Father for his love and concern for me and his signature on my heart.

Hymns of the Saints: No. 459, "Lord, Who Views All People Precious"

Prayer Thought: Thank you, Lord, for loving us despite our flaws and imperfections. Help us to always see the beauty of others in your creation.

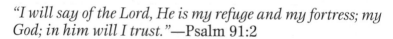

| Saturday **26** June | **Our Greatest Treasures** By Jane Miller Berryville, Arkansas |

"I will say of the Lord, He is my refuge and my fortress; my God; in him will I trust."—Psalm 91:2

As I write this today, the media headline is the news that war has broken out again. The scriptures tell us "There will be wars and rumors of wars." But it doesn't say the wars will be covered on live television for all to see, including our children.

Children today are faced with many challenges and temptations, more so than just one generation ago and much more than two generations ago. I remember what I was confronted with as a teen, and it seems so minimal by comparison. Today just one misjudgment could very well cost a child his or her life.

With alcohol, drugs, sexually transmitted diseases, and now the horrors of all-out war played out in our own living rooms, it's more important than ever to teach our children well. Then we must trust them and their lives to an all-seeing and all-knowing God, who holds us all in God's hand.

Hymns of the Saints: No. 156, "Children of the Heavenly Father"

Prayer Thought: Lord of our lives, into your hands we surrender the most precious gifts you have given us— our children.

| Sunday **27** June | **Committed to God**
By Norma Holman
Wayne, Indiana | |

"Now if the Lamb of God, he being holy, should have need to be baptized by water to fulfill all righteousness, oh, then, how much more need have we, being unholy, to be baptized, even by water."—II Nephi 13:7

Remarks about giving a child to God at a baptismal service stirred my memory of a long-ago experience. My two daughters were very young, and I took them with me on an errand at church. As we were leaving, I had an overwhelming desire to pray, and I gathered the two in my arms, knelt there in that empty church, and literally gave them to God. They both were very quiet and wide-eyed, as if they understood. I promised to be the best mother I could be for their physical and spiritual growth.

This promise was never far from my mind, and I did try my best, and know I often failed. My two lovely daughters now have grandchildren, and I am proud of them. I hope that my promise and dedication of them has guided and protected them in their walk with God through life.

This might sound trivial on paper, but it was one of the most meaningful spiritual experiences of my life. It was as if I had personally met my Lord and said what I wanted for these two precious ones entrusted to me. I was assured that God loved them as much, or more, than I did. I never talked about this experience for fear words would lessen the commitment I had made.

Hymns of the Saints: No. 347, "O Master to All Children Dear"

Prayer Thought: Almighty God, teach us both to commit our children to you and commit ourselves to be living examples of Jesus.

| Monday
28
June | **Trim the Frazzles**
By Maurine Van Eaton
Yakima, Washington | |

"Behold, I give unto you a commandment, that ye suffer none of these things to enter into your heart, for it is better that ye should deny yourselves of these things, wherein ye will take up your cross, than that ye should be cast into hell."—Matthew 5:31 IV

I was having trouble threading a needle to patch a garment that needed mending. I knew I had a good needle, because my mother had used it in mending and quilting. It was a special needle; I had used it many times before and the eye was still the same size, but for some reason the thread refused to go through it.

Then I looked at the end of the thread and saw that it had split into a bundle of frazzles. It was easy for me to understand then why the thread refused to enter the eye. Immediately I trimmed off the frazzled ends.

Sometimes I am like that thread. When I feel like I have frazzles dangling in my life, I have to "trim" them from my mind so I can better focus on prayer, understanding scriptures, planning visits, or on making myself available to do whatever the Lord asks me to do.

Philippians 2:5 reads: "Let the same mind be in you that was in Christ Jesus." And Luke 18:1 says that we should "pray always and not lose hope." So God is telling us to let Christ's mind dwell in our minds. Then we will be more willing to follow the Lord's instructions.

A frazzle can be small and not noticed in our lives to begin with, but it can keep us from being focused on those things that bring us closer to our Lord and Savior, and thus keep us from receiving a greater blessing.

Hymns of the Saints: No. 123, "He Leadeth Me"

Prayer Thought: God of love and mercy, help us trim from our lives the negative thoughts and lesser motives that keep us from receiving the blessings you would have us receive.

| Tuesday **29** June | **Not Alone** By Lois Dayton St. Louis, Missouri | |

"Howl, O gate; cry, O city; thou, whole Palestine, art dissolved; for there shall come from the north a smoke, and none shall be alone in his appointed times."—Isaiah 14:31

Expecting a routine dental appointment to consist of just a simple filling, I was not prepared mentally or physically for a root canal! Having heard horror stories about root canals, but never having experienced one, I was terrified. But the pain that had sent me to the office could not be ignored another moment.

I have problems with "positional vertigo," and when the dentist brought me into an upright position after the procedure, I really "lost it." It took almost an hour before the room, office, and my world stopped spinning and the nausea subsided. No family or friends were close enough or available to pick me up and take me home. The people in the office were reluctant to let me leave, but they had an office full of patients and could not leave for some time.

Whenever I leave home, I pray that I will get out and back again safely, and that day was no different. As a senior citizen, I know my limitations and do not go far from home and "comfortable" territory.

When I started feeling better, they finally let me leave the office. By this time, the traffic is usually terrible. With schools letting out, several large office buildings, and a local hospital sending vehicles out on the road, it was usually very congested. I normally tried to be home before that time.

I said another prayer as I started the engine and cautiously headed home. To my complete amazement, there was no traffic on the road with me at that moment. As I proceeded through each intersection, the lights changed in time to stop all traffic behind me, and there was no traffic immediately in front of me. This was nearly impossible. And there was no traffic within a quarter of a mile, either next to me, in front of me, or behind me! When I needed to make a left turn onto my street, all traffic going in the opposite direction was completely gone.

As I pulled into my garage, I breathed a fervent prayer of thanks and went in and slept for two hours, feeling very well afterward. This may not sound too important in the great scheme of things, but I believe this was definitely a small miracle. I was not alone in the car. I did not come home alone.

Hymns of the Saints: No. 153, "Great Hills May Tremble"

Prayer Thought: Eternal God, we give thanks for moments when we are profoundly aware that you are with us bringing blessing in our time of need.

Wednesday **30** June	**The Hands Tell the Story** By Ward Serig Pensacola, Florida

"And this is the blessing which has been bestowed upon us, that we have been made instruments in the hands of God to bring about this great work."—Alma 14:82

I had never met Gil. I was going through Chicago enroute to a high-school class reunion and had arranged to meet a cousin who had been wanting for years to receive his evangelist's blessing. While driving there, my cousin called my cell phone number and asked if I would consider giving a blessing also to his friend Gil. Gil was a master ironworker in Chicago. Virtually everyone involved in heavy construction in the city knew him and respected him. During the years, he had mentored many young men in the trade, including my cousin. He was no longer able to work his trade and was questioning his usefulness. Gil had also served faithfully as an ordained priest for thirty years.

My first request of Gil as we began to share in preparation for his blessing was "Tell me just who Gil is so I may prepare to share with him in the sacrament of blessing." As he held his aging, but still massive, hands in front of me, his response, which I will never forget, was,

"The hands tell the story." And then he shared with me something of his life, both working his vocation and serving in the ministry. I sensed his self-doubt but also his deep desire to continue to be of service to the Lord, although he could no longer work at his profession.

Gil was assured that in serving with his hands, he had been a molding force in the lives of many young men who are better off today for having been ministered to by his instruction, his love, his kindness, and his example. He was made to know that he would be able to continue bringing ministry to children, to young people, and to older church members because of his love for them and his love for God. God had been shaping him for the present time, not at the end of the line but at the beginning of a beautiful opportunity.

Gil has continued steadfastly in his service of God's people. Virtually every week he is serving, sharing his witness, mentoring young people in the ministry. I count Gil as one of my very good friends, truly "an instrument in the hands of God."

Sing for Peace: No. 44, "Go, My Children"

Prayer Thought: Lord, bless our service to you at every stage of life. Assure us of our worth and lead us to find ways to bring blessing to others always.

July 2004

S	M	T	W	T	F	S
				1	2	3
4	5	6	7	8	9	10
11	12	13	14	15	16	17
18	19	20	21	22	23	24
25	26	27	28	29	30	31

| Thursday **1** July | **A Day with Friends**
By Larry Landsdown
Midwest City, Oklahoma | |

"...as the Lord God of thy fathers hath said unto thee; fear not, neither be discouraged."—Deuteronomy 1:21

Yesterday I went fishing with my neighbor, Bill, and another old friend. We took Bill's pontoon boat to Lake Thunderbird; we took a bucket of chicken for lunch and a cooler of iced-down pop. We were all set for a good day of fishing, but sometimes things don't work out quite as planned. We started having engine trouble before we even got the boat off the trailer. The big engine just would not start. So we hooked up the trolling motor, which ran on a battery. That worked for about half an hour until the battery ran down; then we went back to a little auxiliary five and a half horsepower engine that would run for a while and then die, and we'd have to start it again. So we did get to fish for a little while.

Finally we figured we were finished for the day and headed back to the dock. Because we didn't have a powerful engine to get up any speed, we had to use the winch to get the boat back up on the trailer. The winch cable broke, and we had to repair that. Eventually we got the boat safely loaded, put the top down, bolted it down, and headed for home. Even though we'd had many problems to overcome, we were blessed with a good spirit of fellowship. We still enjoyed the beauty of nature, being at the lake, and the fun of fishing together. We felt that the Lord had watched over us, and I'm so thankful for God's help in our difficulties and frustration.

God always blesses us, even in situations that are disappointing or discouraging. God will help us in all aspects of our lives, including our times at play.

234

Hymns of the Saints: No. 487, "Be with Me, Lord, Where'er I Go"

Prayer Thought: We thank you, Lord, for your presence wherever we are, in times of work and times of play. Restore our weary spirits through time spent with friends and the beauty of your creation.

| Friday **2** July | **Ministry among Broken Lives** By Peggy Michael Cantonment, Florida | |

"Let my word be preached to the bruised and the broken-hearted as well as those enmeshed in sin, longing to repent and follow me."—Doctrine and Covenants 153:9a

For almost two decades, Robert has served as an officer, educator, and chaplain at a federal prison. He has heard many tragic stories, some with no restitution. Some of the sad commentaries are as follows: "My habits have robbed me of my health and my family." "I've lost twenty-five years in useless living, and I can't get it back." "Life has no meaning. I wish I could start over. This time I would do it right." Because of the nature of the law broken, some will have to postpone hope of starting over. One old man declared, "I'm an evil old man, and I know there is a God." He wept bitterly.

Robert approaches each task with skill and compassion. One day during a fierce thunderstorm, a young man collapsed in the yard. Everyone hurried toward shelter, but Robert stopped beside the fallen man and tried in vain to resuscitate him. A number of men inside witnessed this act of mercy and reached out to shake Robert's hand. When his young son died, about a hundred inmates signed a letter of condolence. Daily he tries to make a difference among the broken men of society.

As I iron his white uniform shirts, I pray that not a drop of blood will ever be spilled on them, his or theirs. So far, the Lord has answered my plea, and I pray God will continue to do so.

Sing for Peace: No. 16, "Gentle God, When We Are Driven"

Prayer Thought: May we remember that your love, forgiving God, is greater than our sins.

| Saturday
3
July | **Time to Sell**
By Constance Fant
San Antonio, Texas | |

"Do not, therefore, abandon that confidence of yours; it brings a great reward. For you need endurance, so that when you have done the will of God, you may receive what was promised."—Hebrews 10:35–36 NRSV

My son, David, and I lived in our home twenty-five years. He was never strong but so alive. The latter part of his life, he struggled with terminal cancer. One night he called me into his room and said, "Mother, I'm ready to go home to the Lord. The first one I want to see is Jesus." And in a matter of weeks, he did go home.

I miss him so much, for he was such a blessing to me. There were so many memories in that house that I could hardly bear to leave it and come back in again after David was gone. Family and friends encouraged me to sell, but one dear friend advised me not to be hasty. So I stayed for six months, praying about the decision.

Eventually, I called a real estate broker and asked her to list my property. She came on a Friday and listed it on the computer that afternoon. I knelt in prayer and asked that if I was supposed to sell the house, the Lord would send a buyer right away. The next morning the broker called and asked if she could show the house to potential buyers. They went back to the office and wrote a contract. Within hours, she brought it back to me for my acceptance and signature.

God was with me all the way and answered my prayers as God has many other times. I desire to witness to many people of God's goodness.

Hymns of the Saints: No. 141, "Father, in Thy Mysterious Presence"

Prayer Thought: We praise you, Lord, for your guidance, especially in times of difficult decisions.

Sunday **4** July	**Decision Making** By Heather Osterhaus Dayton, Ohio	

"Lift up your eyes and fix them on the place beyond the horizon to which you are sent. Journey in trust.... The path will not always be easy, the choices will not always be clear, but the cause is sure and the Spirit will bear witness to the truth."—Doctrine and Covenants 161:1a, 7

We are a military family, and moving is a way of life, but this move was not going to be easy. My husband and I traveled from Texas to Ohio to look for a new home for our family. We weren't excited about the prospect of the move, because we were so comfortable in our Texas home. Our family had made wonderful friends at church, work, and school.

It was easier to find a place to live before we had children because there weren't so many considerations. In our effort to find the best fit for our family, we researched the school systems, combed the Internet for rentals, and

237

contacted a number of real estate brokers. After seeking advice from local Community of Christ members, we had come down to two choices. We decided to go to dinner in one of the little towns. As were leaving the restaurant, my husband asked the hostess, "Why should we live here?" Her face lit up and she began to list the many reasons that we had already heard from others as to why this town was a superior place.

She must have sensed that we were tired and fairly stressed over our pending decision. She reached over, touched my arm, and said, "You should pray about it, and it will be clear in the morning. You know, there are really no bad decisions; it's all a matter of what you make of it once you have decided." With her gentle touch, much of my concern melted away and tears streamed down my face. My husband's single question and the caring stranger's thoughtful response reinforced for me the scripture, "Ask and you will receive."

Hymns of the Saints: No. 176, "Teach Me, God, to Wonder"

Prayer Thought: God, as we wander about looking for answers help us remember to ask for guidance. We thank you for always being there to lead us.

Monday **5** July	**Tiny Eyes of Blessing** By Bill Griffin Elkin, North Carolina	

"Nevertheless be of good cheer, for I will lead you along; the kingdom is yours and the blessings thereof are yours; and the riches of eternity are yours."
— Doctrine and Covenants 77:4b

On free afternoons, I enjoy hiking in the national park near our home. One October day I lost track of the time and misjudged how far I was from the trailhead. Dusk gathered swiftly along the high ridge and I was still miles from my car. In the twilight the thick carpet of autumn leaves obscured the footpath, and the blazes painted on the trees had faded since spring. But I hadn't forgotten my Boy Scout training: "Be Prepared."

As night descended on the mountain, I put on my headlamp and turned it on. Every few feet, the beam reflected tiny emerald green sparkles among the leaves. They seemed to line up for me along the trail. Was this an early dew fall? Flecks of mica or some other mineral? I knelt and discovered…spider eyes! Spiders out hunting were leading me in the straight and narrow! In the most humble of God's creatures was a message of his love.

Sing a New Song: No. 50, "Though the Mountains May Fall"

Prayer Thought: Lord, may our steps take us ever deeper into an awareness of your love and mercy.

Sprouts of New Life
By Gerald John Kloss
Philadelphia, Pennsylvania

"Thus saith the Lord God unto these bones; Behold, I will cause breath to enter into you, and ye shall live."

—Ezekiel 37:5

Each summer for the past four years I have enjoyed going to Utah to spend some time with my friend Mike and his family. This has also enabled me to connect with many contacts who have blessed our Latter Day Saint Research Center with many good materials over the past few years.

Mike always plans a tremendous agenda, which has taken us all over the state, and we have visited four of the five national parks there. We have attended the live taping of the radio program *Music and the Spoken Word,* performed by the Mormon Tabernacle Choir on Temple Square, and even attended the Community of Christ re-union in Huntsville.

I have had the opportunity of speaking at our Utah congregations for the past four summers. In July 2002 I spoke at the Ogden congregation and was most blessed by the ministry of Community of Christ people there. The theme that Sunday was "Rooted in Christ." I had prepared my sermon before coming to Utah, and I asked Mike to pull up some plants from his yard that had well-formed roots. This proved to be somewhat difficult, as the summer had been hot and dry. But Mike did manage to pull out a few, and I used these in my sermon.

Afterward I decided to keep these small plants as my Utah souvenirs and brought them home and planted them in a large pot. The plants grew well through the rest of the summer and into the fall. In October I took all of my plants to the church. By January, however, they were mostly dry and nearly dead. So I pruned them, cultivated the soil, and even fertilized it a bit, and by February I noticed one small green blade pushing up through the soil. By April I was delighted that the single blade was a whole clump that I know will continue to grow.

It is likewise with our spiritual lives. We need to nurture them with spiritual disciplines of prayer, scripture study, hymn singing, and the like. It is when we keep the "soil" of our souls nourished that the Lord will bring forth new life.

Sing for Peace: No. 9 (verse 3), "Bring Forth the Kingdom"

Prayer Thought: Almighty Creator, teach us to apply to our lives the principles of wise stewardship of growth— exposure to spiritual nourishment, the sunshine of joy, and the rain of sadness, that we may more wisely bring ministry.

 Prompted by Readiness
By Donna Needham
Carnation, Washington

Wednesday
7
July

"The voice of the Lord is over the waters; the God of glory thunders, the Lord thunders over the mighty waters…. The voice of the Lord strikes with flashes of lightning."
—Psalm 29:4, 7 NIV

I was ordained to be an elder six weeks ago. In those six weeks, the oil vial I received as a gift that day has sat empty on my desk, waiting to be filled. Two days ago the prompting I needed to get some oil for my vial was strong; so I did. The very next day I was called upon for the first time to assist in an administration, and I used that oil.

How often in life I have ignored God's voice and have assumed that the thoughts I have aren't God prompting me. Yet when I listen carefully and respond, God's voice seems clear.

It was that same sort of prompting that got me out of bed in the middle of the night to write this. Perhaps the reason for this won't be as apparent to me as the oil vial, yet I believe there is purpose and a reason for responding to the voice of God.

Hymns of the Saints: No. 179, "Breathe on Me, Breath of God"

Prayer Thought: God, whose voice is for all people, help us to listen and respond when you call us.

| Thursday
8
July | **Reminders of God's Love**
By Jo Ann Townsend
Spokane, Washington | |

"Behold the fowls of the air, for they sow not, neither do they reap, nor gather into barns; yet your heavenly Father feedeth them. Are ye not much better than they? How much more will he not feed you?"—Matthew 6:29 IV

At Samish Island reunion grounds in Washington State there is a bird that will encircle you as you walk through the grass. The groundskeeper told me these birds do this because walking through the grass stirs up the bugs, and the birds can feed on them. The birds are small and very pretty with a stripe of white on their tails.

This past reunion was my first one after about ten years and I was greatly looking forward to the experience. A few days into the week I received news that a loved one at home was ill. Then, over the next two days, my daughter became ill and required two trips to a neighboring town's health clinic to get care for her. My own health was not at its best either. While I was enjoying the fellowship and blessings of the reunion, those health matters weighed heavy on my mind and I decided to go for an early morning walk.

In the quiet and peace of the reunion grounds, I began to walk and pray. Before long, I noticed that several of those pretty birds were encircling me as I walked. I understood the reason, but I chose to believe that God's love was encircling me, bringing me comfort in a time of distress. My burden was lifted and I knew that everything would be OK. And it was.

Hymns of the Saints: No. 130, "How Gentle God's Command"

Prayer Thought: Loving God, it is comforting to know that in times of distress you walk beside us always.

The Last Stitch
By Steve Calvarese
Tulsa, Oklahoma

Friday
9
July

"Then I turned to the Lord God, to seek an answer by prayer and supplication with fasting and sackcloth and ashes. I prayed to the Lord my God and made confession...."
—Daniel 9:3 NRSV

In our Christian education class on the first Sunday of 2003, Edna shared her testimony of answered prayer concerning one of our congregational sisters. She, and many others, had prayed the previous week for Anita's eye surgery to be successful and for the last stitch to come loose.

Anita has had a long history of eye problems; she was going blind, despite a number of surgeries. Her latest surgery, one month before, a new procedure by a specialist in Oklahoma City, helped relieve the high ocular pressure with a tube draining off the excess fluid, which had been causing the high pressure inside her eye. Post-op the surgeon had anticipated that all the stitches inside her eye would fall out naturally as a result of the healing process within a week or two. They did—that is, all but one. The surgeon was contemplating another, somewhat riskier, laser surgery if the last stitch did not come off soon. Edna and others prayed for the last stitch to fall off, and miraculously it did. As soon as the last stitch loosened, the pressure decreased and the eye surgery was declared a success. There was no need for any additional treatment. Anita and Edna both believe that God still answers prayer.

Hymns of the Saints: No. 105, "O Thou God, Who Hearest Prayer"

Prayer Thought: Gracious God, we offer you our humblest thanks, both for your blessings in answer to our prayers of petition and for the faith of so many who hold our needs up to you.

<table>
<tr><td>Saturday
10
July</td><td>**Brought Together in Christ**
By Marlene Brunner
Yuma, Colorado</td><td></td></tr>
</table>

"Sow to yourselves in righteousness, reap in mercy; break up your fallow ground; for it is time to seek the Lord, till he come and rain righteousness upon you."—Hosea 10:12

At the 2002 World Conference, there was some discussion relative to homosexuality and what the church

244

could and should offer to people with this orientation. I was seated in a delegation diagonally across the aisle from a young man who arose on the Conference floor and openly stated that he was homosexual. Although I have never been able to understand this lifestyle, in a sense, I have always felt called by Christ to love all people regardless of how I felt about how they lived their lives.

Just before the start of one of the business sessions, I felt strongly that when this young man came into the conference chamber I should give him a hug and express my love for him as a brother in Christ.

Some time passed before he returned, and I was concerned that I had missed my opportunity. When he finally returned, I hugged him and expressed my love for him as a brother in the faith. He thanked me sincerely and told me how much my hug meant to him.

I am certain that Christ calls us to love all people and not sit in judgment on the way they live their lives.

Sing a New Song: No. 21, "Instruments of Your Peace"

Prayer Thought: Free us, Lord, from all forms of prejudice, that we may see the good in all people. Make us willing to listen to another point of view, and not presume to have all the answers.

Sunday **11** July	**Sharing Our Testimony** By Merna Short Melbourne, Australia

"There are different kinds of gifts, but the same Spirit. There are different kinds of service, but the same Lord. There are different kinds of working, but the same God works all of them in all men."—II Corinthians 12:4–6 NIV

"The kettle's on. Would you like to share a cup of tea or coffee?" This bright invitation came from a neighbor who had set up camp beside us for a couple of days. We folded our chairs and moved onto their site. We each talked about the places we had been, and the reasons we had chosen the equipment for camping according to our needs and restrictions. Relaxing companionably together we exchanged names and where we had come from. It was enjoyable.

That night we invited them into our van for a snack before bed. This time we talked about our occupations and interests. Sharing that one of my interests is writing, I took down the *Daily Bread* and turned to a devotional I had written. The wife read it aloud for us. They were churchgoers themselves. Her voice was full of meaning. I felt blessed to hear the message so alive.

My heart swelled with gratitude for the opportunity given to us, too, to minister in this way. In a brief, chance relationship, maybe we were opening a path for the Lord to move.

Sing for Peace: No. 31, "Lord Jesus, of You I Will Sing"

Prayer Thought: God, may we view all people as precious, sharing your love for them and bringing your blessing into their lives.

<table>
<tr><td>Monday
12
July</td><td>**Loving Obedience**
By Denzil J. West
Independence, Missouri</td><td></td></tr>
</table>

*"For this is the love of God, that we keep his command-
ments; and his commandments are not grievous."*

—I John 5:3

The Great Depression was in full swing when my entire family was baptized: father, mother, brother, cousin,
and me at age ten.

Our dad taught us about the financial law, and he said
that we would be blessed as we kept this law. Money was
not plentiful, but Dad gave my brother and me ten cents
in pennies each week. He reminded us that one cent be-
longed to God in our tithing envelope. I complained that
I could see a movie on Saturday for ten cents, but if I
gave a penny to God for tithing, I wouldn't have enough
money left to go to the movies. Dad just reminded me
that if I saved the other nine cents until next Saturday
that I would have more than enough for a movie. That
was a difficult lesson for this ten year old, but one I still
follow to this day.

Years later when I returned from the marines at the
end of World War II, my mother gave me a little box containing many weekly receipts from the bishop's agent,
each one for one cent tithing. The receipts are long
since gone, but the impact of Dad's teaching remains.
God keeps promises, and when we are obedient, we are
blessed.

Hymns of the Saints: No. 397, "All Things Are Thine"

Prayer Thought: Bless our desires to be faithful, Lord,
and may we joyfully offer our best, that others may
know about you.

Countenance of Joy

By Jeannine Blasick
Monongahela, Pennsylvania

"Every elder, priest, teacher, or deacon, is to be ordained according to the gifts and callings of God unto [them]."
—Doctrine and Covenants 17:12a

I once asked the Lord to show me how people are called to priesthood. In May 1987, I was shown one of many ways God reveals his will to us. While at a prayer meeting, as we sat quietly meditating before the service began, I noticed that an elder seemed troubled, and I remembered how he had looked shortly after being ordained. His face had shown with a countenance of joy in serving Christ. I recalled also seeing this same beauty in the faces of others after their ordination. Then my eyes fell upon each one present, studying them as I followed the circle around the room. I came to my very close friend; again, I saw a special beauty in her countenance as the person in charge spoke to begin the meeting.

This never entered my mind again until two weeks later at another prayer meeting. On the afternoon before going, the Spirit of the Lord came to me in this manner with a tune to words I began to sing "The joy of the Lord is in this place. The glory of the Lord is in this place" repeatedly; it then left me, after which I began to prepare our dinner. After restoring order to my kitchen, I left for church. I didn't think about it again, but partway into the meeting, the same Spirit returned with the words that had been with me earlier that day. As the meeting progressed, my dear friend spoke up saying how she had always desired to have the countenance of the Lord seen in her by others so she could share God's love with them.

Now this was before the cancer surgery she was to have the following week. I then shared openly, in the presence of others, that I had seen the countenance of the Lord upon her face just two weeks before, and was assured that God would be with her during her surgery. She had been diagnosed with a large ovarian tumor. Before the surgery, doctors had prepared her for the worst outcome. She might need a colostomy and ileostomy, and her blood count was extremely high. But her surgery went well, she recovered rapidly, and it was her choice not to have chemo follow-up. She was about to receive a healing blessing because the Spirit had assured me that the "the joy of the Lord" was in this place, and "the glory of the Lord" was also there.

Sing a New Song: No. 11, "Give Thanks"

Prayer Thought: Lord who responds to our asking, we rejoice at your presence in our lives when we seek you.

| Wednesday **14** July | **Interrupted Potential** By Hal McKain Lamoni, Iowa | |

"But for you who revere my name the sun of righteousness shall rise, with healing in its wings. You shall go out leaping like calves from the stall."—Malachi 4:2 NRSV

The little African violet was looking quite sad. Its stems and leaves were uneven—some too long and others too short. I cut off the long stems back to the neck and covered the cut place with soil. The short ones would eventually grow, and with good care, they and new ones would produce a pretty plant. I realized that this African violet would never really reach its full potential. It had been slowed down and had lost the possibility of becoming fully developed. Maybe the problem was that the young plant had missed some important watering days, or an insect had enjoyed it as lunch, or it had received too much water.

I see a similarity in my life and in the lives of some other people. I remember having had some sad, terrifying experiences in my life when I was young that took away an opportunity for good growth that should have occurred at that age. Even in other people, I see flaws in their behavior and realize that possibly something prohibited proper growth at a critical time in their life. I noticed that when two of us "wounded" people were together, it was easy to disturb each other. And when someone came around who was "healed," they could bring peace to an otherwise possibly volatile situation.

What I'm trying to say is that it is so important to understand that living things are sensitive to what goes on around them. And if we feel a personal, spiritual stewardship to provide for maximum human development, we must keep the growing environment positive. It is a beautiful experience to see a disciple of Jesus bring healing to the mind of a human soul. What a wonderful calling it is to be able to bring peace in the human arena.

Hymns of the Saints: No. 109, "Here We Have Come, Dear Lord, to Thee"

Prayer Thought: God of all living things, even in our awareness of interrupted potential, lead us to do all we can to make the most of the potential still present.

"So the last will be first, and the first will be last."
—Matthew 20:16 NIV

As I entered the lobby of my bank, I saw a dad chasing his grinning little son across the floor. The man corralled the boy, at which point the little guy wailed an eardrum-shattering complaint. I prayed a few words for the unhappy child and his sorely tried father. With the raceway cleared, I stepped into line for a teller.

Another woman came up behind me in line, then everyone else in the bank. The father and son joined the end of the queue. The father now held the boy, who was hollering loud enough to shake the roof. I considered letting the man into line in front of me, for everyone's sake. To the woman behind me, I said, "Maybe we should let him in ahead of us? What do you think?"

"Fine with me," she agreed. "Actually, before you came in, he was standing first in line, and then he went running after the toddler."

We stepped to the side and motioned the man forward. He walked by, gripping the unhappy youngster. "Thank you," the father said to us. "You didn't need to do that." A teller smiled in our direction.

The boy continued to squall. A few minutes later, the father completed his banking and turned from the teller. He smiled, nodded at us, and said, "Thank you again, ladies." As he headed toward the door, the boy calmed down.

There in the bank, nobody spoke the words of Jesus in Matthew 20:16, "So the last will be first, and the first will be last." Nobody needed to speak them. The little boy would learn the scripture lesson and the etiquette later. For now, he had examples.

Hymns of the Saints: No. 436, "Go Now Forth into the World"

Prayer Thought: Let us be living examples of your gospel, Lord, wherever we may be.

| Friday **16** July | **Lightning Bug Ring** By Paul McCain Oklahoma City, Oklahoma | |

"But the father said unto his servants, Bring forth the best robe, and put it on him; and put a ring on his finger, and shoes on his feet."—Luke 15:22

When I was five, I attended a birthday party next door. We played one of our favorite games, "Cowboys and Indians," which required us dividing into two teams. That day I was one of the Indians, and several of us had been captured by the cowboys and locked in a small tool shed. The lock consisted of a small board with a nail through the center into the frame around the door, and turned so that it kept the door "locked." Being resourceful, we "busted out" of our confinement by hitting the door on the inside with our shoulders. As I jumped out, I felt the long nail that had held the lock on just moments before, go deep into my bare foot.

Mom called our family doctor and we left immediately to meet him at his office. We arrived some time before he did, and Mom had a very distressed young boy to deal with. Being resourceful, as all mothers have to be, she tried to keep my focus somewhere besides on my foot. In the summer twilight there were fireflies dotting the air near the step that we sat on, so she caught one and pressed its lighted body to the top of one of my fingers to fashion a ring for me.

I still remember two things about that event: yes, the extreme pain, especially as the doctor worked on my foot, but just as much, how special I felt with that gesture of love by my mother. Feeling special covers a lot of pain.

I'm reminded of the prodigal son who, upon returning from his humiliating experience, was given a ring by his father. In the case of the prodigal son, the ring signified a return to a position of authority in the family (the family signet ring was used to seal contracts). In my case the ring sent a similar message to me: I was important.

It took me about forty years to realize why I disliked white cake with white frosting; that was what I had eaten at the birthday party. Now I eat white cake and remember the lightning bug ring.

Sing for Peace: No. 3, "Gather Your Children"

Prayer Thought: Eternal Parent, may we learn from the pain, but focus on the good things in life and the times when we have felt special.

| Saturday **17** July | **Prayer Journaling** By Willa Frey Fairbanks, Alaska | |

"For if you would hearken to the Spirit which teaches a man to pray, you would know that you must pray; for the evil spirit teaches not a man to pray, but teaches him that he must not pray."—II Nephi 14:11

We were introduced to prayer journaling by Evangelist Bob Slasor at a spiritual growth retreat. I had never tried it before and felt reluctant to express my thoughts on paper. I had vowed to never write anything down that I would not want someone else to read. This was the result of having two brothers, one of whom was especially interested in my "private" thoughts so he could tell everyone and thus tease me. So I had to overcome this "life commandment" if I were to successfully write out my thoughts. I was skeptical but decided to try.

Bob introduced the subject, then asked us to separate and write down prayer concerns in our hearts. After about fifteen minutes, he asked us to write what we thought God would say to us about our prayer. This was difficult. I was to write, "Willa, my daughter, I say unto you at this time...." and finish the sentence with the first thought that came into my head. I carefully wrote what I thought God would say in response to my concerns. God would say pretty much the same thing to anyone voicing the same type of concerns, or so I thought. I was skeptical.

At the close of the workshop, Bob asked us to go back and read our prayer journaling and God's answer. I shrugged and proceeded to do so. WOW! The answer hit me between the eyes, and I had a powerful feeling that this was indeed what God was saying to me. I was shaken up but decided to give the whole procedure a chance. That began my prayer journaling experience about ten years ago.

I found that I was more able to stay with my prayers (without my mind wandering) than I had been before. Writing them down helped me to be more explicit and see my concerns more clearly. It taught me the importance of wait time as I sought to know God's plan for me. I'm rather impatient, so this was an important lesson for me to learn. I developed a much closer relationship with God than ever before, one that pointed out specific issues I needed to address. I'm very thankful for this growing experience and highly recommend prayer journaling to everyone, especially if you haven't tried it!

Hymn of the Saints: No. 82, "One Hour with Jesus"

Prayer Thought: Create in us, Lord, a desire to seek your message to us. May we discover a new level of living with your Spirit.

| Sunday
18
July | **Look for the Beautiful**
By Lois Dayton
Arnold, Missouri | |

"...for Zion must increase in beauty, and in holiness; her borders must be enlarged; her stakes must be strengthened; yea, verily I say unto you, Zion must arise and put on her beautiful garments."—Doctrine and Covenants 81:4c

My ninety-two-year-old aunt sold her farm and moved to a senior retirement home. We went to see her, and as I was glancing through the monthly calendar listing activities and programs, I asked her, "Do you play bingo on Thursdays?" "Oh, no," she said, "that's for the *old* ladies!" She was a very devout person, had read her Bible through many times, and had a youthful, positive outlook. She loved children, and they were drawn to her.

A positive attitude, even through adversity, can carry us safely over the speed bumps on the road of life. We must lay our burdens at Jesus' feet and ask him to see us through to the end of our journey. My aunt set an example that I hope to follow. "Look for the beautiful, look for the true," and try to be positive!

Hymns of the Saints: No. 437, "Look for the Beautiful"

Prayer Thought: Eternal God, enable us to look for the best in all situations and not bemoan what we cannot control. Reveal to us the positive, that our lives may be effective.

Revive Us, Lord
By Russell Grinnell
Cookeville, Tennessee

"For thus saith the high and lofty One that inhabiteth eternity, whose name is Holy; I dwell in the high and holy place, with him also that is of a contrite and humble spirit, to revive the spirit of the humble, and to revive the heart of the contrite ones."—Isaiah 57:15

When we lived in Illinois, we liked to go to Devils Backbone Park on the Mississippi River and watch the tugboats pushing barges up and down the river. One spring when heavy rains came and the snow melted in the states above us, the river flooded and came over the banks. For many weeks, trees and all manner of things came floating down the river. Many of these trees had lain rotting along the riverbanks for a long time before the floods came, with little likelihood that they would ever go anywhere. But as the floodwaters rose, they picked up the dead trees. When the water receded, the trees floated back into the river. Those that didn't get caught on something, traveled past several states and on down to the Gulf of Mexico.

We as church members are often a lot like that. For a while, we are willing workers, getting involved in church activities and the programs and goals of the church, but then something happens. Perhaps someone has said something that hurt us, or sickness overtakes us, or we get old and feel we aren't capable of doing anything anymore. So like the rotting trees along the banks, we resign ourselves to wait for death to overtake us and make no effort to take part in church activities because we are too old or too sick or we have some other excuse. We are in need of revival.

We may not be able to do some of the things we did before, but we may find other things that need to be done that we still can do.

Hymns of the Saints: No. 157, "My Life Flows on in Endless Song"

Prayer Thought: God, when the oil in our lamps runs low, help us to see the possibilities for service and realize that opportunities to serve are all around us.

Tuesday **20** July	**Just Ask** By Florence King Feilding, New Zealand

"And I say unto you, Ask, and it shall be given you; seek, and ye shall find; knock, and it shall be opened unto you."—Luke 11:10 IV

During October and November 2002, a woman from the Baptist church visited each church in Feilding asking for people to teach the Bible in the schools. The teachers only have half an hour per week, with not all of the schools wanting them to come in. When there is an opening, teachers must be there to teach.

The response was great. However, with more teachers, this meant that more books were required for the children. Early in February 2003, someone determined that there was no money to pay for the books. Immediately a prayer chain was started. Two days later, a man knocked on the Baptist woman's door. He said that he had heard about the need for money and handed her a check. From then on people kept arriving with money, and because of all this money, a checking account was opened.

The year is divided into two parts, with both halves requiring $540 each. The account was opened with a deposit of $615, with money coming in regularly. Each church was asked to donate a certain amount toward these books.

When people combine in prayer for a great need, miracles always happen.

Sing a New Song: No. 7, "Companions on the Journey"

Prayer Thought: Great God who hears our prayers, may we always put you first in everything, knowing that you will supply all our needs.

Wednesday **21** July	**Encourage Us, Lord** By Barrie Fox Kirkby in Ashfield, England	

"The prayer of faith shall save the sick…. The effectual fervent prayer of a righteous man availeth much."
—James 5:15–16

The other day as I sat reflecting on some of the problems hindering the progress of the church in today's world. I felt myself challenged to accept the fact that we tend to underrate both what we are still capable of doing and what God can still do with us, for us, and through us. I felt myself being challenged to contemplate and accept more fully, the reality of God's power and the numerous ways we are blessed by it.

Imagine the frustration of having the very latest electrical appliances on a desert island where there was no electricity available. Even in our homes, electrical gadgets do not function as they should if we don't know how to handle them or if they are not plugged into a functioning electrical source. Similarly, we need to believe in and in some ways understand how Jesus functions in our lives and to be connected to and alive to the movement of the Spirit.

Some of the sin that so readily creeps into our lives can be likened to the weeds in a garden, or the clouds that block out the sun from our vision, or some of those things that stop an engine from functioning as it should. How true this all seems to be when we really take time to stop and think about it, and yet again I am reminded of the scripture, "The effectual fervent prayer of a righteous [person] availeth much."

Hymns of the Saints: No. 140, "Awake! Ye Saints of God, Awake"

Prayer Thought: God, you have shared with us the good news of your saving grace and love and have called us to promote the message of Christ in our world. Help us to respond to this blessing and challenge.

The Cherry Tree
By Janice Townsend
Spokane, Washington

Thursday
22
July

"Remember this: Whoever sows sparingly will also reap sparingly, and whoever sows generously will also reap generously."—II Corinthians 9:6 NIV

The leaves of the tree were green and healthy, providing shade in the summer and mulch in the winter. Strong, sturdy limbs lifted toward the sky and offered a perfect climbing place for adventurous children. But the fruit of the cherry tree were mostly pit and skin, because the tree was a seedling. It had not been selected because of its good properties or planted intentionally to produce the best harvest. The tree just grew, perhaps from a pit dropped by a bird as it flew over the hillside beside our home.

Our family enjoyed the tree and drank in the beauty of its springtime blossoms. My brother, sisters, and I read books in the shelter of its umbrella-like branches. We used it for a lookout perch in our games of hide-and-seek, and as a place where imagination could take us to the far realms of childish fantasy. Each summer we tried a few of the cherries but they were never very good.

We did nothing to nurture the tree. It was there, part of our lives, and valued for what it was. But now, years later, I recall that tree and wonder why our family so readily accepted what was less than the best—why we deprived ourselves of the greater satisfaction that could have been ours had we intentionally selected and planted a tree of good stock and established variety.

I wonder too if other "seedlings" are still growing in my life, taking up room while not really offering a good harvest. I want to be selective in the things I allow to fill my life. I especially want to weed out those "seedlings" that, while attractive and pleasant, are taking up room that could be more productive, and that might bring forth the harvest most pleasing to our Lord.

Sing for Peace: No. 37, "Were the World to End Tomorrow"

Prayer Thought: Lord, let us be faithful sowers, planting our field of living in ways that will return a rich harvest for your glory.

A Walk to Remember
By Shirley Vallier Remmenga
Fort Collins, Colorado

"...let thy heart cheer thee in the days of thy youth, and walk in the ways of thine heart, and in the sight of thine eyes; but know thou, that for all these things God will bring thee into judgment."—Ecclesiastes 11:9

It was just an ordinary walk—or was it? Bryce and Drew, my six- and four-year-old grandsons, and I were in the mood for a walk. We wandered through the meadow, along the irrigation ditch, crossed it on a plank that served as a bridge, and decided to walk in the ditch itself. Next, we walked along a fencerow and back across the horse pasture north of the house.

We chatted about this and that and about God. We laughed, collected milkweed pods, leaves, sticks, and rocks. When the boys' pockets were so full that they could hardly walk, I let them fill mine. We stopped in a particularly good place for rock collecting, and one of them said, "Grandma Shirley, this is the best walk ever. I'll always remember it!" The other chimed in, "Me, too!" They were a couple of happy, tired boys when we finally made it home.

Now, I'm thinking that they may not always remember this particular walk, but I know I will. It was great fun just being a child again and seeing and experiencing life as they were seeing and experiencing it. I am so grateful for all the little people in my life, for they constantly remind me of the important things—the simple, ordinary, day-to-day relationships we have with nature, loved ones, and God. With them, something as ordinary as a walk becomes a wonderful experience and a valued memory.

Sing for Peace: No. 10, "God of Grace and God of Laughter"

Prayer Thought: God of life and love, thank you for little ones who keep us close to you and to the important things in life. May we never take them for granted.

Saturday **24** July	**Sharing Our Story** By Ralph Holmes Sutton in Ashfield, Nottingamshire, England

"But ye shall receive power, after that the Holy Ghost is come upon you; and ye shall be witnesses unto me both in Jerusalem, and in all Judea, and Samaria, and unto the uttermost part of the earth."—Acts 1:8

I was brought up in a church family that now goes back seven generations. My grandfather, along with two other families, was responsible for organizing our congregation in 1905. From my birth I was encouraged to attend church activities: church school, Zion's League, prayer meetings, preaching services, and all other connected activities.

Two things have been dominant in my life: the church (and subsequently my ministry) and music. The church gave me the opportunity to use my talents to serve God. At eleven years of age I was asked to play the piano for church school. I hadn't even had any formal teaching. At twelve years I played the organ for my first wedding. Because of the encouragement I had from the people of the church many opportunities came my way. My formal training began when I was sixteen years old. I went on to become a teacher of music.

Before I joined the teaching profession I worked as a precision engineer, which brought me into contact with many people with whom I was able to share my testimony. One man I talked to was a deep thinker and read many of our church books. He questioned everything and wanted to know all of the details as well as being convinced of the church's teachings. Although he later joined another denomination he became as good an advocate as one will find for the Community of Christ. Another friend persuaded his own church to set up a stewardship program very similar to ours.

In my profession as a teacher and choral society music director, I have had many opportunities for ministry, being invited to speak at church groups and services in a variety of denominations. This has led to a greater understanding and a better relationship with fellow Christians. Bearing our testimony is seldom easy but whenever we do someone will be blessed, as well as ourselves.

Hymns of the Saints: No. 436, "Go Now Forth into the World"

Prayer Thought: Gracious God, give to us the will and courage to speak for you and to share our blessings with others.

| Sunday **25** July | **Friends** By Shirley S. Case Slater, Missouri | |

"And again I say unto you my friends (for from henceforth I shall call you friends), It is expedient that I give unto you this commandment, that ye become even as my friends in days when I was with them traveling to preach this gospel in my power."—Doctrine and Covenants 83:13a

At a prayer meeting one Sunday evening, the topic of discussion was "friends." There were many wonderful testimonies on the subject and my friend Harold Thayer piped up and said that there are many degrees of friendship. With that I totally agree. Some of my best friends have been people I didn't even know. It sounds crazy, but let me explain.

Last year I had to take a chemotherapy drug called Taxol. This drug takes about eight hours to administer, and it has to be done in a hospital. You sit in a chair with three to four other people in the room doing the same thing. Sometimes we read or sewed or played cards, but most of the time we talked. We shared intimate things about our lives. We shared fears, hopes, and stories about our children. We talked about our churches; the nurses who were inept at inserting needles, and the nurses who were kind; and loves lost because they couldn't deal with the cancer. But mostly we laughed! The laughter was like a good clean rain, cleansing our souls. And we were friends, best friends, savoring each minute with one another like there might not be anymore. And for some, there weren't.

We each realized God would have us love one another as we've never loved before, to accept one another as a dearest brother or sister, and to be friend to all.

Hymns of the Saints: No. 407, "Yesu, Yesu, Fill Us with Your Love"

Prayer Thought: Lord, help us this day to see with your eyes, to listen with your ears, to share you with others, and to laugh with your joy.

Love Thy Neighbor
By LaVerne Cramer
Tomah, Wisconsin

"And thou shalt love the Lord thy God with all thy heart, and with all thy soul, and with all thy mind, and with all thy strength. This is the first commandment. And the second is like this, Thou shalt love thy neighbor as thyself. There is none other commandment greater than these."
—Mark 12:35–36 IV

Mark says "Love thy neighbor." What does this scripture mean to you? I have a modern-day example of what it means to me. Our daughter, Ina Mae, shared the following story with me. John, her husband, works as director of computer operations. One of John's employees had cancer. He came to work with a tube in his chest. Because of his sickness, he missed many days of work and wasn't able to fulfill his workload. After some time, John's boss wanted John to force the man with cancer to take long-term disability and replace him at work.

John couldn't bring himself to force the man out, because this dying man wanted to work and was doing the best he could. Instead John took on the extra load himself. He would work on Saturdays and come back in the evenings to work. John carried this extra load for two years, so that the dying man could keep working whenever he was able to, until God took this special employee home on November 4. I wonder, is this what Christ meant when he said, "Bear ye one another's burdens"?

Hymns of the Saints: No. 369, "Bear Each Other's Burdens"

Prayer Thought: Lord, we thank you for the added strength you give us daily to help us carry another person's burden.

We Are Never Lost
By Faye Williams
Kennett, Missouri

"Hold up my goings in thy paths, that my footsteps slip not. I have called upon thee, for thou wilt hear, O God, my speech, and incline thine ear unto me."—Psalm 17:5–6

While traveling with some friends, my sister-in-law realized she must have taken a wrong turn and was not on the right road. She stopped and said to an elderly gentleman, "We are lost." He replied, "No, you are not lost; I know exactly where you are." He then gave them directions to help set them back on the right road.

We should be aware that we are never lost. God knows exactly where we are at all times. We should feel secure in knowing that God can always lead us in the right direction, if we will only ask. How wonderful to know that the Lord is there for us no matter how many wrong turns we make in life.

Hymns of the Saints: No. 331, "Father, Who in Jesus Found Us"

Prayer Thought: Our kind and loving God, help us remember to follow the teachings of your word, knowing that by doing so, we will make the choices that will keep us on the right path of life.

Parental Guidance
By Jim Edwards
Sparta, Wisconsin

"...care for the soul, and for the life of the soul, and seek the face of the Lord always, that in patience ye may possess your souls, and ye shall have eternal life."
—Doctrine and Covenants 98:5j

We are all aware that home is a vital influence in raising God's servants. All major institutions in society (school, government, religion), are highly dependent on the institution of family. We have also observed that as we leave home and family, we do not always use our agency wisely, both in terms of our lifestyles and in our time involvements. However, the fact that organized religion continues to exist and the vast majority of children are brought up, baptized, confirmed, and continue to be active in religious affiliations is a testimony to the truth of Proverbs 22:6.

My sisters and I were raised by parents who provided Christlike examples through their services to their fellow beings and to their God. All of my siblings and I are active servants in our church, communities, professions, and volunteer organizations. Our parents have also influenced the lives of many people outside our family.

Doctrine and Covenants 68:4c instructs parents to "teach their children to pray, and to walk uprightly before the Lord." The world has always needed the example of good parents who teach their children about a life given to Christ, as portrayed in the scriptures, and a relationship with God through the Holy Spirit. Parents who teach their children to pray and to study scripture are a real blessing.

A life of service has created a sense of fulfillment and joy for me, a joy that exceeds any riches lost or any elements of inconvenience that may be experienced in the process.

Hymns of the Saints: No. 379, "Thou Must Be True Thyself"

Prayer Thought: Gracious God, we are thankful for the blessings of loving parents, and brothers and sisters of the faith who teach and guide us in pathways of service. We are further thankful for the joy and fulfillment that come from serving you and our fellow beings.

Thursday **29** July	**The Lord Will Supply** By Ethel Knackstedt Kansas City, Kansas	

"Teach me your way, O Lord, that I may walk in your truth; give me an undivided heart to revere your name. I give thanks to you, O Lord my God, with my whole heart, and I will glorify your name forever."

—Psalm 86:11–12 NRSV

Many years ago, when our children were small, I received an anonymous letter with a $20 bill tucked inside. It was a letter of encouragement, one that told me that the Lord was aware of my anxieties and concerns and that God was pleased with my dedication.

Now, with a young family and the operation of a household, money was tight but we certainly weren't destitute. I was so taken aback with the gift that I called my pastor's wife. I told her what had happened, and that I felt so unworthy of it: others needed it a lot more than I did. She kindly listened and then she said, "Ethel, someone has been impressed to send you the money, and they know you will use it wisely. Accept it and be thankful."

To this day I have never known who my benefactor was, but it has prompted my giving in many ways. Our giving over the years has been in increments of $20 bills. We were once aware of a family who lived out of town and had a need. We agreed on an amount and mailed the money to them.

We needed a brake job on our car and were prepared to pay the amount called for, but when we took the car in, the mechanic informed us that the rear brakes were fine; we only needed to replace the front brakes. The difference in price was the exact amount we had sent to our friends.

Even though I never knew who my benefactor was, I have a feeling that their gift was multiplied many, many times. All I know is that it has borne fruit in my life and in the lives of my loved ones.

Hymns of the Saints: No. 125, "My Shepherd Will Supply My Need"

Prayer Thought: Great Provider, may we be ever willing to share with those in need, even as we have been blessed by the kindness of others.

 Deeds of Love
By Isabelle Saxton
Cheyenne, Wyoming

Friday **30** July

"The faithful will abound with blessings, but one who is in a hurry to be rich will not go unpunished."
—Proverbs 28:20 NRSV

The summer of 2002 brought a big change in my life. I became ill, so I could not do some things I was used to doing. It had been an important part of my life to help people in a variety of ways. Suddenly I was on the other end of things. Wonderful neighbors, church family, and relatives came to my aid. All that was done for me was amazing: food brought in, shopping, rides to the doctor, just coming to be with me, to name a few. I quickly learned that a person needs to be a good receiver, not just a good giver.

A friend knew I wanted painting done, so she recommended Rick, a professional painter, who soon became my friend. He sanded and painted all the trim on the outside of the house and shop, and caulked outside and inside the house. His beautiful, caring spirit brightened my days. Each morning before he started work, he came in to check on me and visit a bit. The morning before he finished, I told him to please sit down; I had something I needed to say. I said, "Rick, I want you to know you have been a blessing to me, not only doing fine professional work, but how you see little things to do to help out. You are a very important part of my healing."

In his quiet way, he answered, "Thank you for saying that. No one has ever said that to me before."

I mentioned to him that he had my house looking super, and now I needed the dirty windows washed. A week later, he and his wife came and washed all the windows, inside and out. What a joy to look out clean windows to view my flower garden that a neighbor was taking care of while I couldn't.

There were several unusual incidents, too numerous to relate, that happened during those two months of illness. God was with me, and through them all, the blessings outweighed the pain.

Hymns of the Saints: No. 8, "You May Sing of the Beauty"

Prayer Thought: Merciful God, we offer our profound thanks for both friends and strangers who have blessed our lives when we have had need. May we return their loving acts as we are able.

Through the Generations
By Emma Strickland
Grafton, Australia

"I have no greater joy than to hear that my children walk in truth. Beloved, thou doest faithfully whatsoever thou doest to the brethren, and to strangers."—III John 4–5

In the early 1870s, missionaries from America visited the east coast of Australia and held meetings at a small township on the Manning River. A family of McLaughlins became interested, and out of the twelve brothers and sisters, eight became baptized members, and the other four always had a yen for the gospel. These young people found it difficult to change their faith, as their father used to lock up the horse saddles so they couldn't attend meetings. This did not hinder two of the younger men; they just rode bareback! One was my father.

After my father married my mother, she soon became a member. They had ten children, of whom I am the youngest. Only one brother and I are left now, but I am proud to say that we were all baptized into the latter-day light.

Hymns of the Saints: No. 477, "We've a Story to Tell to the Nations"

Prayer Thought: God of all generations, show us how to instill in those who follow us an appreciation for the determination of our forebears to follow their conscience. May we value our faith anew.

August 2004

S	M	T	W	T	F	S
1	2	3	4	5	6	7
8	9	10	11	12	13	14
15	16	17	18	19	20	21
22	23	24	25	26	27	28
29	30	31				

| Sunday
1
August | **Smile Power**
By Helen M. Green
Toledo, Ohio | |

"You have made known to me the ways of life; you will make me full of gladness with your presence."
—Acts 2:28 NRSV

I have a friend whose countenance always reflects joy. A contemporary, she has experienced good and bad events in her life, yet I have never seen her when she wasn't smiling. Early in our relationship, she was a strong influence on my own desire to wear a "happy face." We are told that it takes far more muscles to frown than to smile, so I reason that I don't have to work so hard to smile.

One day as I paused for a stop sign, the garbage pickup crew came around the corner. I thought of the tremendous service they render to our community. It is a thankless job and never pleasant in any kind of weather. I smiled at them as the truck crossed in front of me, and the two men in the cab showed broad grins as they held up their thumbs in approval. Those grins carried me the rest of the day. They also caused me to say a thank-you prayer for the work they do and a request that their day would be pleasant.

We are all connected. How much better to exchange smiles than scowls.

Sing for Peace: No. 23, "We Are Called to Be Peacemakers"

Prayer Thought: Lord, help us to appreciate the many humble workers who do the dirty jobs, the tiresome work, the unpraised service that makes our lives better. May we be willing to make the lives of others better also.

Are You Sharing Your Witness?

By Dorene Kilburn
St. Paul's Station, Ontario,
Canada

"I will give thanks to the Lord with my whole heart; I will tell all of your wonderful deeds; I will be glad and exult in you; I will sing praises to your name, O Most High."
—Psalm 9:1–2 NRSV

"Are you sharing your witness?" The person who put that question to me at a workshop my husband and I attended is someone whose friendship I value enormously. She took me by surprise, and for a moment, I thought she was talking to someone behind me—or maybe that's what I wanted to think! I told her Orme reminds me periodically that I often pass up opportunities to witness of what God has done in my life, beginning with answering the prayer of countless family friends for a tiny baby who was critically ill and wasn't expected to live.

I know, but I don't always act on the knowledge that God will guide us to those occasions where we can witness of his involvement in our lives. I know, too, that when we share a testimony of our own experiences, no one can refute it—it is our experience! And I also know that sharing God's blessings in our lives can reinforce another's faith. Or perhaps it can be the beginning of a journey of discovery, and a commitment to follow Jesus. God can make disciples with our help.

Hymns of the Saints: No. 470, "Tell It! Tell It Out with Gladness"

Prayer Thought: Lord of our lives, help us to put aside our reluctance at times to speak for you. May we try to take every opportunity you give us to share our testimony of your blessings in our lives.

<table>
<tr><td>Tuesday
3
August</td><td>**First Prayers**
By Susan Miller
North Wales, United Kingdom</td><td></td></tr>
</table>

"And blessed are all the pure in heart; for they shall see God."—Matthew 5:10 IV

I was searching bookstores for a little book on children's prayers. My daughter was turning three and I wanted some prayers that I could teach her both at dinner and at bedtime. The standard "God is great, God is good, Let us thank him for our food, Amen" from my recollection seemed too basic. I wanted something a bit more creative!

Needless to say, I didn't find what I was looking for in conventional bookstores, so I stopped at a Christian bookshop. They had exactly what I wanted. In the meantime, we had been starting off with a simple dinner grace that our daughter could repeat after us: "Dear God, thank you for the food; thank you for our blessings, Amen." She was timid, but she would repeat each word carefully with her head bowed, eyes closed, and hands in position.

Now that I had these books, though, I could teach her to say a perfectly rhymed little prayer, and it would be so much better! Before I got the chance, though, Madison taught us. It was dinnertime and her dad said, "OK, let's say prayers." Madison chirped, "I'll do prayers, Daddy," and with no help from us she bowed her head, closed her eyes, positioned her hands, and said in such a sweet voice, "Dear God, thank you for the food; thank you for my family, and thank you for Jesus, Amen."

Our mouths dropped—where did this come from? We hadn't taught her to thank God for her family or for Jesus, but out of the mouth of this little one came a most perfect prayer. Madison loves to "do prayers" now. And the books I bought? They lay on her bookshelf, not needed. Our daughter is writing her own.

Hymns of the Saints: No. 223, "Jesus Loves the Little Children"

Prayer Thought: Heavenly Parent, thank you for continuing to astound us through our children.

| Wednesday **4** August | **Cheerios on the Carpet**
 By Denzil J. West
 Independence, Missouri | |

"People brought babies to Jesus, hoping he might touch them. When the disciples saw it, they shooed them off. Jesus called them back. 'Let these children alone. Don't get between them and me. These children are the kingdom's pride and joy.'"—Luke 18:15–16 TM

The people in our congregation are getting older, and it doesn't take a rocket scientist to figure that out. When I speak with others I think I still sound the same, for I basically feel the same. But while recently looking at our congregations's twenty-year-old yearbook, I realized that my picture looked much different from what I see in the mirror.

What I am saying is that our congregation looks more and more like a senior citizen organization. This does have some advantages, though. Our brothers and sisters are richly acquainted with the scriptures, and their years of experience make them a wonderful blessing to each of us.

But last Wednesday evening, at our mid-week prayer service, while there was a lull in the testimonies, I noticed two Cheerios on the carpet, under a pew.

My mind raced back to the previous Sunday. I couldn't remember any small children being present at church. Mulling this over, I felt a lump of sadness in my heart. Having the joy of grandchildren in my life made me wonder how we might, once again, hear the sweet sound of a baby's cry in our congregation.

This will be my personal quest. Why? Because last Wednesday night I saw two Cheerios on the carpet, under a pew, and I missed the presence of little ones among us.

Hymns of the Saints: No. 348, "We Bring Our Children, Lord, to Thee"

Prayer Thought: Gracious God who welcomes children, may our houses of worship know the cries of little ones, and may we learn to welcome them into our presence, for they represent eternal promise and continuing life.

| Thursday **5** August | **Heavenly Example** By Luther M. Beal Beals Island, Maine | |

"Carry each other's burdens, in this way you will fulfill the law of Christ."—Galatians 6:2 NIV

I was fortunate to be born and raised near family members living in our small fishing village. Those who moved away were able to return often, and traditionally, the family gathered for holidays and reunions. Our small congregation was a very close extended family. These good people influenced me for all my days, and I am constantly reminded of the religious guidance, by example, that they set in their daily lives. Growing up, I heard so many stories of my two grandmothers helping and caring for those who were sick or less fortunate than we were.

Memories of my mother and father serving those not in our immediate family, plus providing a safe, loving environment for my brother and me, will last a lifetime. There were times when all four of us would be sick, and my mother would put aside her discomfort and misery, and leave her sickbed to attend to my father, brother, and me. She was a strong worker in her church, community, and family.

Recently she has suffered devastating health problems and now requires assistance in many ways. My father has become her caregiver and has taken on many of the duties that she once performed. She is often concerned that by caring for her, he will be unable to do the things he loves and is still able to enjoy. His response is that it is payback time, and he *is* doing what he loves.

In my church school classes, I learned that doing for others will bring good things to us in return. I have seen this in my parents' example, and in so many other instances in my life. I believe that Jesus' life was an example of loving and caring for others. What a wonderful world this would be if all could live their lives according to this heavenly example.

Hymns of the Saints: No. 424, "Send Me Forth, O Blessed Master"

Prayer Thought: Master of our lives, lead us to find joy in lifting the burdens of others. May others then find you through our example.

Unexpected Gift

By Diane F. Schwartz
Las Vegas, Nevada

"Giving thanks always for all things unto God and the Father in the name of our Lord Jesus Christ."
—Ephesians 5:20

I sent a testimony to *Daily Bread* that was published as the August 6 selection in the 2001 issue. It was about a darling little boy I met at a softball game. I received a wonderful letter from another *Daily Bread* writer about what I had written, but I hadn't really noticed the date for which it was selected. We had moved in May 2001, and between painting the interior of the house we were selling and the interior of the house we were buying, plus moving, we were nearly worn out. Needless to say, I got behind on my reading.

Much later, when I was reading through the 2001 *Daily Bread*, I came upon this writing. That's when I first noticed the date that it appeared. I had sent in a scripture verse and a hymn selection, but had left the title blank. I never title what I write; I figure the *Daily Bread* staff can do a better job of that. I was surprised to see that it was titled "Never Forgotten." Truer words were never written, because August 6 was my favorite grandpa's birthday, and I will never forget my bright-eyed round little grandpa.

Sometimes we receive small gifts that are so meaningful, like the title of that writing. I am thankful for such thoughtfulness and for the writings in *Daily Bread*. I can often identify with some of the writers without seeing their names, simply by reading what they have written.

Hymns of the Saints: No. 184, "God Who Gives to Life Its Goodness"

Prayer Thought: God of blessing, we offer our deepest thanks for those unexpected gifts that grace our lives from time to time and that make us know that you are aware of our needs.

| Saturday **7** August | **Perfected in Christ**
By Janie S. Qualls
Lake City, Arkansas | |

"I am confident of this, that the one who began a good work among you will bring it to completion by the day of Jesus Christ."—Philippians 1:6 NRSV

The highway between Lake City and Jonesboro is being widened to four lanes. There are bright orange barrels and "under construction" signs everywhere. Sometimes there is a detour. The signs remind me of my life. I feel I have been under construction all my life, with a few detours thrown in. Someday the rough edges, flaws, and imperfections will be perfected in Christ.

Traffic doesn't stop while a road is under construction. Life, too, goes on while we struggle and learn life's lessons, which will serve us well. The Master Workman will change our lives into ever-increasing value for his sake. When his work in us is complete, we shall be like him, perfectly conformed to his likeness.

Hymns of the Saints: No. 174, "O Christ, My Lord, Create in Me"

Prayer Thought: Great Creator, may we be willing to place ourselves in your hands, that you may form us more nearly in your Son's likeness. Perfect us, to bring blessing and to fulfill our calling.

<table>
<tr><td>Sunday
8
August</td><td>**Ignored**
By Roberta Dieterman
Caledonia, Michigan</td><td></td></tr>
</table>

"For I pray continually for them by day, and my eyes water my pillow by night because of them; I cry to my God in faith, and I know he will hear my cry...."
—II Nephi 15:4

When I was younger I used to laugh at my grandmother because she was such a "people watcher." She planned her bus trips to the doctor's office or for shopping so she would have extra time at her stops to watch and meet people.

Now that I'm my grandmother's age, I find myself enjoying "people watching" too. Many times it affords me a visual lesson in life. One day, while at the mall waiting and "watching," I noticed a man with two boys who were about seven or eight years of age. He did a lot of talking and laughing with one, yet appeared to almost ignore the other. The boy tugged on his sleeve a few times and started to talk to him, but the man would say, "Wait just a minute." I watched the trio for fifteen or twenty minutes. After several attempts to get the man's attention, the boy's body language changed and he didn't make any more attempts to communicate.

I admit I have no idea what was going on in their lives, but that little boy reminded me of just how fortunate I am that I can always count on my heavenly Father to listen to me and to respond to those times when I "tug on his sleeve." God is always fair in his attention to his children. We are all equal in God's sight. What a wonderful comfort that is. I can only imagine how I would feel if God chose to ignore me and put me on hold when I was in need.

The trio moved on, but the one boy walked a few steps behind the other two. I said a quiet prayer for the three of them, and I know God listened.

Sing for Peace: No. 3, "Gather Your Children"

Prayer Thought: Patient God, we are grateful that through the power of your Spirit, we know you listen when we share our needs and longings with you. May we, in turn, listen to others, and especially to our children.

| Monday
9
August | **Enabled to Hear**
By Penny McCurdy
Independence, Missouri | |

"May the Lord repay you [Ruth] for what you have done. May you be richly rewarded by the Lord, the God of Israel, under whose wings you have come to take refuge."
—Ruth 2:12 NRSV

One day as I was watering my flowers, I heard the phone ringing. I quickly thought that I didn't remember ever hearing the phone ring from my backyard while water was running from the hose. This puzzled me, but I went to the house, picked up the silent phone, and only heard the dial tone. As I replaced the receiver and turned away, the phone rang. I picked it up, and a nurse from a local hospital asked if I would be available to pick up a friend from the emergency room. Of course I said I could do that. I changed clothes and left immediately for the hospital. When I arrived it wasn't long before my friend was ready for discharge, and I took her home.

In thinking about this whole event, I can only say that God works in wondrous ways. I was very sure I heard the phone ringing from the yard, even with the water running. That in itself is an improbability. To me, this was an act of God so my friend's needs could be met.

If we, as followers of our Lord, trust him fully for all our needs, our needs will be met, even if at times it seems impossible. I desire to trust God for all my needs, and I know with assurance that God will lead me wherever he desires me to serve him or my fellow travelers.

Hymns of the Saints: No. 457, "My Lord, I Know That All My Life"

Prayer Thought: Tune our minds, hearts, and ears to listen for the many ways you call us to service, Lord.

Tuesday **10** August	**God's Balance of Nature** By Larry Carroll Glen Easton, West Virginia

"And the locusts went up over all the land of Egypt, and rested in all the coasts of Egypt; very grievous were they.... For they covered the face of the whole earth."
—Exodus 10:14–15

During the past several years, Asian lady beetles have infested this area. They are a breed of ladybug imported from Asia. They were evidently brought to the United States to control aphids on pecan trees.

But like the gypsy moth before them, they escaped to other areas of the country. They have since multiplied and become a serious pest, invading people's houses and becoming almost impossible to get rid of.

The Asian lady beetles show how we humans can upset God's balance of nature. God created all things with a particular purpose, each in a place where it functions best. So often, humans determine that they have a better idea. Would it not be best to respect and follow God's plan?

Hymns of the Saints: No. 402, "God in His Love for Us"

Prayer Thought: Almighty Creator, may we thirst to know the wonders of your creation and more greatly appreciate the intended purpose of all things.

| Wednesday **11** August | **On Aging** By Olevia Huntsman Bald Knob, Arkansas | |

"Do not cast me off in the time of old age; forsake me not when my strength is spent."—Psalm 71:9 RSV

My mother-in-law is feeling the effects of her age. She has hands that will not cooperate when she tries to do small tasks, even to feed herself. Because of this problem of "shaky hands" she cannot put the drops in her eyes to control her glaucoma. She has always been a hard worker and very self-sufficient, but now feels she is a "burden" because she has to have assistance.

Recently, I took her to her ophthalmologist to have her eyes checked. I realized after listening to her conversation with the assistant that she was looking for an alternative to the drops. She was willing to undergo surgery so that she wouldn't cause others what she felt was a burden. The doctor assured her that surgery was far too risky a procedure, when medication would control the disease. He understood her fears and reaffirmed her value and worth as a person.

No one wants to be a burden to others; none of us wants to lose our independence. It is frightening to realize that one day we may be unable to perform the tasks we do so easily today. It is hard to reconcile the aging of the physical self with the inner self who feels as capable as ever. There are many elderly people in our world who suffer from feelings of unworthiness. I pray that we may be more sensitive to the needs of our aged relatives and friends so they can feel a sense of purpose throughout the remainder of their lives.

Hymns of the Saints: No. 465, "We Thank Thee, God, for Eyes to See"

Prayer Thought: Lord, show us how to value those who are older and who are no longer independent. May we learn how to validate their worth as people who still have much to offer.

Thursday **12** August	**When a Stranger Prayed** By Karen Anne Smith Ludington, Michigan	

"And he hath put a new song in my mouth, even praise unto our God; many shall see it and fear, and shall trust in the Lord."—Psalm 40:3

Even as the restaurant's shift manager, I was expected to chip in and help my crew with pre-close cleanup, and so I found myself sweeping an almost empty lobby just minutes before locking up. The only customers left were two delightful little girls with their neatly groomed dad. Wanting them to feel welcomed and not rushed, I smiled and said, "Hi." This afforded the gentleman an opportunity to use the restroom while I watched his girls.

When the man returned, he and I chatted. I really didn't have time to visit but was more concerned with his feelings than saving five minutes on my close. Besides, it had been a hard day and I really needed a little respite.

The conversation turned to my job and I had to admit that I was seriously burned out; I could not lie. But I also shared my love of writing. When I'm sitting at my word processor, stress melts away and I can smile again. This stranger seemed so positive and supportive that my enthusiasm just bubbled over. I told him of my dream to write stories with Christian themes for the science fiction and fantasy crowd. I felt that it would be a way to reach some people who would not be open to more conventional witnessing.

I suddenly realized I had to get moving. If I wasted too much time, my crew would be working late and labor costs would skyrocket, so I tried to excuse myself. My new friend grasped both of my hands, and before I knew what was happening, he began to pray. Right there in the middle of the restaurant's lobby, he prayed that the Holy Spirit would support and guide me in my dream to write in Jesus' name.

Ever since that night I have thanked God for the very special gift of a stranger's prayer. The memory of it has encouraged me to persevere, and I am happy to report that my first fantasy story has sold to a magazine that features science fiction stories with Christian themes.

Hymns of the Saints: No. 382, "God Forgave My Sin in Jesus' Name"

Prayer Thought: Help us, God, to gratefully accept ministry from strangers and to freely testify of the Holy Spirit as opportunity arises.

| Friday
13
August | **Praise and**
Thanksgiving
By Janice Townsend
Spokane, Washington | |

"Blessed be the name of our God; let us sing to his praise, let us give thanks to his holy name, for he works righteousness forever."—Alma 14:88

Her face showed the marks of a long life, yet the bright blue eyes were young and lively as she reached out lovingly to clasp my hand. The robe she wore was made of coarse cotton. It revealed her calling as a nun—one who had chosen to give her life to Christ and who was committed to service and ministry.

"May I pray for you?" she asked as she stood by my hospital bed. I felt strengthened and encouraged by the words she spoke on my behalf as we bowed together before our Lord. A brief conversation followed; then she left me with this admonition: "When you pray, remember to thank and praise God. God likes to have you do that."

In the months since my encounter with this compassionate woman, I have not forgotten her or her wise counsel. Indeed, I have felt a continual litany of praise and thanksgiving arising in my heart because of God's goodness to me. And I do not neglect to tell God so. Rich moments of personal worship are mine as I tell God how grateful I am and how "great-ful" God is.

Sing a New Song: No. 33, "Lord, I Lift Your Name on High"

Prayer Thought: Almighty God, thanks and praise be to you—for who you are and what you do. May we never fail to tell you how grateful we are for your loving kindness.

Saturday **14** August	**A Gift of Love** By Lillian Bayless Kirby Blue Springs, Missouri	

"Give to him that asketh of thee; and from him that would borrow of thee, turn not thou away."—Matthew 5:44 IV

My shopping for the week was completed and my groceries were packed in the trunk of my car. I was tired and wanted to return home to my family. Then I heard a weary voice calling to me. I recognized the woman as one who had, years before, cleaned my house several times a month. She hung her head in shame as she asked me for money to buy her family dinner for that night. It was the end of the month, and she had come up short.

I reached into my wallet and gave her the last of my money—a twenty-dollar bill. She promised to come out to my house and help me with my ironing the next week. I gave her a hug and sent her on her way.

After arriving home, I put away all my groceries and quickly started dinner for my own family of seven. My daughter Sharon approached me as I stood at the stove. I had given her one of my "next-to-new" purses earlier that day. She was laughing and said, "Thanks for the money, Mom!" She told me that she had found a twenty-dollar bill in a side pocket of the purse. She happily put it into a pocket of my apron as a gift of love.

All that we put into the lives of others comes back into our own.

Hymns of the Saints: No. 388, "Brothers and Sisters of Mine"

Prayer Thought: May we not hesitate, Lord, to share what we have with those who have nothing. Teach us to trust you to care for us when we do so.

One Out of Five
By Shirley Vallier Remmenga
Fort Collins, Colorado

"For this very reason, you must make every effort to support your faith with goodness, and goodness with knowledge, and knowledge with self-control, and self-control with endurance, and endurance with godliness, and godliness with mutual affection, and mutual affection with love."
—II Peter 1:5–7 NSV

The thick dust swirled around me and pieces of gravel bounced against my legs when the pickup truck flew past. I saw it speeding toward me, so I turned my back and covered my nose and mouth to keep from inhaling so much dust and to prevent the loose gravel from hitting my face. The day was hot, and the season was drier than usual. I probably should have decided to walk in the fields instead of on the road for those very reasons. But there I was.

After the dust settled, I resumed my walk. In the length of that mile, four more vehicles met and passed me, three of them in a great hurry, with no regard for me at all. The other driver slowed down, waved, and kicked up no gravel whatsoever. I acknowledged his kindness by smiling and waving to him. What he did made me feel thankful and happy even though I was covered with dust.

I began thinking about what I had just experienced and decided that one out of five was quite a good percentage. Anyone who has mailed or handed out a survey to be returned the following week would be delighted if 20 percent of the surveys were returned, I presume. I know the World Church would celebrate if 20 percent of its members would pay their tithing. What if one out of five people really pursued peace and justice? It would be a different world, a better world, I'm thinking. Would that all of us could be counted in the 20 percent who respond with kindness and respect—the one out of five who lives the gospel of Jesus Christ each day.

Hymns of the Saints: No. 389, "If Suddenly upon the Street"

Prayer Thought: Lord, we thank you for the kindness of others. Help us to be among those who live out Christ's gospel in their daily lives.

| Monday **16** August | **Blessed by the Sacrament** By Mark E. Megee East Windsor, New Jersey | |

"Look especially to the sacraments to enrich the spiritual life of the body. Seek for greater understanding of my purposes in these sacred rites and prepare to receive a renewed confirmation of the presence of my Spirit in your experiences of worship."

—Doctrine and Covenants 158:11c

How often do we "go through" the sacraments and never truly sit back and realize their blessings? We prepare the emblems as priesthood or sit in the pews waiting for the emblems to be blessed and served. We sometimes join in song as they are being prepared. We watch.

The true call of the sacraments is to be involved. "Now in this moment," I guess one could say. A real wakeup call to me was at Deer Park campground when church president Grant McMurray was our guest speaker. We were asked to take our emblems from the building and go out into the park to make our peace and, when ready, serve ourselves. We were taken out of the fast-paced service that we here in North America have gotten so used to. Instead of having it served assembly-line style, we were sent out. And out we went, each one accepting the sacrament when he or she felt ready.

It was quiet in the park that morning despite all the people scattered about, silently meditating on the enormity of the sacrament's meaning. We had been sent out, but then we returned to hear the morning message. Although it was a quiet time, we had each shared the moment together. The sacrament blessed *us;* then we were sent forth to take the message to others.

Sing a New Song: No. 8, "Eat This Bread"

Prayer Thought: Eternal God, may we never mindlessly partake of the sacrament simply as a familiar ritual, but truly contemplate the depth of our commitment.

<table>
<tr><td>Tuesday
17
August</td><td>**Hear and Obey**
By Lois Bourgonje
Porcupine Plain,
Saskatchewan, Canada</td><td>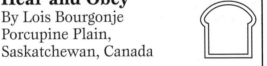</td></tr>
</table>

"O remember, my son, and learn wisdom in your youth; learn in your youth to keep the commandments of God, and cry to God for your support."—Alma 17:68

One day my husband needed to go to the dentist. When he got there, the dentist decided that she needed to split a wisdom tooth in order to pull it, but another tooth wouldn't take the anesthetic and go numb. My husband said to pull it anyway. What an experience! I was waiting in a store across the street, and when he came in he actually looked yellow in color. He said, "Let's go home." I tried to talk him into waiting before driving, but he wanted to go.

My husband drove slowly down the road and I was wondering how I could help him. It entered my mind, *You can pray for him, and as you pray, touch him.* I feared he would think I was foolish if I touched him, so I silently prayed. Again it came to me, *As you pray, touch him.* These thoughts were so strong! So I laid my hand on his knee, and I prayed. Immediately the car sped up, and at the twelve-mile corner he stopped the car and got out. I thought he was having problems, but he had taken out the dressing and everything was fine.

When we got home I thought all he would eat was soup, but he said he could eat a meal. That night he attended a Lion's Club meeting, and everything remained fine. How blessed he was on that day and the days following!

Hymns of the Saints: No. 60, "Now Thank We All Our God"

Prayer Thought: Loving God, we rejoice at your instruction and blessing. We are grateful that you hear our prayers and bless us when we have need.

Clutter
By Eileen Turner
Portland, Oregon

"Finally, brethren, whatever is true, whatever is honorable, whatever is just, whatever is pure, whatever is lovely, whatever is gracious, if there is any excellence, if there is anything worthy of praise, think about these things. What you have learned and received and heard and seen in me, do; and the God of peace will be with you."
—Philippians 4:8–9 RSV

Clutter has a way of keeping us from getting a job done. It creates a fog of the mind. We all know the feeling of losing something. It's there somewhere in all that clutter! So we begin to sort through the mess, and if we're lucky, we find what we've been looking for. Then, and only then, are we able to focus on the task at hand.

On the hillside behind my home stood an old maple tree. Its branches were touching my roof, and when the wind blew, the branches swept across the roof and gutters. I decided to have the tree removed, since I had perhaps twenty-five others, and this one would not be missed. While the workmen were there, I also had some other tree sprouts taken out. To my amazement, their removal opened up a vista of mountain and sky. The sun now could reach the path below.

Sometimes we need to weed out the clutter or debris that gets in the way of productive labor. And when we do, we can see more clearly what needs to be done, what path to take. God has work for us to do. We just need to prepare the way so we are ready and can put our fingers on the tools we need for the task.

Sing a New Song: No. 32, "Lord, I Give You"

Prayer Thought: Clear our vision, Lord, of all that surrounds us—our possessions, our activities, and the people with whom we associate. Help us reevaluate what to keep and what to let go, that we might move forward in the work to which you have called us.

Thursday **19** August	**Reshaped by the Future** By Peggy Michael Cantonment, Florida	

"But now, O Lord, thou art our Father; we are the clay, and thou our potter; and we all are the work of thy hand."
—Isaiah 64:8

At reunion, we were each given a ball of clay. Even before we received instructions, people began coaxing shapes from the mass. Planet Earth emerged with new boundaries. One person formed a cup and saucer, another crafted pliable dentures. A tomato worm crept from nimble fingers. A husband made a sugar cube for his wife's cup. Vessels of various shapes emerged. One created an ear of corn. It was delightful to glance around at the interesting creations. Then we got serious.

We were asked to form an object that told something about ourselves, and powerful testimonies emerged from the clay. Many made hearts that told diverse stories. One worshiper showed us a heart with holes in it. He said, "This is my heart. It has holes in it because it is empty and broken. I suffer because dear friends who have shared the gospel since my youth no longer walk with me."

One young man fashioned his clay into a big question mark, laid it on his book, and gazed at it. We all did some soul-searching, for discomfort had come among us. But as we poured out our feelings to one another, a subtle change came over us. There was hope, for we realized that God was still in this work. The young man with the question mark began to reshape his clay. This time he formed a rocket that pointed skyward. He seemed to catch the new resolve that dwelled within us.

I witnessed a new beginning in our church at that service. Truly the Lord is reshaping our lives and making us into a joyful, hopeful people.

Sing for Peace: No. 38, "Christ Has Called Us to New Visions"

Prayer Thought: Reshape us, our Creator, into what you need us to be to bring hope and joy to those around us.

| Friday
20
August | **Kindness Cools Anger**
By Jane Miller
Berryville, Arkansas | |

"The end of a matter is better than its beginning, and patience is better than pride. Do not be quickly provoked in your spirit, for anger resides in the lap of fools."
—Ecclesiastes 7:8–9 NIV

I was stuck in traffic again. The lane I was trying to turn into was so long that it couldn't get through the light before it turned red. And the line was so long that I couldn't even get into the lane; the cars just kept coming. It was so frustrating.

We hear so much these days about road rage. So many times it results in violence because it is so hard for drivers to curb their anger. Of course *I* would never let *my* anger get out of control. Not *me*!

However, I could feel myself getting angrier as one green light after another changed to red. I was talking to myself as I voiced my frustration. Then I noticed a woman stopping a car-length behind the car in front of her. When the light turned green, she smiled at me and motioned me to go ahead. She let me into the lane, and I mouthed a thank-you as I slipped into line ahead of her.

More humble and a lot ashamed I vowed to try a little harder next time to remember that there are some nice people left out there and to hold my temper in check in those frustrating situations.

Sing for Peace: No. 16, "Gentle God, When We Are Driven"

Prayer Thought: Enable us to cool our anger, Lord, in frustrating situations. May we not think only of ourselves, but show kindness to those around us.

| Saturday **21** August | **Faulty Expectations** By Don Richardson Osceola, Iowa | |

"My Spirit is reaching out to numerous souls even now and there are many who will respond if you, my people, will bear affirmative testimony of my love and my desires for all to come unto me."—Doctrine and Covenants 153:9b

One hot summer day, my wife and I stopped to get a cone of soft ice cream. As we waited in line, we noticed that the clerk was new. She asked questions, as she was learning her job. The customer ahead of us ordered a medium-size cone. The new clerk made a cone and showed it to her supervisor. The supervisor immediately threw it into the garbage, saying it was too large and that if the customer came back again he would expect the medium cone to be that size. So the clerk filled a new cone and gave it to the customer. It seemed like such a waste. An explanation to the customer would have satisfied him and saved the store a little money.

In a time when people are in such great need, do we treat them like that? Afraid that if we testify to them of Jesus, they will expect more from us the next time they see us? Shouldn't we be more like Jesus, who gave everything, even his very life, for each person? Giving of what we have, physically and spiritually, will make our neighborhoods and communities more like families.

Sing for Peace: No. 15, "Put Peace into Each Other's Hands"

Prayer Thought: Merciful God, teach us to treat others with kindness and to live out Christ's example wherever we may be. May others be able to expect the best from us.

| Sunday **22** August | **An "Extra" Twenty-Dollar Bill** By Ruth Andrews Vreeland Albuquerque, New Mexico | |

"But the fruit of the Spirit is love, joy, peace, long-suffering, gentleness, goodness, faith, meekness, temperance; against such there is no law."—Galatians 5:22–23

In our adult class one Sunday, the lesson focused on allowing the Holy Spirit to show us when and where others were in need, and how to join God in his work, which is ever around us. I decided to take my son out for lunch that day, and because my husband was out of town, it was just the two of us. I found an ATM, and when it was time to request the amount of cash needed, I absent-mindedly hit the button that said, "$40 Fast Cash." After getting the cash in my hands, I stared blankly at the amount. It had been my habit for years to get only twenty dollars in cash at a time. Why did I take out forty dollars? Oh well, I thought, maybe the

297

extra twenty dollars will come in handy for lunches this week. I stashed it in my purse for later.

After lunch I dropped my son off at the house and decided to get a few things at a nearby store. Once there, I put the few things from my list in the cart and then wandered over to the clothing section, though I didn't need any new clothes. I passed a young woman, about twenty years of age, who was shopping with an older woman, and I overheard a bit of their conversation. It was clear the young woman was truly in need and the older woman was trying to be of assistance. The response from the younger woman led me to believe she was waiting for her absent father to "come back home" and then they'd have money to buy the things she and her siblings needed. Until that happened, she didn't feel she could afford to spend any money, as they had so little.

The Holy Spirit didn't just *rest* on me at that moment but *completely filled* me. I was overcome and went weak in the knees as God told me in a clear voice that the "extra" twenty dollars I had in my purse was *needed* by this young woman. I felt prompted by the Holy Spirit to give her the money. Now, I am not the kind of person who gives money away, but of course, I obeyed—how could I not? After all, it wasn't really *my* money; it was God's "extra" twenty dollars. I was just in a place where God was working, and learning to be in tune with that.

The young woman was tearfully grateful, and though twenty dollars won't change her life, it gave her the message that God is watching out for her. And I told her God was, as I placed the money in her hand.

Sing for Peace: No. 27, "I Am Standing Waiting"

Prayer Thought: Lord, increase our awareness of those around us who are in need, and may we listen to the voice of your Spirit as you prompt us to help.

Innumerable Services
By Frances Hurst Booth
Prescott, Arizona

"[Jesus] knew they were laying for him and said, 'Show me a coin. Now, this engraving, who does it look like and what does it say?' 'Caesar,' they said. Jesus said, 'Then give Caesar what is his and give God what is his.'"

—Luke 20:23–25 TM

For income tax verification, acknowledgments for charitable giving usually state, "No goods or services have been received by the giver." Personally, I find that giving in the exercise of one's stewardship brings innumerable returns and "services"—worship experiences that nourish the soul; the sacraments; relationships with our brothers and sisters worldwide; personal encounters with leaders; spiritual and financial counseling, and more.

Although these services are available to all without charge, the act of giving brings me the deeper satisfaction of being part of a broader goal—spreading the gospel and the establishment of God's kingdom on earth.

Hymns of the Saints: No. 416, "May We Who Know the Joyful Sound"

Prayer Thought: As receivers of so much that uplifts us, Lord, prompt us to participate in whatever way we can in the innumerable services offered through the church.

Daily Insight
By Helen L. Lynn
Carlsbad, New Mexico

"Fight the good fight of faith, lay hold on eternal life, whereunto thou art also called, and hast professed a good profession before many witnesses."—I Timothy 6:12

The testimonies in *Daily Bread* mean so much to me. As I read one each day I'm reminded that the glory of each morning is that it offers us the chance to begin again.

I greatly appreciate the creative talents of the writers and the willingness they have to share with the world. Many times the devotion will hold a special message just for me. Sometimes it will be one of guidance, comfort, or encouragement. It may offer some insight I need at that particular time regarding a problem I may be struggling with. It never ceases to amaze me how God meets our needs in ways we could never even imagine.

Living by faith is a fairly new experience for me but I discover that the more I trust God to meet my every need, the stronger my faith becomes. It's awesome to be aware of how very much God loves each one of us unconditionally. It's not as if God takes all the care and problems away, yet when they are turned over to him, in faith believing, they are easier to solve. Tough decisions become easier and much less complicated to make, while the right decisions are more obvious. A calm, sweet spirit of peace comes to me that lets me know God is with me.

I pray to be and grow more like Jesus so I can dwell with him, not only in this life, but in the life to come.

Hymns of the Saints: No. 199, "He Lives in Us! Immortal King!"

Prayer Thought: God, we thank you for your available presence in all aspects of our lives, whether through the testimonies of others, or in our decision making. May we seek your presence daily.

Wednesday **25** August	**Reach Out and Touch** By Merna Short Melbourne, Australia	

"For in the gospel a righteousness from God is revealed, a righteousness that is by faith from first to last, just as it is written: 'The righteous will live by faith.'"
—Romans 1:17 NIV

"The story of the woman touching the hem of Jesus' garment has always meant a lot to me," she said. "The analogy is reaching out in faith and reaching for Christ—a double healing. I had an experience recently that increased its significance. My daughter was in hospital. I was sent for during a procedure. 'It's all right,' I assured her as they worked on her. She put out her hand and held my hem. A peace came over her. This touched me deeply.

"Later I was in my apartment. A man had died that day. His family had arrived too late. I awoke suddenly, scared stiff. I was so fearful I might have lost my daughter. I felt I needed to reach out and touch—a physical thing. I ran my hand along the hem of my nightgown. In my heart I said, *I'm reaching out, Christ.* A warmth filled my whole body. The scripture of the parent's faith and the answer, 'Your daughter will be healed,' was so strong, all fear left me."

Hymns of the Saints: No.167, "Jesus, the Very Thought of Thee"

Prayer Thought: Lord, we reach out to touch you for your healing presence, knowing you are eternally there.

Thursday **26** August	**I Need Directions** By Gerald John Kloss Philadelphia, Pennsylvania	

"Through thy precepts I get understanding; therefore I hate every false way. Thy word is a lamp unto my feet, and a light unto my path."—Psalm 119:104–105

I am extremely fortunate to have the opportunity to travel throughout the states of Pennsylvania, New Jersey, and Maryland teaching a wonderful graduate-level course for teachers called "Dimensions of Learning." I am delighted with the many wonderful contacts I have made and to see the positive impact on so many classrooms. When I travel to places new to me I usually get good directions from the program organizers or from the Internet.

Recently I taught a class in Sewell, New Jersey, which is close to the Woodbury congregation of our church. Because I had been to the Woodbury church so many times, I decided I didn't need any directions to find the location. I hadn't been to Woodbury in about two years and didn't realize that a new highway had made my old way of going no longer workable. I finally had to bring out the map, which thankfully I had included in my materials for the first session. The map helped me, and I was able to make it to the training site with enough time to set up for the course.

I often think of the many times when we try to go it alone through life. Thinking that we are in charge, we bypass the use of scripture, prayer, and other spiritual disciplines only to discover that we are lost somewhere and then need to find our way back and include the Lord in our lives.

Hymns of the Saints: No. 311, "Guide Us, O Thou Great Jehovah"

Prayer Thought: Lord God, help us to always turn to you first as the source for direction in our lives.

| Friday **27** August | **Gift of Presence** By Ardith Lancaster Paisley, Florida | |

"Come to me, all who labor and are heavy laden, and I will give you rest. Take my yoke upon you, and learn from me; for I am gentle and lowly in heart, and you will find rest for your souls. For my yoke is easy, and my burden light."
—Matthew 11:28–30 RSV

During Easter week, I wanted so much to show my appreciation for the wonderful gift God gave us through his Son, Jesus Christ. In going back over those last days of his earthly life through reading the scriptural accounts, it didn't seem enough to just say thank you. I thought there must be something more that I could do.

As I spent more and more time in prayer about it, I became aware that God was giving me a gift of presence. It is not what God might tell us, it *is* God, it is *Jesus*—it is *being with* them, in their presence, that strengthens and enables us to become consecrated personalities who can be used to bring blessings to others. That is how we discover what we can actually do for God, to give him the gift of fulfilling our purpose.

My husband, Arnold, had a grandmother who never received anything without giving something in return. Once when I wanted Arnold to take something to her,

303

he said, "No, Grandma can't afford it." He meant that he didn't want to have her give him something in return, because she had so little to begin with.

God is like Arnold's grandmother—we can't give God anything without him giving us more in return. However, God can "afford" it, and truly wants to give us his special gift of presence. So I guess I'll keep on trying to give God my gift—not to receive a gift from him in return, but to pass along that gift of presence.

Sing a New Song: No. 31, "Lord, Help Me to Know Your Presence"

Prayer Thought: Greatest Giver of all, teach us how to give the gift of our presence in the lives of those who need our attention.

Saturday 28 August	A Whole New Life By Ferryl Cash Troy, Kansas	

"O Lord, you have searched me and you know me. You know when I sit and when I rise; you perceive my thoughts from afar."—Psalm 139:1–2 NIV

The fall of 2002 brought another change in our lives—Don and I had our last child leave for college to attend Graceland University. I knew it was the normal order of life for our children to grow up and leave home. It was a time I had looked forward to and yet dreaded at the same time, for I had thrived on the busy schedule of our children's activities. But how would I fill my time now that everyone was gone?

I was terrified that loneliness would overtake me and I would rattle around our empty house with nothing to do. Yet at the same time I was looking forward to being able to catch up on projects that had been left undone for years. I am not one to sit idle for long. I labeled those pictures that had been piling up in boxes and put them in albums. I pulled material scraps that I'd saved for years from closets and sewed them into quilts. I crocheted unused yarn into afghans.

I didn't think it would ever be possible, but I was actually enjoying the free time and coming home to a quiet house. And many weekends or weeknights we traveled to Graceland to see the plays our sons were involved in, the dance team and choir that our daughter participated in, or to visit our three children, daughter-in-law, and grandchild.

Our schedule has slowed down a little, but other activities have helped to fill in the gaps. This is a new time to enjoy in our lives. It is the way things are meant to be. It is wonderful how God helps us adjust to whatever changes come to us.

Hymns of the Saints: No. 177, "O God, in Restless Living"

Prayer Thought: Bringer of blessing, work with our restless spirits that we may find calm and a whole new vision of what life can be at each stage.

"Fear thou not; for I am with thee; be not dismayed; for I am thy God; I will strengthen thee; yea, I will help thee; yea, I will uphold thee with the right hand of my righteousness."—Isaiah 41:10

Pictures and talk of war lay heavy on my heart. It was a distressing time without an end in sight. That morning I decided to do other things and not turn on the television. It was a refreshing time to work in the yard. I decided I'd better plant a cutting given to me by a neighbor, before it was too late.

I often put food out in my backyard for birds and other animals who might come on the scene, so I thought the raucous calling from the high line above my house was from a big black crow. They often would sit and scold for a handout. Was I surprised to see a green bird! It was a parrot, talking for all it was worth. It answered me in its own language for some time. I went in the house to get something for it.

Knowing that parrots ate fruit, I cut an apple into large pieces. When I returned it was still there—now lower in a large bush, but too high for me to hand the apple. When I put a piece on the bush, the piece was buried in leaves. I looked for a lower place, but high enough for the parrot to feel safe. The top of a nearby but lower bush proved to be perfect. It was thrilling to see the parrot fly down and start eating. It even let me put more apple there while it was eating.

After watching it awhile, I decided to try to take its picture. I went in to get my camera, and was thrilled to find it still there when I came out. The parrot let me take several pictures and even move up close, without exhibiting any fear. I was so close I could have stroked its back, but I didn't want to alarm it. It was gorgeous, with a fuchsia head and big collar. When it moved its head, each feather rippled. It was a work of art. One could not help but appreciate it as a beautiful handiwork of the Creator. It stayed until it had eaten all the apple, and my spirit was lifted. I felt it truly had been a blessing from the Lord.

Hymns of the Saints: No. 52, "This Is My Father's World"

Prayer Thought: We thank you, Lord, for reminding us of your love and creative power through the beautiful creatures of your creation.

| Monday **30** August | **Making Bread** By Shirley Botting Wiarton, Ontario, Canada | |

"And the second [commandment] is like this, Thou shalt love thy neighbor as thyself...."—Mark 12:36 IV

Last summer my husband, Ed, and I took our motor home on the ferry to Manitoulin Island, in Lake Huron. We go there every summer for part of July and August. We stop in Providence Bay at the farm home of our friends, Lyle and Sharon Dewars. They welcome us anytime; they are such good friends.

While we were staying there Sharon asked me if I would please "pan" and bake the bread Lyle had mixed earlier in the day. The bread was for the next day at the church bake sale. Sharon was busy taking care of her two granddaughters and didn't have time to help. Because I bake bread all the time, I was very glad to form the loaves and put it in the oven.

It made me feel good to do something in return for their hospitality. We got the bread looked after. I love to help whenever I can.

Hymns of the Saints: No. 415, "Help Us Express Your Love"

Prayer Thought: Lord, help us to joyfully offer service to others. May we be your hands and feet, and thereby show your love.

Tuesday **31** August	**A Life Together** By Phyllis Elliott Florissant, Missouri	

"The righteous walk in integrity—happy are the children who follow them!"—Proverbs 20:7 NRSV

In September 2002, my husband, Jim, and I celebrated our fiftieth wedding anniversary. We had the actual celebration in August because most of our children could come home then. Our youngest was unable to come because of medical problems. We decided to have only our relatives and hold it in our own home because our own medical conditions caused us to tire easily.

Some of our family had gone the evening before to see a Cardinals baseball game. Our children had ordered a cake and brought all the food in, so I wouldn't have to do any cooking. There were twenty-one of us for the day. We took lots of pictures and made an audiotape of memories. We reminisced about things we had done, places we had lived, trips we had taken, and activities and friends from the past. Something one person would remember, would jog someone else's memory of other things. All the children had taken part in children's choir, Christmas plays, morning services, and youth groups at church.

Our congregation sent us flowers to commemorate the day, and just by chance they were the colors from our wedding! We are thankful for the good life we've had and for our wonderful, loving family.

Hymns of the Saints: No. 368, "O Perfect Love"

Prayer Thought: God of all our years, we give thanks for occasions of celebration in our lives, and for our families and friends who make those celebrations possible.

September 2004

S	M	T	W	T	F	S
			1	2	3	4
5	6	7	8	9	10	11
12	13	14	15	16	17	18
19	20	21	22	23	24	25
26	27	28	29	30		

A Celebration of Life
By Marlene Brunner
Yuma, Colorado

"Strength and honor are her clothing; and she shall rejoice in time to come.... She looketh well to the ways of her household, and eateth not the bread of idleness."
—Proverbs 31:25, 27

Since the fall of 1998 I have led a widows' support group called "The Widows' Might." Ina, a former Baptist pastor's wife, widowed for twenty-six years at the time, was a part of this group from the very first. Ina never missed a meeting until she became ill with brain cancer in early 2002. She remained alert and aware of what was taking place, but could only leave her house with great difficulty.

Ina requested that three of the local pastors—Presbyterian, Methodist, and myself representing the Community of Christ—conduct a celebration-of-life service on her behalf. She planned the entire service and arranged how each of us should participate.

A service of this nature on behalf of a person who was still alive was a first-time experience for me. It was most unusual to have the person whose life we were celebrating actually be in the congregation. It did give the honoree the privilege of hearing all the nice things that were said about her and the effect she had had on all of us. It was truly a beautiful service and one I would highly recommend if circumstances permit.

Ina died in August 2002, but she and her gracious beauty will never be forgotten by all who were privileged to have known and loved her.

Sing for Peace: No. 12, "Of All the Spirit's Gifts to Me"

Prayer Thought: While we yet live, Lord, may our life be a celebration of all that is good—of your creation, of people, of our abilities and opportunities.

| Thursday **2** September | **Gift of the Hummingbird** By Judy Oetting Levasy, Missouri | |

"If ye then, being evil, know how to give good gifts unto your children, how much more shall your heavenly Father give good gifts, through the Holy Spirit, to them that ask."
—Luke 11:14 IV

In the early morning I am often gifted with the presence of ruby-throated hummingbirds at nectar feeders close to my picture window. So when my three young granddaughters came to visit overnight, I woke them early, as they wanted to see the birds I'd told them were the smallest in the United States.

They lined up on their knees with their noses pressed against the glass and waited with expectation. I was concerned, however, that the "hummers" might be intimidated by this new scene on my side of the window. I sent a prayerful plea to God, who knows when a sparrow falls and has a special love for little children: "Lord, let them see the wonders of your love through your creations."

I am always awed at how quickly prayers can be answered. Not only did a hummingbird come to the feeder; it came to the window and hovered in front of one little wide-eyed girl at a time. Tears came to my eyes when the hummingbird finally left and the three girls turned in unison, faces radiant with joy, and said together, "Grandma, did you see that?"

312

This experience made such an impact on them that whenever they visit they rush to the window to see if the hummingbird is there. It has also impacted me with the resolve to spend more time sharing with them the wondrous love of such a caring Creator.

Hymns of the Saints: No. 52, "This Is My Father's World"

Prayer Thought: Eternal Creator, even as we are thrilled by creatures great and small, may we one day have the greater joy of being in your presence.

| Friday
3
September | **Sportsmanship**
By Helen M. Green
Toledo, Ohio | |

"Blessed are the merciful, for they will receive mercy. Blessed are the pure in heart, for they will see God."
—Matthew 5:7–8 NRSV

Last year during a women's soccer tournament at nearby Bowling Green State University, one of the players collapsed on the field and died. Activities were suspended for the day, and that particular game between the two competing universities was rescheduled. Because the girl who died loved sports and was committed to her team and the game, her grieving parents felt the best way to honor her memory was to continue the games as scheduled. They were present at the next game, which was between the two schools that were playing at the time of her death.

In a touching tribute at the beginning of the game, the competition was dedicated to the girl's memory. At that time, the opposing players walked over to the BGSU team and presented each player with a long-stemmed rose, accompanied by a genuine hug. There were tears on each side as the girls' expressions revealed giving and receiving compassion. The game that followed was one of utmost sportsmanship. Participants and viewers experienced a unique twist to competition that could only be defined as Zionic outreach. It can *still* happen.

Sing for Peace: No. 6, "We Are People of God's Peace"

Prayer Thought: Universal Lord, we are bound by the compassion that binds all people in times of stress and loss. Help us to develop this fruit of the Spirit as we work toward universal peace.

 Blessed to Be a Blessing
Saturday 4 September
By Enid Stubbart DeBarthe
Lamoni, Iowa

"Let the little children come to me; do not stop them; for it is to such as these that the kingdom of God belongs."
—Mark 10:14 NRSV

It is my privilege to attend a Lamoni-area rural congregation known as the "Blooming" (Bloomington) Community of Christ, which recently expanded its parking lot and plans to double the size of its sanctuary. Rows of chairs in the aisle and rows of chairs in front of the pews will not always seat the congregation, which ranges from infants to aged adults. Ninety-year-old Joe can't hear but keeps involved as the "balloon man," who is surrounded after church by toddlers and young children begging for their balloon animals.

Ours is a congregation blessed with quite young children playing interlude music on the piano or violin, and sharing in reading scripture, offering prayer from the pulpit, and taking up the offering. When our quite young Keeley Brunner shared "up front" I could not hold back the tears.

You see, she and I were in a hospital in Des Moines at the same time several months ago. I spent a week in intensive care, not expected to survive an aortic aneurysm. Keeley had a ruptured appendix and was also in critical condition. Elders came from Lamoni daily to administer to both of us. And Keeley's father always included me in his visits, even when I was barely conscious of his presence. My surgeon signed my medical record, "The most amazing woman I ever met," because my aorta did not rupture even at ten centimeters, when most aortic aneurysms start bleeding at five.

To share with Keeley under the ministry of her father, High Priest Kevin Brunner, in congregational worship services seemed almost a resurrection experience. And to see some twenty to thirty children and youth gathered on the platform, presenting a worship service, is indeed a blessing. That blessing was even more notable when Bloomington children and youth presented a drama and music program at Lamoni Community of Christ.

Hymns of the Saints: No. 156, "Children of the Heavenly Father"

Prayer Thought: Lord who blessed the children, teach us to know our children's worth and to celebrate their gifts, that they may develop their potential and always serve your community.

| Sunday
5
September | **No Stranger to Jesus**
By Jean Cottle
Alta Loma, California | |

"Be not forgetful to entertain strangers; for thereby some have entertained angels unawares."—Hebrews 13:2

One Sunday morning Brother Jim discovered a homeless man behind our church building. The man—I'll call him John—had spent the night there. He had a duffel bag, a bike, a dog, and a guitar. John had long hair tied back in a ponytail and a bushy, ginger-colored beard. His clothes were rumpled but fairly clean.

Brother Jim introduced himself and chatted in a friendly way with John for a while. Then he invited the homeless man to come inside and worship with us. John accepted the invitation. We don't often have strangers visit our congregation but when they do they are always welcome.

After the opening hymn and the invocation, Brother Jim introduced John to the congregation. He briefly explained the stranger's presence. Then he told us that John had written a song. With a little encouragement and persuasion, John played his guitar and sang his song to the congregation. The homeless stranger had a beautiful voice and his song was inspiring. He seemed to enjoy being part of our worship service, and we enjoyed having him there. John was a stranger to us but I knew that Jesus knew him well.

Hymns of the Saints: No. 171, "Help Us Accept Each Other"

Prayer Thought: Creator of each person, help us to remember that you know and love us all equally, regardless of our circumstances. Remind us to do likewise.

| Monday **6** September | **What Song Shall We Sing?** By Florence King Feilding, New Zealand | |

"See that ye love one another; cease to be covetous; learn to impart one to another as the gospel requires; cease to be idle; cease to be unclean; cease to find fault one with another; cease to sleep longer than needed; retire to thy bed early, that ye may not be weary; arise early, that your bodies and your minds may be invigorated."

—Doctrine and Covenants 85:38a–b

In the palm tree next door to me there are many sparrows' nests. This tree could be between fifty and sixty years old. Every morning I am awakened by birdsong as the birds sing in unison. These are songs of joy as they welcome the new day.

However, at evening, when they are starting to settle down for the night, they sing a very different kind of song. I call it their "squabble song." It is almost as though they are fighting. I can imagine them saying to each other, "Move over; that's my place on the branch."

I sometimes smile to myself, thinking how like human beings these birds are. Whenever everything is going all right, we are happy. But as soon as something upsets us, we get annoyed and start to quarrel among ourselves. If we could only keep the song of joy within us, how much richer our lives would be.

Hymns of the Saints: No. 29, "With Happy Voices Ringing"

Prayer Thought: May our hearts be uplifted in songs of praise and thanksgiving to you, almighty God, that our work may be light and our relationships, a joy.

317

<table>
<tr><td>Tuesday
7
September</td><td>**What Prayer Can Do**
By Geraldine Billings Greer
Mesa, Arizona</td><td></td></tr>
</table>

"Call unto me, and I will answer thee, and show thee great and mighty things, which thou knowest not."
—Jeremiah 33:3

One morning shortly after the beginning of the school year, I went to the library to check out some visual aid equipment. When I stepped inside, I noticed that the librarian was talking to a freshman girl. When they saw me, the girl started to leave. The librarian told her that she didn't need to go. Then the girl said in the most angry tone I had ever heard, "I hate her."

This really upset me. I couldn't understand why she felt this way. I didn't have her in class; I was teaching seniors. I didn't even have her in study hall. As far as I could recall that was the first time I had ever seen her.

I remembered that in the scriptures we are told to pray for our enemies. So I began to earnestly pray for her. I prayed as I have never prayed before.

One morning in the spring, shortly before the end of the school year, I was sitting at my desk preparing for the day's classes, when the girl from the library came in. To say that I was surprised would be putting it mildly. She explained that they were having a test that day in freshman English class over the play *Romeo and Juliet*. She said that she had read it, but just couldn't understand it. A friend had told her I was an authority on Shakespeare and that if she asked, I would explain it to her. I assured her I wasn't an authority, but that I would help her. So I sat down with her and explained the play and answered her questions. When the bell rang for the beginning of class, I wished her luck.

From then on every time she saw me, she would stop and talk; sometimes she came into my room to ask for help. I never found out why she hated me, but I felt as if I had a friend. One morning near the end of her junior year, she came into my room and asked if the rumor was true that I was retiring at the end of the year. I told her that I hadn't made up my mind, but that I was thinking about it. Then she begged me to stay one more year because she had been looking forward to being in my class her senior year. What a difference from "I hate her" to "please stay one more year"!

Now I know that prayer can change people, if we just forget our feelings and put our trust in God.

Sing for Peace: No. 36, "Called by Christ to Love Each Other"

Prayer Thought: Turn our thoughts instantly to prayer, Lord, when we appear to have a problem with another person. We pray for you to work with everyone involved in any relationship difficulty.

| Wednesday **8** September | **May We Hold Hands Today?** By Gerald John Kloss Philadelphia, Pennsylvania | |

"And they, continuing daily with one accord in the temple, and breaking bread from house to house, did eat their meat with gladness and singleness of heart, praising God, and having favor with all the people."—Acts 2:46–47

In September 2002 I had the delightful experience of coming on board at the Philadelphia Christian Academy as the teacher for grades three and four. Working at a private academy is a joy and a pleasure, as there is so much I can do with a small group of children. Having worked for close to thirty years in the Philadelphia public school system as a teacher, administrator, and teacher-trainer, I loved the opportunity to read the scriptures with the children and pray as needed.

One afternoon when I was becoming overwhelmed with the negative behavior of one of my students, I decided to pray. I had all of the children join me in a circle prayer of support. I asked the child who was to be prayed for to sit in the middle, and we each prayed for him. I specifically prayed and included the positive behavior that I longed to see. We all placed our hands on the head of this child and joined forces in our support. I was amazed at the results. I realized that my emotion had been defused because I was actually touching the person of concern and praying with others who were doing the same.

The impact lasted in the lives of the children. The behavior of the child we prayed for did improve. But I also was delighted when at lunch one day, as we were all sitting to eat together, one of the children noticed that the table was round and remarked that this must be a lunch table for a circle of prayer support. This child asked if we could join hands and pray for a concern he had for his dad, who was in Iraq and desperately missed by this child. We did pray, and then each day since, we have had additional prayer requests at the lunch table.

How wonderful to see the children focusing on feeding their spirits first!

Hymns of the Saints: No. 81, "Father Almighty, Grant to Us Thy Blessing"

Prayer Thought: Lord God, as we connect our prayers with those of others may we truly feel your power and presence.

Emblems of Love
By Janie S. Qualls
Lake City, Arkansas

"But concerning love of the brethren you have no need to have any one write to you, for you yourselves have been taught by God to love one another.... But we exhort you, brethren, to do so more and more...."
—I Thessalonians 4:9–10 RSV

After Mother's death I realized why she didn't use the pillowcases I had embellished or the dishcloths I'd crocheted for her. They were there in her chest with the afghans my daughter and sister had crocheted for her. She had considered them to be tokens of our love for her and put them in the chest for safekeeping.

We are to love one another. Little acts of love are often appreciated more than we realize; the smallest act of kindness can make a big difference in someone's life.

All are created with the ability to bring joy to others. This can be accomplished in so many ways. We can bring joy to others in ways that are uniquely ours. When we lighten another's burden, we lighten our own.

Hymns of the Saints: No. 404, "I Would Be True"

Prayer Thought: God of compassion, show us the myriad ways of expressing our love for those around us. May we model an uplifting love for all your children.

"God is love. Whoever lives in love lives in God, and God in him."—I John 4:16 NIV

We had been out late, and on arriving home we checked messages on our phone. A thoughtful, loving church friend had left one: "Our son-in-law has rung to say the airlines have cheap inter-capital fares. I thought you might be interested."

We went online on the computer to check. There were some seats available for half the normal price. We excitedly rang our son and his family on the other side of the country. They had just moved from a desert town to the city. "Is it too soon to visit? Shall we try to come?"

"Yes! Come." they answered.

I'm writing this as we fly over to be with them, anticipating family sharing and meeting again with the church members in that area. What joy! And all because someone cared.

Hymns of the Saints: No. 64, "O Jesus, the Giver of All We Enjoy"

Prayer Thought: We are so grateful, Lord, when the thoughtfulness of others touches our lives in a special way. May we find joy in being thoughtful of others.

| Saturday **11** September | **Pursuing Peace through Love** By Luther M. Beal Beals Island, Maine | |

"I pray that out of his glorious riches [God] may strengthen you with power through his Spirit in your inner being, so that Christ may dwell in your hearts through faith."
—Ephesians 3:16–17 NIV

Early in my formal education, I read and was taught about ancient religions believing that God sent tragedies to punish his children. We studied of rituals, sacrifices, and prayers to keep God from inflicting such retribution. I was comforted by my church school lessons assuring me "God is love." I grew to adulthood believing in a God who cared, loved, and provided help in times of need. We learned about the teachings of Jesus, which support the principle of a loving God.

When horrific terrorists' acts befell our nation and the world, the statements of two of our nation's religious leaders shocked me. I could hardly believe the reports that they blamed the events on God's retribution for the actions of certain people. The thought that God would cause such suffering to punish his people for their belief or sexual preference caused me great distress. I could not imagine worshiping a God who punished those who disagreed with the political teachings and philosophies of these internationally known religious leaders.

This experience caused me to renew my appreciation and gratitude for a religious community teaching love, peace, tolerance, and understanding. We should never take our Christian family for granted. Today, I appreciate even more the joy that comes from association with the Community of Christ.

Sing a New Song: No. 21, "Instruments of Your Peace"

Prayer Thought: Join us together, Lord, in bonds of love and appreciation for the gifts of everyone. May we leave judgment in your courts.

<table>
<tr><td>Sunday
12
September</td><td>**Definite Ideas**
By Mary Twinn
Collinsville, Illinois</td><td></td></tr>
</table>

"[God] has rescued us from the power of darkness and transferred us into the kingdom of his beloved Son, in whom we have redemption, the forgiveness of sins."
—Colossians 1:13–14 NRSV

My co-worker and I had been assigned in pediatrics to care for children with upper respiratory infections, and our attention was focused on a four-year-old boy who wanted to be held and rocked.

He had definite ideas about who he wanted to hold him. He looked at my co-worker, a black woman, and said, "I don't want the one with the black face on it!" Then he looked at me and said, "And I don't want the one with the crooked face on it!"

The one "with the black face on it" picked him up, sat down, and began to rock, and he snuggled contentedly into her lap and fell asleep.

What is cute, funny, and acceptable in a little one, however, for the very reason that it is natural, childlike behavior, ceases to be cute, funny, and acceptable as he grows older. Then it becomes prejudice and bigotry.

There are too many people today who still hang on to what is ugly, cruel, and destructive. One cannot help but wonder how such feelings and behaviors can still exist. Yet they do, and in our post-9/11 world their evil is almost beyond belief!

Still we cannot doubt that the power of God and goodness and love are far greater and that these will and *must* surely prevail.

Sing for Peace: No. 17, "To Live at Peace with Others"

Prayer Thought: Creator and divine Parent of every race and people, help us to so live that the world might see in us the transforming power of your love.

| Monday
13
September | **Unwavering Faith**
By Shirley S. Case
Slater, Missouri | |

"Wherefore, there must be faith; and if there must be faith, there must also be hope; and if there must be hope, there must also be charity; and except you have charity, you can in no wise be saved in the kingdom of God."

—Moroni 10:15

As a child I grew up in my grandmother's home. What a blessing to have lived there! My grandmother had about every kind of cancer possible at different times in her life, and as I look back on those days I realize that the faith she had in God was totally unwavering. Many a night I lay in my bed listening to her prayers as she asked God to grant her life long enough to "raise the little girls—they need me," as she would say. And I never doubted for a minute that she would.

From the time I was five years old, she taught me faith in God, which she said was strength for every trial in life. She taught us to pray and told us stories about Jesus and his love for us. You could just *feel* that love as she told it. She was 4'11" and 150 pounds, her spirit was strong, and her steps were sure because they were grounded in Christ. She lived to be seventy-two, dying of

325

bone cancer. She was the example of committing her life to helping and caring for others, and she trusted God to provide for our needs. God never let us down.

We had few worldly possessions but we were rich in love for each other and for those we encountered in life. I am so thankful for the loving care God had for us as children, and for being raised in the best place possible—the home of my grandmother, Ara Belle—teacher of faith in God and healer of broken souls.

Hymns of the Saints: No. 120, "In Heavenly Love Abiding"

Prayer Thought: Merciful God, we thank you for those in our lives who have taught us an unwavering faith in your awareness of our needs. We offer you our lives, that you may use us to bring hope to others.

Tuesday **14** September	**More Than a Stained-Glass Window** By Barrie Fox Kirkby in Ashfield, England	

"We believe in Jesus Christ, the Son of God, who created heaven and earth, and all things, who shall come down among the children of men."—Mosiah 2:4

Even highly literate people are reckoned to only be able to absorb about 20 percent of what they hear in a connected discourse. It is said, however, that if the discourse is illustrated by some visual material, the percentage may well be, in some cases, as much as tripled. That observation perhaps should cause us to realize how important it is to attempt to let people see, as well as hear, what we believe Jesus has done and is doing in our lives.

Sometimes, but perhaps not often enough, we reflect on what our congregation is achieving in its endeavors to bring people to Christ. This thought, however, certainly came to mind when I read about the words that had been put on the exterior notice board of a church—words that didn't appear to quite say what I am sure was intended. The quite elaborately presented wording simply said, "Don't let worry kill you off. Let the church help." Now, there's a thought to contemplate!

As I think about this, I am challenged anew to realize that Jesus has to be so much more than a figure in a stained-glass window or a picture on the wall at church. Years ago, according to the New Testament, he was breathtakingly involved in the lives of people. Today, through the presence and power of the Spirit, Jesus is still alive and active in the lives of people who accept him as their Lord.

Hymns of the Saints: No. 224, "O Jesus Christ, to Thee May Hymns Be Rising"

Prayer Thought: Life-giving Lord, become real to us as we read the scriptures, offer our prayers, and meditate on what you would have us do in this life. Come alive in our hearts!

| Wednesday **15** September | **Complacency** By Eileen Turner Portland, Oregon | |

"I consider that the sufferings of this present time are not worth comparing with the glory that is to be revealed to us."—Romans 8:18 RSV

The first American slaying in more than a decade in Lebanon occurred in November 2002. Bonnie Witherall and her husband, Gary, had committed themselves to serve as Christian missionaries at a medical clinic in the Lebanese seaport city of Sidon. Bonnie worked at a church-affiliated medical clinic for Palestinian women from a nearby refugee camp, where there was extreme poverty and hopelessness. The evening before her murder, she had given her testimony in Arabic for the first time—not an easy feat. They were beautiful words, and they were her last words for those she had come to serve. She found joy in everything she did, sharing her faith and friendship.

When Gary returned to the States for a memorial to honor Bonnie's mission, he said, "One thing I have to deal with when I come back to America is sleepy churches and happy Christians." He called upon Christians everywhere to leave behind their "lukewarm lives" and open their eyes to the world's suffering.

Sometimes we become so self-involved and complacent with what we have that we overlook the desperate conditions and circumstances of others in our world. If our message is to love one another, maybe we should widen our boundaries.

Sing a New Song: No. 28, "Let Justice Roll like a River"

Prayer Thought: Lord, move and shake us from our apathy and the sense that we can do nothing. Reveal to us the ministry we can give daily in your name to give others hope.

"Offer hospitality to one another without grumbling."
—I Peter 4:9 NIV

On a Wednesday evening in the winter of 2002, our city experienced a severe ice storm, and thousands of residents in our area lost heat and electricity. By Thursday morning, our house temperature had dropped to 49 degrees. When I got up, cold air collected under my wheelchair, numbing my legs. I returned to bed. I covered myself with a blanket and quilt in an effort to keep warm. My daughter left to search for a place that had heat. An hour later, she returned without success.

Then we called the Salvation Army shelter. They had room for us but we could not bring our dog or bird. Next I called a good friend who was an animal lover. She owned a cat and dog. I asked her, "Do you have heat?"

"Yes. My husband bought the last available generator this morning. We have heat and electricity."

"I need a favor. We can stay at the Salvation Army shelter but we can't take our pets, and we won't leave them here to freeze. Will you baby-sit our Pomeranian and parakeet?" I asked.

"What are the sleeping arrangements there?" she asked.

"I'll be sleeping in my wheelchair while Lynda uses a cot," I replied.

"You and your pets are welcome here. We only have one bedroom, but we'll fix a bed for Lynda on the couch. You can sleep in your wheelchair here as easily as at the shelter. And we have a safe place for the bird away from the cat," she responded.

Soon my friend and her husband arrived at our house to help with the move. After packing the car with my medical supplies and some clothes, they were ready for me. I sat in my wheelchair as all three of them took me down the icy ramp and helped me into the car. Then the animals were loaded, and we followed our rescuers to their home.

Two dogs, one bird, one cat, and four adults lived together for three days. On Saturday our heat and electricity were restored. By that afternoon the house was warm and we returned home.

This couple willingly opened their dwelling to our family, providing a warm abode and food. My daughter, pets, and I were blessed by these followers of Christ, and we thank God for them.

Hymns of the Saints: No. 78, "We Thank You, Lord, for Strength of Arm"

Prayer Thought: Lord who owned nothing, we are rich indeed when blessed by the generosity of friends. May we open our hearts to others in time of need.

Friday **17** September	**Family Bonds** By Neta Minthorn Nelsen Beaverton, Oregon	

"Only, live your life in a manner worthy of the gospel of Christ, so that, whether I come and see you or am absent and hear about you, I will know that you are standing firm in one spirit, striving side by side with one mind for the faith of the gospel."—Philippians 1:27 NRSV

Seven of us live together, and soon there will be eight. We sometimes have breakfast together, and we all eat at the table; it's a big one. Sharing is a way of life in our home. Someone needs a diaper changed, another wants a question answered, and still another likes to follow his G.G. (grandfather) to the garage to "see what he's doin'." Sharing the laundry, dirty dishes, house cleaning, and many other household tasks are ways of loving—together. When Guy, the hamster, is turned loose by little hands, we scamper to catch him to protect him from dangers, or if the milk jug goes dry, someone is ready to go for a new one. The family dog, Violet, likes our togetherness. She is let outdoors whenever needed, but wants to be with the family too.

Our family shares different religions. We all go to church when the time is right to do that. Sometimes one person must go to a meeting and needs to have the smaller children stay at home. We take turns watching the young ones. Working hours vary, and then the small children are watched and cared for also. It's a togetherness of hearts we share. I am glad that we share the love of Jesus Christ in our home. I love our family, all three generations.

Sing a New Song: No. 34, "Make Me a Channel of Your Peace"

Prayer Thought: Bind cords of love around our hearts, Lord, when we share life in one household. Melt tensions, and help us give respite to one another.

<table>
<tr><td>Saturday
18
September</td><td>**Clearing the Rubble**
By Janie Fehrenbacher
Broken Arrow, Oklahoma</td><td></td></tr>
</table>

"Meanwhile the people in Judah said, 'The strength of the laborers is giving out, and there is so much rubble that we cannot rebuild the wall.'"—Nehemiah 4:10 NIV

I am gaining a new appreciation for the Old Testament, for as it has been pointed out to me, that is the Bible that Jesus knew. When I came across this scripture it touched a chord in my soul. How many times do we feel burdened and tired? Not just physically, but within our minds and spirits?

Perhaps that is because there seems to be so much "rubble" in our daily living, and that rubble is piled so high it has become difficult for some of us to "see" over it. We easily become discouraged when others do not react to or visualize the spiritual "truths" we hold dear. We become so intense over the concepts we personally "see," that we cannot see the long-range possibilities in the viewpoints of others in our circles of influence. If we have learned anything since September 11, 2001, it is that when people are so driven to "see" only their own perspectives, the rights and hopes of others are infringed upon. Are we not similar to the ancient Hebrews, who could not imagine rebuilding the wall?

If we get too caught up in our own needs and wants, there is little time left to extend the gift of friendship, to feed the hungry (hungry for love and acceptance…not just food), the call to reach out by listening and accepting a need to communicate or "vent." Our strength is driven by the Spirit of Christ, who calls us to be kinder, more loving, more imaginative, more adventurous, more skilled, and more understanding in our relationships.

Strength begets strength. One disciple can help another, and that person can touch yet another. We are not in this alone. Christ calls us to follow him, even when we are tired, discouraged, and depressed. For we simply do not walk alone when Christ is by our side.

Hymns of the Saints: No. 392, "Go, Make of All Disciples"

Prayer Thought: God of strength and vision, open our eyes to the rubble in our lives and give us the strength to clear it away. Then empower us to build a new life, rich in ministry.

| Sunday **19** September | **A Trip to Remember**
By Melba Jean Dixon
Farwell, Michigan | |

"Upon the wings of his Spirit has my body been carried away upon exceedingly high mountains. And my eyes have beheld great things."—II Nephi 3:40–41

La Buena Fe, Honduras, has held a special place in my heart for a very long time. John Blumenschein, a doctor from Independence, Missouri, brought his family to that lovely valley near Lake Yojoa in 1957. He built a health clinic there, and began to serve the needy people of the area. After only one year, Dr. Blumenschein died of cancer, and his wife, Marian, carried on the work. Many people served there during the years that followed.

In the sixties my sister, Gail, fresh out of the "San" school of nursing in Independence, went there to serve. Gail and a classmate, Beverly Thompson, from the Yukon, Canada, lived at La Buena Fe for one year. Their tales of hardships and illnesses were far exceeded by stories of the happiness and joy they experienced with the people they soon grew to love.

Gail's tales of adventure greatly influenced my son, Mark, to become a physician with a desire to serve in Third World countries. As Mark made plans to embark on his second trip to Central America with the Health Ministries team, he invited other family members to go along. With the approval of team director Ron Edwards, my husband and I, and four other family members including Gail, made the journey. We nonmedical people found plenty of work to do.

Photos and descriptions had not prepared me for the breathtaking beauty of the lush countryside and the serene valleys surrounded by majestic mountains. Our trip continued to Guatemala, where we saw an active volcano. I viewed with awe and wonder another part of God's majestic creation.

Yet nature in all its beauty failed to surpass the love and compassion I experienced as I interacted with the people we met on our journey in Central America. No body of water, no towering mountain, could compare with the absolute beauty I saw in the eyes of the children God created. My life has been enriched, and I am grateful.

Sing a New Song: No. 40, "Now Sing to Our God"

Prayer Thought: Loving Creator, whether near or far away, may we learn to appreciate the wonders of your world and the spirits of your precious people.

Unfamiliar Difficulties
By Don Richardson
Osceola, Iowa

"Look at the birds of the air: they neither sow nor reap nor gather into barns, and yet your heavenly Father feeds them. Are you not of more value than they?"
—Matthew 6:26 RSV

I was visiting with an eighth grader about her previous day's absence from school. She was living with an aunt and uncle. She told me that if I had listened to the TV news two nights before, I would know why she had been absent. Her mother had been arrested and was in jail, and her father, who had abducted her at one time, was about to be released from jail.

As with most of us, I could not fathom the depth of her problems. I was raised by "goodly parents." Situations like this were not part of my growing-up years. I found it hard to respond appropriately to a young teenager facing such a horrendous life because of her parents.

When terrible situations enter our lives, situations beyond anything we have ever experienced, we can turn to the one Source that is always constant. The scriptures remind us of God's greatness and loving concern even for those whose lives are in constant upheaval. Gratitude should fill our hearts if we have had the good fortune of being raised by loving parents, especially ones who taught us of Jesus and tried to live their lives according to their understanding of him.

When we find ourselves asked for counsel in unfamiliar situations, we can pray for God's guidance before we speak. We can also pray for those who have not been as fortunate, for we know that the Lord loves us all equally.

Sing for Peace: No. 13, "God of the Sparrow"

Prayer Thought: Compassionate God, grant us insight when we are facing unfamiliar difficulties in people's lives. Show us how to offer hope to those who struggle daily with problems beyond our imagining.

Tuesday **21** September	**The Sugar Maples** By June Russell Independence, Missouri	

"The righteous flourish like the palm tree, and grow like a cedar in Lebanon. They are planted in the house of the Lord; they flourish in the courts of our God. In old age they still produce fruit."—Psalm 92:12–14 NRSV

The big old sugar maples on our street bring me such joy each fall when they burst forth into bright gold and red. Their beauty almost takes my breath away. Now, as their leaves are beginning to drop, I notice that they have become rather spindly, having lost branches in ice storms the past few years. Before long, we will lose some of them. I am glad to see that several new ones are growing in some of the yards in our neighborhood.

How like our own lives! Just as a maple tree is planted, grows to maturity, gives shade and shelter to birds, animals, and humans, and then each year displays its beauty, so also we are born, grow up, take our place in the world, and (we hope) make a contribution to the world around us.

My prayer for each of us is that even though the ice storms of our lives may leave us depleted, like the sugar maples, we may still bring joy, delight, encouragement, and warmth to those whose lives we touch.

Hymns of the Saints: No. 14, "For Beauty of Meadows"

Prayer Thought: Creator of life's colors, remove the habits in our lives that hold us back from sharing the beauty you have placed there to bless others. May we seek to bring blessing as long as we can.

Wednesday
22
September

Little Joys
By Roberta Dieterman
Caledonia, Michigan

"Thou shalt thank the Lord thy God in all things."
—Doctrine and Covenants 59:2d

It was near the end of vacation and I was sitting on the balcony, looking out over the Gulf of Mexico. It was a beautiful morning, and there were a lot of people walking the beach. I was looking forward to going home, but was sad at leaving the sunshine and warm temperatures for my cold, snowy home.

Then something caught my eye out in the water, so I grabbed my binoculars and saw such a wonderful sight that all I could say was WOW! A dolphin—its entire body—came out of the water in a graceful arch, not just once, but three times. No one on the beach seemed to notice. I couldn't believe my luck at looking out at the exact moment. What a thrill. I thanked God for this gift of his creation.

Like the people on the beach, many times I'm not looking in the right place and I miss those surprises that are all around me—a baby's first steps, a bright red cardinal against a snowy background, seeing friends greet each other. Little joys are all around us—sunsets, sunrises, a harvest moon. All these things cause me to stop and say, "Thank you, God, for letting me witness those little surprises you tuck into the fabric of our lives."

Hymns of the Saints: No. 65, "God of the Earth, the Sky, the Sea"

Prayer Thought: Lord of all life, pull us away from life's distractions to notice the little joys all around us—creatures of the seas, butterflies on the wind, fields of wheat—things that we, with all our knowledge, cannot create.

Thursday **23** September	**A Stranger No More** By Dennis D. Grewal Creston, British Columbia, Canada	

"Now therefore ye are no more strangers and foreigners, but fellow citizens with the saints, and of the household of God."—Ephesians 2:19

In the summer of 2002 our family went to Missouri to take our older daughter for her first year of university. We stayed with relatives outside Independence. One evening my wife was busy visiting her sister and I decided to go for a long walk. Beautiful rolling hills and unique countryside reminded me of our great Creator.

Suddenly a car stopped behind me. An elderly gentleman rolled his window down and said, "You must be a stranger here." When I told him why we were there, he said, "Now that your daughter is in Missouri we will see you more often." I had a wonderful visit with this man. We talked for a long time. When I said good-bye to him we were no longer strangers.

Sometimes an encounter with strangers can give us completely different views, and with loving and kind words a stranger can become a good friend.

Hymns of the Saints: No. 485, "Blest Be the Tie that Binds"

Prayer Thought: Lord, join our hearts to those we do not know who long to share their lives with us or who may need our ministry. Grant us wisdom in such encounters.

<table>
<tr><td>Friday
24
September</td><td>**Sustained through All Things**
By Herbert W. Rotchford
Springfield, Illinois</td><td></td></tr>
</table>

"Peter therefore was kept in prison; but prayer was made without ceasing of the church unto God for him."

—Acts 12:5

When I was ten years old, I was in a hit-and-run accident. I was unconscious for forty-one days. My mother sat at my bedside every day praying for her "little boy" to live. There had been extensive head injuries and several brain operations. Sometime after the second operation, the doctors and nurses finally convinced her that if I were to live I would be a "vegetable." Mom told me that she stopped praying for me to live and prayed, "Lord, if he will truly be only a vegetable, I would rather he die. But thy will be done, not mine."

Within a few days I awoke when a nun jiggled my big toe. I told her to go away, to leave me alone; I wanted to sleep. She told me I had been sleeping for forty-one days, and didn't I think that was long enough? I was kept in the hospital for several more days before being discharged. I resumed my paper route a week later.

This was the first of several episodes in my life when I believe that God heard prayers and intervened to save my life. During the time I was unconscious and in my recuperation, I don't remember feeling any pain. I remember playing ball in a beautiful green field—laughing, running, and romping with my friends. Where had I been? Why didn't I feel any pain? I have amazed doctors with my recovery from heart attacks, bladder surgery for cancer, and the chemotherapy that followed. They were further amazed when I was diagnosed with prostate cancer and underwent the full thirty-nine radiation treatments without any serious side effects, even though I have diabetes.

The night before I was to have double by-pass surgery, the elders came to the hospital and administered to me. I knew without a doubt that everything was going to be all right before they left. That was in June 1978.

Gradually I realized that God is looking out for me and has been throughout my life. Through the highs and lows, he has been there patiently waiting for me to call out to him. All my troubles are not over, but I have faith that his Spirit will give me the needed strength and guidance to weather the storms of life.

Hymns of the Saints: No. 457, "My Lord, I Know That All My Life"

Prayer Thought: God of blessing, we thank you for your sustaining hand through all the trials of life. We pray to be uplifted that we might offer our service in your name.

| Saturday
25
September | **Trust in the Lord**
By Ethel Knackstedt
Kansas City, Kansas | |

"Trust in the Lord with all thine heart; and lean not unto thine own understanding."—Proverbs 3:5

In March 1980 our daughter, Jeanette, was facing serious leg surgery and would need to be hospitalized for several weeks. Since we lived in Ottawa, Ontario, and she had a seventeen-month-old son, she decided to bring him to Kansas City for our older daughter to care for while she was in the hospital. I was working part-time, and the plan was that I would take him back home and care for her and little Bryce until she was able to assume some of those responsibilities.

After Jeanette left Kansas City for Toronto where the surgery would be performed, I had the strong feeling that I should be with her for the surgery, a feeling that would not go away. My husband, Lloyd, had been off work for several months because of foot surgery, and his company had been on strike for three months. Our available cash was almost gone, and my part-time job only paid for a few groceries.

We talked it over and decided I needed to go. After buying my plane ticket and leaving some cash for Lloyd, not knowing when the strike would end, I left with $100 in my purse. I didn't know where I would stay or for how long; I just knew I had to be there.

As the plane taxied down the runway I said a silent prayer: "Lord, I praise you for getting me this far, and I'll trust you for whatever is to come."

My son-in-law met me at the airport and informed me that he was staying with a friend of his and there would be no room for me there. As we arrived at the hospital the elders were there, administering to Jeanette. After they finished their prayers and introductions were made, my daughter asked them if they knew where I might stay. They conferred and told us of a church family who would have room and lived near a bus line. One of the elders called the family and they agreed to house me. With my limited funds I would probably be staying a very short time.

I ended up staying eleven days, and during that time Jeanette was in surgery three times. After the third time I knew it was OK for me to go. My hosts had been so wonderful; I was touched by their generosity.

I called my husband to tell him I would be home in a couple of days. I asked him if the strike had been settled and he said no, but when I arrived home on Saturday he said the strike had been settled the previous day and that he would be going back to work on Monday. I was awed by the Lord's timing.

Hymns of the Saints: No. 187, "Great Is Thy Faithfulness"

Prayer Thought: Faithful God, help us to never doubt your trustworthiness. You know of our needs before we tell you. You only want our hearts.

Sunday **26** September	**One Hour of Spiritual Bonding** By Helen Lents Independence, Missouri

"Love each other like brothers and sisters....Be patient when trouble comes, and pray at all times."
　　　　—Romans 12:10, 12 New Century Version

The corkboard was filled with prayer request envelopes—petitions, praise, pleas, longings, and needs. Each one represented a soul precious to God and one of my fellow beings.

As I glanced at the names I realized that many were just names to me—there had not been opportunity to connect faces and names. We were here at a silent retreat, and so were not to speak but to experience spiritual bonding through openness to God's Holy Spirit among us. I tentatively took my first envelope down, quietly read the prayer request, and bowed my head in prayer for this child of God, one also known to me. This was a privilege as I shared my personal response to this request of a friend.

Next, two envelopes were clipped together, one unsealed and the other sealed; the name was not familiar to me. As I read the request in the open envelope and bowed my head in prayer I wondered if I could really pray effectively for this person—and surely not for that which had been chosen to be kept private. The words flowed smoothly and freely as my unuttered but sincere prayer was offered for this person's concern. I felt assured that I was being led by the Holy Spirit in understanding to some degree the needs of this request.

That experience continued for the entire group of approximately twenty prayer requests. I truly felt both the impress of God's Spirit and a bonding with the sisters and brothers whom I shall continue to uphold in my prayers.

Hymns of the Saints: No. 312, "Let Us Pray for One Another"

Prayer Thought: Eternal God, we thank you for the power of your Holy Spirit to overcome our lack of knowledge and to lead us in prayer for the sake of others.

| Monday **27** September | **Life Lessons on Roller Skates** By Paul McCain Oklahoma City, Oklahoma | |

"Therefore, my son, see that you are merciful to your brethren; deal justly, judge righteously, and do good continually; and if you do all these things, then shall you receive your reward."—Alma 19:78

As a young teenager in Henryetta, Oklahoma, many of us kids enjoyed roller skating. At first, for a year or two, someone would bring a portable skating rink to town, set it up for a month or so, and then take it somewhere else. Apparently someone then decided that it had caught on enough to put a rink there permanently.

I remember what a challenge it was to learn to skate, at first hanging onto the rail, and going around time after time. While I was motionless against the rail, screwing up my courage, the fright of having to mix with all those fast skaters was somewhat overwhelming.

After getting just a little skill, and being a risk-taker, I would then venture out onto the main floor into the crowd of more advanced skaters.

Once I got a little way into the crowd, I could then see only those people in front of me, and, somehow without concern, those across the floor. I couldn't see those coming up behind me at all, and I soon learned that the only ones who really mattered were those fairly near to me. Because I moved quite slowly at first, there seemed to be a vacuum in front of me, sort of like the driver in rush-hour traffic going ten miles slower than everyone else. I was able to relax some, then, and work on technique and not falling down.

Somewhere along the way I learned an important life lesson; it applied to roller skating then, and later to many other facets of life—school, work, relationships. The lesson, of course, is that I have too often looked at the immensity of a task and shook with some fear at the undertaking. Then, on realizing that I only had to deal with a small part of it at one time, I lost some of the anxiety and was able to focus energy where it was needed, not worrying about all those other aspects. I believe that the Lord does not give me more than I can handle, but I also believe that he expects me to learn the skills to break large tasks into smaller, more manageable ones.

Life can be overwhelming; we live in uncertain times with many things pressing on us. If we are to deal with them we must not waste time on the ones we cannot have a reasonable effect on, and concentrate on those that the Spirit reveals are ours to deal with.

Hymns of the Saints: No. 197, "Let God Be God"

Prayer Thought: Lord, may we not be overwhelmed by the immensity of your call to us. Let us learn the small tasks, put our newfound skills together, and move out in your Spirit to fulfill our call.

<table>
<tr><td>Tuesday
28
September</td><td>**Just a Little Gray Fox**
By Shirley Vallier Remmenga
Fort Collins, Colorado</td><td></td></tr>
</table>

"I, the Lord, have called you in righteousness; I will take hold of your hand. I will keep you and will make you to be a covenant for the people and a light for the Gentiles."
—Isaiah 42:6 NIV

"O Lord, I'm so tired and so frustrated, please help me," I prayed as I left church and started for home. The hour was late, the meeting had been long, and it hadn't gone that well. Not that we hadn't covered a lot of important topics that needed to be addressed. It was just, it seemed to me, that nothing had been resolved and our time had been wasted.

As I turned the corner onto Vine Drive, a pair of shiny eyes appeared in the light from my headlights. A small gray fox scurried away and ran into the weeds along the road. It was a beautiful little creature with a slim body and a big furry tail. It had been feasting on a carcass that lay in the middle of the road—a victim of a previous vehicle. I had only a glimpse of this little fox, but that glimpse changed my mood. Suddenly, I was no longer exhausted and troubled. In fact, I felt good and I smiled. I have not seen that many foxes in this part of Colorado so it was a real treat to see one. I drove on home with a song in my heart and it came to me that maybe the meeting hadn't been such a waste after all.

A little fox on a dark night; a woman discouraged and tired; a God who answered a prayer—a little incident with a great ending.

Hymns of the Saints: No. 185, "Lord of All Hopefulness"

Prayer Thought: How often, Lord, you bless our lives in unexpected ways. Help us to be aware of your blessings and to rejoice in them.

| Wednesday **29** September | **The Call of Zion** By Charlotte Jones Sherman Oaks, California | |

"Heed the urgent call to become a global family united in the name of the Christ, committed in love to one another, seeking the kingdom for which you yearn and to which you have always been summoned. That kingdom shall be a peaceable one and it shall be known as Zion."
—Doctrine and Covenants 161:6b

Recently I had an unusual experience when I attended the memorial service for a friend's brother. It was at a town some distance away, at a Mormon "meeting house." During the service they spoke of beliefs held in common with our church, the Community of Christ. It was good to not have to explain certain concepts.

After the service we shared food and conversation. I appreciated the warm reception I received and was impressed with the viable congregational life that nurtured my friend and welcomed an outsider like me. The table where I sat had several who were converts. It was good to be able to discuss the basic beliefs we held in common, but sad that the differences kept the message of Christ from being spread as well as it might be if we were united.

Our move to mingle with other churches is encouraging. The message of Christ can go forward through the uniqueness of our church, so that the inspiration of our prophet can serve as a leavening agent and be instrumental in spreading the gospel. It is exciting to consider and a goal to foster with God's direction.

Sing for Peace: No. 9, "Bring Forth the Kingdom"

Prayer Thought: God, we open ourselves to the direction of your Spirit, that the gospel of Christ may be spread through your wisdom. Show us how to break down barriers with other Christians.

| Thursday **30** September | **Peaceful Hills** By Clara Covert Ottawa, Ontario, Canada | |

"And he shall judge among the nations, and shall rebuke many people; and they shall beat their swords into ploughshares, and their spears into pruning hooks; nation shall not lift up sword against nation, neither shall they learn war anymore."—Isaiah 2:4

Each autumn hundreds of people tour through the Gatineau Hills of eastern Québec to view the trees in their fall splendor. As I traveled with a busload of seniors along the winding roads through the hills, the view from the wide windows was breathtaking—the bright scarlet of maples and the gold and yellow of poplars contrasted with the green conifers.

The main stop on our trip was at Champlain Lookout, where we left the bus and wandered around. The splendor of God's creation filled the air with wonder and tranquility.

Unlike some places in the world, there were no rumbling war tanks breaking a path through the trees, no marching boots crushing the late-blooming flowers. Instead, as we silently reentered the bus, we knew we were experiencing the unsullied greatness of God's work.

Hymns of the Saints: No. 315, "This Is My Song"

Prayer Thought: Creator God, may we always be aware of the beauty of your creation, and work to preserve freedom, if we have it, so that others in need of release may come and go in peace.

October 2004

S	M	T	W	T	F	S
					1	2
3	4	5	6	7	8	9
10	11	12	13	14	15	16
17	18	19	20	21	22	23
24	25	26	27	28	29	30
31						

Beauty in All Things
By Faye Williams
Kennett, Missouri

"Rejoice evermore. Pray without ceasing. In everything give thanks; for this is the will of God in Christ Jesus concerning you."—I Thessalonians 5:16–18

During a recent ice storm, our town was without power for several hours and some parts were out for days. As I looked out at the devastation of broken trees and power lines, it was hard to find something positive about the situation.

It is sometimes difficult to find blessings in the midst of destruction. I could only think, "This is the day the Lord hath made; we will rejoice and be glad in it." Another scripture also came to mind: "In all things give thanks."

We took many pictures and shared the beauty by sending them to our daughters out of town. In the midst of such beauty, one could forget the problems of the storm.

Hymns of the Saints: No. 172, "God, Who Touchest Earth with Beauty"

Prayer Thought: We thank you, Lord, for helping us by bringing to mind positive circumstances in times of trouble.

Gas Leak
By LaVerne Cramer
Tomah, Wisconsin

"Humble yourselves therefore under the mighty hand of God, so that he may exalt you in due time. Cast all your anxiety on him, because he cares for you."
—I Peter 5:6–7 NRSV

It was a very cold night in January. My husband, Lloyd, had just returned home from a basketball game and was putting the car in the garage when Bob and his wife just happened to be walking by our home. They smelled gas outside, and Bob ran into our garage to tell Lloyd. Lloyd can't smell, so he never noticed it; they came in and our son John called the Hot Line for Gas Leaks.

A man came around ten o'clock and checked our basement. He said his tester showed there was gas coming into the basement, but the smell was stronger outside. He would have to call the crew; it was too dangerous to let it go all night. Four or five trucks came, and the crews worked all night. Around 8:00 a.m. they were finally finished. As I thought about the danger we had been in, I remembered how I had prayed that morning for God's protection, never realizing that God had protected and spared our lives.

I wonder how many times God takes care of us unknown to us. That favorite old hymn "God Will Take Care of You" certainly became a reality that night to me.

Hymns of the Saints: No. 148, "Where Wilt Thou Put Thy Trust?"

Prayer Thought: We thank you, God, for the daily blessing of life itself. May we show our appreciation by living life as fully as possible on behalf of others.

"Be of good courage, and he shall strengthen your heart, all ye that hope in the Lord."—Psalm 31:24

Many are rejoicing over the release of POWs in Iraq. Many testify to praying for just such an event and give thanks to God, as they should. But what about the prayers of others that went unanswered when their sons or daughters were killed in this war? Many cry out, "Where was God then? Why didn't he protect my son (or daughter)?"

I can remember feeling this way when as a child I prayed for my mother's healing from Parkinson's disease. I clearly remember that many of my prayers had been answered, so why not this one? Why are some prayers answered and others seemingly ignored? What kind of a God is that?

My parents, especially my mother, tried to help me as I struggled with this issue. They pointed out that God has never promised us that we would be free of pain, problems, or anxiety. God has promised to walk with us through them, supplying us with the necessary strength and direction to handle them and the courage to move forward.

My mother's testimony was a life filled with many rich blessings. She never suffered from common ills that many of us go through such as colds, flu, and the like. She easily and quickly delivered her babies with very little pain. She did fall easily so we tried to watch so we could be there to help. Once, while visiting, she fell off a porch toward a patch of thorny bushes ten feet below. Before she reached them, she told of feeling a pair of strong arms lift her free of them and lay her gently on the ground. We were blessed by this event also, for we realized that God was there.

What about the loss of a child, a spouse, or other loved one? While these are very painful experiences, Mom pointed out that the length of a life is not what is important, but how that life is lived. Have we found and followed Christ?

Through pain and suffering we have the opportunity to grow and strengthen our spiritual lives and perhaps help others along the way. My mom did. May we always remember that we do not walk alone; God is there.

Sing for Peace: No. 44, "Go, My Children"

Prayer Thought: Help us, Lord, to realize that we never walk alone and to look to you for the strength we need in times of difficulty.

Monday **4** October	**Childhood Innocence** By Mark E. Megee East Windsor, New Jersey	

"Stand fast therefore in the liberty wherewith Christ hath made us free, and be not entangled again with the yoke of bondage."—Galatians 5:1

The innocence of children—Jesus spoke of it two thousand years ago. It must seem so far away to our children these days, in a world where most kids are exposed to things we could not even comprehend when we were growing up. What have we done with the innocence of our children?

It's still there. It's just buried a bit. A recent trip to a playground with our six kids showed me that it just needed to be dusted off. Looking around the park, we had kids on swings and slides and climbing trees. They were helping each other climb and pushing each other on the swings. They were still the same innocent children that they were when they were toddlers, despite the world's attempt to bury them in the muck we call society. It just had to be brushed off.

The same has to be done with adults. Let's dust off the things that weigh us down and keep us from being that innocent child that God made years ago. Jesus is bidding us to join him.

Hymns of the Saints: No. 186, "Creator of Sunrises"

Prayer Thought: Cleanse us with your Spirit, forgiving God, that we may rediscover the joy and innocence we see in our children.

Tuesday **5** October	**A Compelling Spirit** By Jeannine Blasick Monongahela, Pennsylvania	

"It is my will that my priesthood be made up of those who have an abiding faith and desire to serve me with all their hearts, in humility and with great devotion."
—Doctrine and Covenants 156:8a

In the summer of 2002 while at reunion, we had the privilege of receiving the ministry of Apostle Linda Booth. The more she shared with us the more I related to her and felt a closeness, so that I was able to share with her. It concerned my calling to the office of priest.

Having been blessed with the gift of dreams and visions, I related the following dream. The setting was in our home long before the calling of women to priesthood had been presented. My doorbell rang. When I went to answer it I saw no one, but sensed a powerful presence. A voice asked if this was the house of a priest. I answered, "No, it is not." The voice asked again, "Is this the house of a priest?" Again I answered, "No, it is not." But the third time the voice declared, "This is the house of a priest." On awakening, the same powerful spirit remained with me most of that day.

On pondering the meaning, I felt it had to be for my husband. I gave it no more thought until 1984 when the revelation came for women to be called. If indeed the call were for my husband, he would have had the experience. I now knew it was for me. So I waited for those in authority to come to me.

Ten years passed, when my cousin, who had not known of my dream, asked an elder why I had never been called and was told that I had been rejected because my husband had not attended for years and probably would not support me. This was the hurt I shared with Apostle Booth. She said, "Why, you have fallen through the cracks," and advised me to make it a matter of prayer as to whom I should tell. I did just that for two months, and then felt a compelling need to share it with our pastor.

Soon after this my husband and I left for a trip to the Smoky Mountains. On returning home I was scheduled for a stress test but failed it, was admitted to the hospital for a heart catheterization, and failed it. Three days later I had bypass surgery. For the next two months I was unable to attend church, but when I wanted to go my husband offered to drive. He's been attending now for three-and-a-half months. He has been generous in buying things for the church, such as two new flags and a new church seal. He also bought a microwave and a kitchen storage cabinet.

I've since been called to the office of priest. My husband supports me and is a changed individual. He wanted nothing to do with the church for thirty-seven years. One thing I learned through the words of the apostle is, "It's not whether we are worthy of being called, but whether we have a desire to serve." This caused me to share my experience with my pastor. I'm in my seventy-fifth year of life and feel like Grandma Moses beginning a new career.

Hymns of the Saints: No. 362, "A Diligent and Grateful Heart"

Prayer Thought: God of revelation, continue to draw us to you through the inspiration of your Spirit. May we joyfully prepare ourselves to serve your people wherever we may be.

| Wednesday **6** October | **So Full of Life** By Diane F. Schwartz Las Vegas, Nevada | |

"A new commandment I give unto you, That ye love one another; as I have loved you, that ye also love one another."—John 13:34

In October last year, our women's scripture group hosted a small birthday party for one of our members who is in a care facility. Margaret was going to be ninety.

It is always so wonderful to see her. Because of a stroke several years ago, her speech is limited and she is in a wheelchair, yet despite these problems, her mind is sharp and her light blue eyes are beautiful and full of life. She loves to laugh so we tell her stories and sometimes jokes. We go to minister to her, but we are the beneficiaries. I can remember clearly from a few years ago the first time she took my hand and pulled me close so she could whisper, "I love you," to me. I didn't even really know Margaret when I first started visiting her to take her the sacrament, but she has become an important part of my life, and I have grown to love her.

I have always found the love of God shining clearly from the eyes of the very old and the very young—one so new from God and so full of innocence, and the other nearing the return to their Creator and so full of wisdom. They each have something to teach us, and I receive great joy from being in the presence of both.

Sing a New Song: No. 11, "Give Thanks"

Prayer Thought: Lord, remind us that those who are confined by their physical disabilities need to be loved and to know they are not forgotten. May we also allow them to minister to us.

Thursday **7** October	**All Things Are Spiritual** By Louita Clothier Lamoni, Iowa	

"The elements are eternal, and spirit and element, inseparably connected, receiveth a fullness of joy."
—Doctrine and Covenants 90:5e

I love the outdoors, and walking is one of my favorite sources of refreshment and energy. It is my time for meditation, problem solving, and creative ideas. If I feel in a sociable mood, I walk in town. If I'm more introspective and meditative, I walk the Railtrail, a woodsy green "tunnel," east to the Interstate. But most often my steps take me to open country. It has been on the rural roads around Lamoni that I have been the most strongly touched by God's presence, and where I have had some illuminating life-changing experiences.

There the wide sky stretches over me from horizon to horizon. There I can peer through layers of sun-rimmed clouds, feeling as if I am seeing into all eternity. Often my thoughts turn to prayer, and I find myself a mile down the road, not remembering how I got there.

On ordinary days I see ordinary fields and trees. Other times when my spirit is awakened, I walk feeling completely surrounded and filled by love, a kind of cosmic love. On those days it is as though every leaf on every tree and every bird that sings is a manifestation of God's love, that God's Spirit is in all things and through all things.

Surely that is how God would have us see all of life. The word came to the early church "...verily I say unto you, that *all things unto me are spiritual*" (Doctrine and Covenants 28:9). This tells me that God's indwelling presence is in all of creation; that there is no realm of life that is beyond God's sovereignty, and that our mission is to all of creation, to all of life.

Hymns of the Saints: No. 49, "Earth and All Stars"

Prayer Thought: Creator of all that is, our hearts are filled with praise beyond our ability to express for all you have created and for our part in it.

| Friday **8** October | **Keeping Our Balance** By Roberta Dieterman Caledonia, Michigan | |

"Preserve sound judgment and discernment, do not let them out of your sight…. Then you will go on your way in safety, and your foot will not stumble."—Proverbs 3: 21, 23

While passing a local church I read the following on their sign: "A stumble can prevent a fall." It reminded me of one winter day when I was walking on an ice-covered sidewalk and lost my footing. After a few seconds of fancy and comic footwork, I regained my solid footing.

While it was embarrassing, it could have been worse if I had fallen.

It did remind me of how often I've "stumbled" with a new task or office at church. There were times I took jobs I wasn't prepared for, and in the learning process I stumbled. Fortunately there were people who came to my aid and helped me get back on solid ground. Helping each other when we stumble on life's path is what God wants us to do. I'm very thankful for those people in my life who have been there to help steady me when I've been unsure of myself.

New situations need not cause us to stumble; there are those whose support we can call on when the need arises. Although it's true a stumble can prevent a fall, sometimes we do fall, but we are assured there will always be the hand of God to help put us back on our feet.

Hymns of the Saints: No. 439, "Teach Me, My God and King"

Prayer Thought: We thank you, Lord, for your help when we've stumbled and fallen and for those who are there to set us on the right path once again.

| Saturday **9** October | **Offering Praise** By Norma Holman Wayne City, Illinois | |

"Sing praises to the Lord, for he has done gloriously; let this be known in all the earth. Shout aloud and sing for joy…."—Isaiah 12:5–6 NRSV

I have been concerned that I seem to be unable to show praise to God in the joyous manner I have seen in others. I feel it, think it, say it, pray it, but never seem able to demonstrate the spiritual joy I feel. My daughter told me it is like a child lifting outstretched arms to be held, as we reach our hands and hearts to our heavenly Parent.

Our congregation sponsored a well-known gospel quartet in our Family Life Center, and my attention was drawn to a young adult man with obvious physical disabilities. He was so joyous, enthralled, and totally immersed in the praise music. He seemed to need to look at his right foot to get it to tap the way he wanted, and his face would beam when he got it right. Evidently he couldn't clap with his left arm, but moved his right hand and arm with enthusiasm. A few times he was able to move his shoulders with the rhythm, and in one high moment his arm was raised and tears streamed down his face. I left feeling I had seen true praise in that young man.

I desire to praise God and his creation with magnificent attributes, and I now know God understands my heart, even when I am unable to express it. I may never feel the joy of worship and praise the same as that young man, just as I could never preach, sing, or play an instrument. But we each have our own gifts, because that's the way God made us.

Sing a New Song: No. 38, "Mighty God, Transforming God!"

Prayer Thought: Transform us, mighty God, that we might offer praise in whatever way we can for the power of your Spirit in our lives.

Mystical Moment
By Charles Kornman
Grand Junction, Colorado

"And we have the word of the prophets made more certain, and you will do well to pay attention to it, as to a light shining in a dark place, until the day dawns and the morning star rises in your hearts."—II Peter 1:19 NIV

It was one of those mystical, magical moments when time stood still, and it is frozen forever in my memory. Dawn was just beginning its invasion of a mountain valley. I stood hidden in the willows bordering Quartz Creek in Colorado. Mountain trout are cunning creatures, and I had just cast my fly upstream, letting it float downstream. A movement captured my attention. A doe and her fawn were suddenly standing in the stream. The doe stood there, flicking her ears, probably listening for danger. The fawn frolicked around her as it danced in total freedom. Birds began their welcome to the dawn.

Daylight was casting its incredible glow over all of that beautiful part of creation. The mother-offspring addition to the magic of that moment was clearly, to me, an act of God. The angels and I were the only audience in that incredible moment. I stood, frozen in wonder, praying that no fish would take my fly. None did. Mother and child moved about on their deer business. I stood there, marveling at God's creative genius, little knowing that that "frozen" moment was part of God's healing magic to melt an ice-bound heart.

Hymns of the Saints: No. 69, "Creation Flows Unceasingly"

Prayer Thought: Incredible Creator, we humbly give thanks for the mystical moments of life, when you reach through all that hardens our hearts to touch us once again.

The Power of Prayer
By JoAnn Townsend
Spokane, Washington

"Be afflicted for nothing; but in everything by prayer and supplication with thanksgiving let your requests be made known unto God. And the peace of God, which passeth all understanding, shall keep your hearts and minds through Christ Jesus."—Philippians 4:6–7

I was taking care of a new young mother who, a few hours earlier, had delivered a premature baby. The neonatal intensive care physician came into the room to update her and her family on the baby girl's condition. The baby was unstable, and the doctor tried to prepare the young parents for the worst. Despair seemed to fill the room.

After the doctor left, I asked the mother if she would like someone from a church or the hospital chaplain to come and say a prayer for the baby. She responded she didn't want anyone called. Silently I said my own prayer. Later, when I went back into the room, her family was talking about the power of prayer and the many people they knew who would pray for her. Because the baby was so fragile, the mother had not yet been allowed to touch her, but it was mentioned that she could just lay her hand alongside her and send loving energy to her. The young mother's eyes lit up. Her countenance became filled with hope, and she couldn't wait to see her little girl.

Later I wondered what it must be like to have no understanding of the love of a heavenly Father and the power of prayer. Too many people live their lives in loneliness and despair. A simple message of a loving God and prayer can be life changing.

Hymns of the Saints: No. 213, "I Sought the Lord"

Prayer Thought: Eternal God, help us bring your peace and healing love to a world in need.

Tuesday **12** October	**Faith of a Child** By L. Joyce Wilcox La Mesa, California	

"And so great was the faith of Enoch, that he led the people of God, and their enemies came to battle against them, and he spake the word of the Lord, and the earth trembled, and the mountains fled, even according to his command."
—Genesis 7:15 IV

Nathan, our grandson, was so excited about his baptism February 16, 2003. He wanted to be baptized at the beginning of the service, but I explained that it wasn't the right time in the service. The worship proceeded and he sang his solo. When he finished we proceeded down the steps of the font in the El Cajon church. As I finished the words and laid him down into a "watery grave" and brought him up, it was a beautiful spiritual experience for us and the congregation, as they expressed to me afterward.

The next month there was a business meeting, and Nathan was sitting beside me. I called to his attention that he was now a member and to pay close attention to the business at hand. He is a studious child. Three projects of importance had to be attended to that were going to cost several thousand dollars. Nathan whispered in my ear, "Grandma, my dad owes me $121, and when he pays me I am going to give it to the church to help pay." I was deeply touched that he felt his responsibility as a member.

His father attends another church but comes to ours on special occasions. His father gave the closing prayer the morning of Nathan's baptism, and the Spirit touched him so that he had to end his prayer quickly. I know he is kind and attends reunions with his family, and sometimes prayer service, and he prays and testifies. We all pray he will come every Sunday with his family.

Hymns of the Saints: No. 151, "Every Good and Perfect Gift"

Prayer Thought: God, may we put our trust always in your power to transform lives. Guide us on the path of discipleship.

Wednesday
13
October

Breath of Life
By Lillian Bayless Kirby
Blue Springs, Missouri

"Make a joyful noise unto the Lord, all ye lands. Serve the Lord with gladness; come before his presence with singing."—Psalm 100:1–2

Our small church choir contributed a ministry of music to the worship services several times a month. Some of the singers had years of vocal training and could read music very well. But most of the choir members were novice singers with untrained voices. A camaraderie developed as we sang easy and familiar music.

That innocent happiness all changed when a professional music major and director moved into our area and decided to attend our congregation. As choir director, as time passed he chose more difficult music for us to learn and perform. We were even challenged to present a "Tenebrae" service on Good Friday to a large congregation.

Our enthusiastic leader concentrated especially on the choir's breathing techniques. He emphasized harmony, not only of correct notes, but coordination of our breathing together at the proper time. Our "warm-ups" consisted of opening our mouths, breathing in through our mouths, humming, and breathing out slowly. His techniques eventually whipped a small rag-tag choir into a unit that could sing as one voice. We were now equipped with the spice that savored our singing.

Our leader always ended our practice sessions in humble and fervent prayer. He also developed a more relaxed attitude, and the Holy Spirit shone through his directing. We knew that God had indeed blessed us as we learned to be followers and as we chose to serve Christ through the ministry of good music.

Hymns of the Saints: No. 179, "Breathe on Me, Breath of God"

Prayer Thought: Creative God, may we joyfully breathe in our blessings as we consciously breathe out our prayers to you. May we be energized to develop our gifts and not settle to give second-best service.

Thursday **14** October	**Cast Your Bread** By Wallace Van Eaton Yakima, Washington	

"Cast thy bread upon the waters; for thou shalt find it after many days."—Ecclesiastes 11:1

Some time ago I read in *Reader's Digest* of a woman who went to purchase a painting from an artist. His response was, "That is the tenth painting I have sold, so take the purchase price and give it to your church or to a charity of your choice."

I make spinning wheels, and I liked this idea, but I wanted to have control over where the money went. When I sold the next tenth wheel I would put it toward painting the church or some other need. Occasionally I have given a wheel to someone whom I thought deserving.

Not long ago I made a wheel for a woman who, when it was finished, couldn't pay for it. Her house had burned and her husband had failed to pay the premium on the insurance, so I gave her the wheel. Another woman wanted a wheel in the worst way but couldn't afford it, so I gave another of the tenth wheels to her. There was such a to do from her family to think that someone would just give her something so valuable.

A woman who received one of my first wheels as a gift now, several years later, goes to spinning demonstrations, and those attending ask her, "Where did you get your wheel?" She lets them spin on it, and in some cases I get orders for more wheels. It is from her appreciation and thankfulness that she gladly refers them to me.

It isn't always the remuneration that counts. Sometimes the gratitude shown is worth more than anything money can buy.

Hymns of the Saints: No. 397, "All Things Are Thine"

Prayer Thought: Lord of creation, we humbly thank you for our abilities, whatever they may be, to create things that can be shared with others.

<table>
<tr><td>Friday
15
October</td><td>**The Blessing of Forgiveness**
By Merna Short
Melbourne, Australia</td><td></td></tr>
</table>

"Beloved, let us love one another; for love is of God; and everyone that loveth is born of God, and knoweth God."

—I John 4:7

A misunderstanding with a very dear friend had caused a dreadful hurt. Presumption and lack of communication on each of our parts was the cause. I felt miserable. I thought, *If I don't deal with this, the hurt won't go away. Instead it will fester and get worse.* "How can I approach this, Lord?" I pondered.

For a couple of days, until I could approach the situation with a healing attitude, I kept my distance. While walking one evening in the fresh air, I felt I could leave antagonism behind. Our friendship was of too great a value for me to hesitate any longer. Retracing my steps, I saw my friend coming toward me.

"I need to see what's wrong," she said.

"I'm glad you've come," I responded. "I was coming to see you."

"I'm deeply sorry for what occurred," she said.

We had each been working from a different assumption. We let the healing begin from that moment, without spoiling it with recriminations.

I am so grateful for the scriptures and teachings of the church that foster right relationships, the joy of healing, and the freedom of the Spirit that this brings into our lives.

Sing for Peace: No. 18, "God! When Human Bonds Are Broken"

Prayer Thought: Teacher of healing and forgivenss, may

we always seek wholeness in our relationships with others. Bring the peace and understanding that can only come from your Spirit into our lives.

<table>
<tr><td>Saturday
16
October</td><td>**No Time to Pray**
By Grace Andrews
Independence, Missouri</td><td></td></tr>
</table>

"Thus the Lord works with his power in all cases among the children of men, extending the arm of mercy toward them that put their trust in him."—Mosiah 13:27

I was at the roller rink at every possible opportunity. A fairly typical teenager, full of energy, I loved to skate. Apparently, I was proficient enough to be approached by those in charge of the rink and urged to go "professional," which I never pursued. This was fun for me—but I had other goals and didn't want skating to occupy my life.

One night, as I automatically skated hand in hand with a friend, we were engaged in conversation. Suddenly, a small boy fell crosswise in front of us and lay on the floor, his terrified face turned toward us. It was too late for us to react. I panicked and closed my eyes, knowing my skates were going to smash into his head. But, amazingly, no collision occurred.

A moment later, I opened my eyes and realized my partner was still skating beside me and that we had covered the distance to the other end of the rink without incident. We turned around to see the small boy still lying on the floor, now in back of us, in the very same position. I asked my friend, "What happened?" He shook his head in disbelief and said, "I don't know—I closed my eyes. I knew we were going to hit him. How could we have missed?"

We spun around and skated back to the little boy, helping him to his feet. I asked, "What just happened? How did we avoid hitting you?" Disbelief was written all over his face, as he replied, "I don't know—I closed my eyes." So, what happened? I will never know. But the reality of that experience has followed me all my life. I have never forgotten that wonderful experience on roller skates one night.

When it's too late to pray, and too late to stop our momentum, sometimes a power unseen steps between us, and the danger or hurt we might have caused. Thanks be to God.

Sing a New Song: No. 16, "How Majestic Is Your Name"

Prayer Thought: Marvelous God, we offer hearts full of thanksgiving for times when you have acted with mercy beyond our comprehension.

| Sunday **17** October | **Seeing with Jesus' Eyes** By Charles Brockway San Jose, California | |

"I pray that the God of our Lord Jesus Christ, the Father of glory, may give you a spirit of wisdom and revelation as you come to know him, so that, with the eyes of your heart enlightened, you may know what is the hope to which he has called you...."—Ephesians 1:17–18 NRSV

My wife, Edith, and I were living in Taiwan on a two-year church assignment there. We had been coached by Apostle Sekine to accept the people there just as they were and to be very open to them. For the most part this was not a problem for us. We had both had years of experience in being accepting of people. But living in an utterly foreign environment did present its problems.

We were glad to eventually return to our home in California, feeling that despite some stresses and difficulties, we had been sustained by the Good Spirit while in Taiwan.

One afternoon I was walking along a street in Taipei. I must have been tired and a little out-of-sorts that day. I saw a man and thought, "That's a peculiar-looking person." Soon after that I looked at another man and had the same thought. Then I realized that I really didn't want to be putting people down in my thoughts because of how they looked. As I continued on my way I said a brief silent prayer, "Lord, help me to see these people through the eyes of Jesus."

A presumptuous request, perhaps, but it worked. I experienced an immediate change of attitude, and no more that day did I look at someone and think, "How strange." And in reflecting later on that experience, I realized that in that situation, *I* was the strange-looking person on that street.

Hymns of the Saints: No. 370, "Eternal God, Whose Power Upholds"

Prayer Thought: Our concept of beauty is so often limited, Lord, to those who look or think as we do. Grant us new eyes, that we may see as you do.

<table>
<tr><td>Monday
18
October</td><td>**Science Upholds Faith**
By Lois Dayton
Arnold, Missouri</td><td></td></tr>
</table>

"Devote yourselves to prayer, being watchful and thankful. And pray for us, too, that God may open a door for our message, so that we may proclaim the mystery of Christ, for which I am in chains."—Colossians 4:2–3 NIV

While browsing through our local weekend newspaper, I found a wonderful article about some scientific studies of the power of prayer in healing. This is something that people of faith have known about and believed in for years, but medical science had been dubious and frequently derisive about something so very intangible.

Many studies are now under way, not to prove that God exists but that the power of prayer promotes healing *and* improves longevity. I can personally testify to that. I've had cardiac bypass surgery, carotid artery surgery, and many fairly serious conditions. Prayer intervention and administrations have brought me through to enjoy a good quality of life. I'm enjoying my children, grandchildren, and great-grandchildren, only through the grace of God and prayer!

The newspaper article was so enlightening that I wanted to share it with some people who did not usually get the paper. I was trying to figure out how I could get someone to go on the Internet or how to scan some copies. I even thought I might go to a local store where there was a copy machine. You can imagine my disbelief followed by joyful wonderment when I found two more copies of that same section in the stack of paper I hadn't looked at yet! If the machinery that assembles the sections of the paper before delivery had malfunctioned, why was it with this particular section? I knew then that I was supposed to share this with some people, plus with those who read *Daily Bread*!

Sing for Peace: No. 33, "Heal Me, Hands of Jesus"

Prayer Thought: Creator of our minds and bodies, why are we amazed that prayer has the power to heal? Grant us power to trust in your healing touch as we seek you out daily.

| Tuesday **19** October | **God Called You** By Denzil J. West Independence, Missouri | |

"Choose you this day whom ye will serve;... but as for me and my house, we will serve the Lord."—Joshua 24:15

The first time we attended the Southeast Illinois Reunion at Brush Creek we met a beautiful couple, Myra and Harley Throgmorton of Sparta, Illinois.

The first day, Harley gathered all the boys and girls together at the lake's edge and offered to teach any who wanted to learn, how to fish. Harley had a number of poles, bait, and lines and showed the children how to bait their hooks. The next day Harley invited two or three for special training, coupled with spiritual guidance. This happened over and over until each child had experienced Harley's deep love and personal guidance.

As the reunion week continued it was noted that Harley would call out to one of his fishing students, "Hey! There was a call for you." "Who was it?" was the child's reply. "You can find out who called you by reading Jeremiah 33:3," Harley replied.

The youngster would hurry to the cabin and read, "Call unto me and I will answer thee, and show thee great and mighty things, which thou knowest not."

By this time Harley had prepared each boy and girl for a new spiritual awareness. These young people returned home with a new vigor to follow the Lord Jesus' call.

Hymns of the Saints: No. 391, "Jesus Is Calling"

Prayer Thought: Precious God, when you call us, help us to hear you and gladly respond to your request.

| Wednesday **20** October | **A Lasting Heritage** By Janice Townsend Spokane, Washington | |

"Be careful, and watch yourselves closely so that you do not forget the things your eyes have seen or let them slip from your heart as long as you live. Teach them to your children and to their children after them."
—Deuteronomy 4:9 NIV

I closed the notebook with a snap, glad that the time-consuming job was over. My afternoon had been spent compiling a list of the many keepsake items in our home that have been handed down through the years by past members of our family. The list contained a brief description of the source and history of each item. This was my way of ensuring that our children will know and appreciate the family heritage that is theirs.

Preserving memorabilia and stories of those who came before is important to me. I want our family to know and remember their forebear, David Rife, who came from Switzerland in the 1700s and lived out his devotion to the Lord as a Mennonite minister. I want them to know about William Gillet, an English rector in the 1600s; about his son Jonathan who brought a 1599 Geneva edition Bible to New England and faithfully recorded family information in it; about Puritan Richard

Risley, one of the founders of the Commonwealth of Connecticut; about the Sweets, who followed Roger Williams to Providence, Rhode Island. I want my children to know about the Thorps, the Littles, the Christiansons, and all those good people who loved and served the Lord as Sunday school teachers, church builders, civic leaders, and faithful followers.

Both in my birth family and in my church family, I have received a rich heritage of faith. I regard it as a sacred trust that I will do my best to share with all.

Hymns of the Saints: No. 433, "Faith of Our Fathers"

Prayer Thought: Quicken our minds, God, that we may perceive which things in life have true and lasting value. Help us to lovingly preserve them and pass them on to future generations.

| Thursday **21** October | **Just a Pile of Stones** By Dorothy Cross Paisley, Florida | |

"Ye also, as lively stones, are built up a spiritual house, an holy priesthood, to offer up spiritual sacrifices, acceptable to God by Jesus Christ. Wherefore also it is contained in the scripture, Behold, I lay in Sion a chief cornerstone, elect, precious; and he that believeth on him shall not be confounded."—I Peter 2:5–6

Once, we had the man who built our house in Littleton, New Hampshire, do some work at our camp in Vermont. As he was pointing up the stonework of the fireplace he accidentally struck the stone that determined the integrity of the whole fireplace. He called me in Littleton to tell me that the whole fireplace structure had fallen down.

He said, "I'll build it back up." And he did. By the time I got out there late that afternoon, he was just cleaning up after finishing it. I don't remember whether we ever told my husband. Not wanting to tell him may be the reason this man got it done so fast.

This incident made me realize the importance of the cornerstone. Without Christ and his sacrifice there would be no structure to the church or to our faith. We would be just like a pile of stones, without form or purpose.

Hymns of the Saints: No. 136, "How Firm a Foundation"

Prayer Thought: Lord, we thank you for being the foundation of our faith, and for enabling us to work together to share your teachings.

<table>
<tr><td>Friday
22
October</td><td>**Close at Hand**
By Paul McCain
Oklahoma City, Oklahoma</td><td></td></tr>
</table>

"God has entrusted you with these things which are sacred, which he has kept sacred, and also which he will keep and preserve for a wise purpose in him that he may show forth his power to future generations."—Alma 17:45

Juli was such a cute baby and little girl. She doesn't like us to show the video (transferred from Super 8 film) of her picking up Easter eggs and dropping some because the strap on her makeshift basket broke and she had trouble keeping the eggs in it; but she was so cute. She was born in Tulsa, and about ten days after, she was blessed in Woodward, Oklahoma, about ninety miles from where we lived. Shortly after she turned eight, she was the first person to be baptized in the new Enid, Oklahoma, church.

Like so many, though, as a young adult, she had some rebellious years and didn't attend church. Some time after I moved back to Oklahoma in 1995, Juli decided to return to church. Our granddaughter Rachel had been born, and it was a delight to have Juli attend again. I know that the music director (now our pastor) was thrilled, because Juli plays piano, and it's more than an educated guess that many prayers went up on the matter. My wife, Janet, has been Rachel's Sunday school teacher and, when the two of them are missing at the same time, you can expect them to be found together at the playground, or checking out some of nature's creations.

Juli, husband Steve, Rachel, and new grandbaby Rebecca recently moved into the housing addition where Janet and I live. When Janet and I go for a walk, we can stop by their house just to check in.

Janet and I had the privilege of performing Rebecca's baby blessing. How wonderful it is for the two of us to be involved in their lives in such special ways. Rachel will turn eight soon, and although I was looking forward to baptizing her, I'll gladly let Juli, by then a newly ordained priest, baptize her daughter. Maybe Janet and I will get to confirm her.

I know now why some people have moved across the nation to live near their children and grandchildren; there's no way to describe how good it feels to have them "close at hand." It's great to see the Lord work in people, and it's especially sweet to see him work in those we hold so dear. It must be a joy to God's heart when we are "close at hand" also.

Hymns of the Saints: No. 447, "Would You Bless Our Homes"

Prayer Thought: Eternal Parent, we understand as earthly parents the joy of having our children close, though that is not always possible. May we find ways to keep close to one another and to you.

"And he shall turn the heart of the fathers to the children, and the heart of the children to their fathers...."
—Malachi 4:6

I am a member of Community of Christ because of a friend—not my personal friend, but a friend none-theless. Many years ago in Wheeling, West Virginia, a young man was riding the trolley car home from his work in the steel mill. This young man was asked by his friend, "Lou, what church do you belong to?" Lou responded, "Why, I'm a Lutheran." His friend then asked him, "Well, why don't you join a church that is named after Jesus Christ?" to which Lou replied, "Maybe I will."

In responding to this invitation, my grandfather, Louis A. Serig, did become a member of this church. He married a church member from Ohio, Amelia Ebeling, and they raised their nine children in this faith. "Grandpa Serig" as we called him was pastor of the church for several years before he passed away more than fifty years ago.

My mother's family was not of this faith, but Mother joined the church and was a faithful member. Although she died before my fifth birthday I can still remember the smell of bread and sweet rolls baking on Saturday mornings. I was sharing this memory with a sister in the family a few years ago, and she told me that Mother would sell some of those baked goods around the neighborhood each Saturday, and that was where she got the money to put in the offering on Sunday morning.

Several years after I was married, Dad sent each of his four sons a copy of the prayer that Grandpa prayed at Mother's funeral. It is still one of my most treasured possessions. It was a brief prayer and it included the following paragraph: "We beseech thee, dear Lord, in behalf of those that mourn—the father and mother, sister, brothers, husband, and the four little boys who shall miss their mama's care. May they at this time receive thy consideration. We realize the burden will rest heavily upon these little fellows. May thou in thine infinite wisdom open avenues for their best good and welfare."

I can truly testify that God in his "infinite wisdom" has fulfilled Grandpa's prayer many times over. I have experienced again and again in my life God's presence and blessing to the point where I can declare with Job, "I know that my Redeemer lives."

Hymns of the Saints: No. 60, "Now Thank We All Our God"

Prayer Thought: God of all generations, we offer our thanks for the remarkable ways you have been present for us throughout our lives. May we turn to you always for guidance.

| Sunday **24** October | **A Very Special Light**
By Dorene Kilburn
St. Paul's Station, Ontario, Canada | |

"You are the light of the world. A city built upon a hill cannot be hid."—Matthew 5:14 NRSV

A dear friend of ours just died. Her passing leaves an enormous void in our lives and in the lives of all those who knew her, but she will continue to inspire us through our memories of her life of true discipleship.

Sue had a positive attitude about everything. We attended the open house for her eightieth birthday, and as we left, she said, "See you at my eighty-fifth!" Then breast cancer was diagnosed just a few months before her eighty-fifth birthday. That she just saw as an "inconvenience"—she had a mastectomy two weeks before the planned open house, and still was able to celebrate another milestone among her friends.

Though not a member of our faith community, Sue was a true disciple of Christ. She was active in her church and supported all sorts of worthy causes, both financially and with hard work, anything from improving the environment to supporting projects that made the quality of life better for disadvantaged children in far-off lands. She even visited these children when she was in her seventies! Sue always put her concerns for others ahead of concerns for herself.

When the cancer returned and began to spread throughout her body, she had to go into hospital, and her first words to any visitors were "How are you?" She was an inspiration to all in the selfless life she lived, and she was an inspiration in her dying, too. She had requested that the choir sing "On Eagle's Wings" at the service of celebration of her life. These were words of assurance that Sue believed with her whole heart. She was and will continue to be a light on our path of discipleship.

Sing a New Song: No. 41, "On Eagle's Wings"

Prayer Thought: Loving God, we give ourselves to you in service. May we shine like the sun so that others will see Jesus and find the joy we experience in following him.

"Behold, we count them happy which endure."

—James 5:11

Relishing a contented state of happiness, Martha and I reflected back over the religious experiences that brought us together in 2002. Because we both pray for spiritual direction and then promise to follow that inspiration when it comes, we enjoy backtracking how we feel that we were led to each other.

We met as senior adults in January 2002 at Community of Christ's weeklong reunion on Grand Cayman Island. We remember the moment we met at the food table, spread with special island food for the potluck. We both immediately felt that we wanted to stay always in the presence of the other. It was a surprising and great feeling! We both had lost our wonderful spouses and were still experiencing the grief and loneliness. Even with all of our family and church friends helping us, we still had times of strong sorrow.

Neither of us had ever been to Grand Cayman. In addition, this was the first time that Grant McMurray, president of Community of Christ, had been the guest minister. In Arizona, friends had asked Martha some months before if she wanted to go to the reunion. When the terrorist attack came on September 11, she still felt she should go; it was an opportunity she did not want to forfeit. Martha was struggling with leaving her job of seventeen years at Whispering Pines, the church's campground, but felt it would be good to be in a completely different environment. This proved to be a wonderful change.

I had everything scheduled to go on vacation to Cancun, Mexico, over Thanksgiving 2001 with my daughter Barbara and granddaughter Hali-Rose. However, a case of the shingles affected my shoulder and the doctor said I could not go. This shut the door to Cancun and opened the door to the church reunion in Grand Cayman in late January.

When we met at the food table at reunion, we looked at each other over our plates of food, expressed our goodwill, and just kept talking and smiling. We had gone to church reunions when we were young and had attended Graceland College at different times.

In the next few months, many other rich experiences happened that prepared us for our wedding on November 30, 2002. And yes, Grant McMurray even officiated at the sacrament. It was held at Graceland's Cheville Chapel, which meant so much to us! We are so thankful for the positive impact the Community of Christ and Graceland University have had on our lives. We have been blessed!

Hymns of the Saints: No. 351, "Redeeming Grace Has Touched Our Lives"

Prayer Thought: Gracious God, we offer profound thanks for the way you work in our lives when we open doors of opportunity. May we seek your guidance throughout our lives, and have the courage to follow it.

Tuesday **26** October	**Where Two or Three Are Gathered** By Charlotte Jones Sherman Oaks, California

"For where two or three are gathered together in my name, there am I in the midst of them."—Matthew 18:20

Today I had a humbling experience. Bringing Communion to three people gave me an opportunity to share in the company of the Holy Spirit in a way that touched me and made the all-encompassing love of God evident.

Two of the incidents involved members of the Catholic faith. On one visit the shut-in's caretaker knelt with me as the prayer was said over the bread and wine. At the end I saw she crossed herself and said some words I could not hear, showing the depth of her emotion. The first time I asked her if she wished to join us, she declined. But the next time, she partook of the emblems and has continued doing so. I don't remember seeing her kneel before, but this time she knelt and crossed herself. I felt she had truly worshiped with us and was blessed. She thanked me for including her.

On my next visit the Catholic woman was a patient in the same room as the person to whom I brought Communion. The first time I asked if she wished to join us, she declined. Then afterward, when invited to join us, she did so, except once when she was very ill. Tonight when she was asked, she said yes, because the last two times had helped her so much.

It has been a blessing to be able to share Communion with others, and to feel the Spirit of Christ touching souls and meeting needs.

Hymns of the Saints: No. 2, "Met in Thy Sacred Name, O Lord"

Prayer Thought: We thank you, Lord, for blessing us when even two or three come together in your name, by being present and meeting the needs of each one.

<table>
<tr><td>Wednesday
27
October</td><td>**Discards**
By Larry Carroll
Glen Easton, West Virginia</td><td></td></tr>
</table>

"Lay not up for yourselves treasure upon earth, where moth and rust doth corrupt, and where thieves break through and steal."—Matthew 6:19

One day in 2002, as I was walking around my property, I noticed a stack of moldy old papers inside an outbuilding. Not wanting others to see this unsightly mess, I decided to discard the papers.

As I lifted them, I was appalled at what I saw disintegrating in my hands—a collection of *Saints' Heralds* from the early 1950s through the early 1960s. What had caused these magazines to come to this condition? They had lain neglected and exposed to the elements for years, and now they were no more.

How senseless it is to leave things where the elements can destroy them! We must each ask ourselves: How many gifts and talents are we allowing to go to waste that we should be sharing with others?

Hymns of the Saints: No. 465, "We Thank Thee, God, for Eyes to See"

Prayer Thought: Lord, may we not allow our gifts and talents to lie idle and waste away. Inspire us to use them daily, that we may bring blessing wherever we go.

The Child Within
By Olevia Huntsman
Bald Knob, Arkansas

"It is good to give thanks unto the Lord, and to sing praises unto thy name, O Most High."—Psalm 92:1

On this January day I sit staring out on the snowy-white world at the campground where we are staying. The snowflakes are coming down fast and furiously. I dread even the thought of getting out and going anywhere. Then I notice my neighbors, all bundled in layers of clothing, coming out of their motor home. They immediately start building two small snowmen on their picnic table. They snap pictures of each other standing beside them. To my surprise the husband lies down on the ground and begins to move his arms back and forth, making a snow angel, as the wife snaps more photos. I find myself laughing out loud as I am caught up in the joy of the moment. It is so good to see this couple, who are probably in their late sixties, celebrating the child that still resides within them.

I look into the mirror and am caught off guard by the woman who stares back at me. I don't feel any different inside than when I was a young person, but there is the evidence in that image. Sometimes we think we have to conform to that image, forgetting that we can still find joy in the simple pleasures we enjoyed as a child.

On this cold winter day, I have been transported back to a simpler time—when my only worry was whether the snow would give us a "snow day" when there was no school, and hoping for enough snow to build a snowman and have a snowball fight. Children have faith that all will be right in their world, and I am thankful today for that reminder.

Hymns of the Saints: No. 184, "God Who Gives to Life Its Goodness"

Prayer Thought: Creator of snowflakes and simple joys, thank you for the faith and pleasures of childhood that still lie deep within us. Remind us that we can have the joy of a child no matter our age.

Friday **29** October	**The Grass Is Already Green** By Gerald John Kloss Philadelphia, Pennsylvania	

"And God said, Let the earth put forth vegetation…. And it was so…. And God saw that it was good."
—Genesis 1:11–12 RSV

Today was Communion Sunday. As we begin each worship service in our congregation we take time to mention both reasons for praise and petition in our lives. It is heartwarming to hear our members reflect first on the ways God has blessed them. One wonderful woman, Barbara, has recently had a recurrence of cancer, and so she has up and down days. It is so good to see a smile coming from her despite her situation. We all love this dear woman and pray often for her.

After the service this morning, I was talking with her about the beautiful April day we were having. She replied that it was nice outside, but then commented that it was supposed to get cold later today and snow tomorrow. After the winter we have had here in the northeast, snow has become a "bad" word. As Barbara said this, I turned to her and commented, "Oh, that's OK, because the grass is already green." She turned and smiled at me and added that this was just like the current situation with her soul—her grass was already green.

God had clearly touched her and had established roots and spiritual growth, so that no matter what befell her life, even cancer, the grass of her life with God was already green. I left church truly wondering who had preached the sermon that day.

Hymns of the Saints: No. 280, "Now the Green Blade Rises"

Prayer Thought: Gracious Redeemer, reveal to us the green grass in our lives that we so often fail to see, so that when life's snows come, we will know there is life underneath.

| Saturday **30** October | **October Night** By Helen M. Green Toledo, Ohio | |

"And I, God, made two great lights; the greater light to rule the day, and the lesser light to rule the night; and the greater light was the sun, and the lesser light was the moon…the moon to rule over the night and to divide the light from the darkness."—Genesis 1:19–20 IV

A recent survey revealed that Halloween has exceeded Christmas in the display of seasonal decorations. One October night as I took leave of a friend's home, I commented on the enormous inflated pumpkin on a lawn down the street. In the same neighborhood could be seen gigantic illuminated ghosts and witches riding broomsticks (suspended by invisible wires).

But as I pulled away from that section of the city and drove through nonresidential streets where there was little light pollution, I looked up and beheld a magnificent harvest moon that God had hung in the sky overhead. Perfect in symmetry with shadings that revealed dimension to the earth's only natural satellite, it was untethered to any earthly power source. All the lighted, inflated symbols of Halloween paled by comparison.

No matter how many years I carry on my body, I never cease to be awed by God's creative craftsmanship; nor do I cease to be grateful for the senses that allow me to experience God's handiwork.

Hymns of the Saints: No. 196, "The Lord Our God Alone Is Strong"

Prayer Thought: Creator of worlds spinning through space, we thank you for the world we know best and for sight, touch, and sound that allow us to experience what you have designed to sustain and bless us.

| Sunday **31** October | **Taught to Make Peace** By Jane McDonald Eldridge, Iowa | |

"Become a people of the Temple—those who see violence but proclaim peace, who feel conflict yet extend the hand of reconciliation, who encounter broken spirits and find pathways for healing."—Doctrine and Covenants 161:2a

It was a rare warm night in Iowa for Halloween. Parents took advantage of the pleasant evening to stroll with their children in the neighborhood. Homeowners also joined in the fun by sitting outside on their porches, greeting each other and the parade of children.

I had spent an hour hearing "trick or treat" from ghosts and goblins, Power Rangers and princesses. The next young fellow bounding up my sidewalk was dressed in camouflage—an army costume complete with a painted face. But instead of the usual Halloween salutation, this young boy announced, "Make peace not war!"

Surprised and smiling at him, I offered the boy some candy. I waved to his mother, who was walking with him. His statement of peace was precious. I admire the home where this theme is taught and children are guided by loving parents.

Hymns of the Saints: No. 452, "For the Healing of the Nations"

Prayer Thought: Almighty God, show us how to promote healthy ways to deal with conflict in our neighborhoods, families, and nations. Lead us in our efforts to start where we are by loving others and teaching peace.

November 2004

S	M	T	W	T	F	S
	1	2	3	4	5	6
7	8	9	10	11	12	13
14	15	16	17	18	19	20
21	22	23	24	25	26	27
28	29	30				

| Monday
1
November | **Strength for the Journey**
By Vivian Parker
Escatawpa, Mississippi | |

"Surely goodness and mercy shall follow me all the days of my life; and I will dwell in the house of the Lord forever."
—Psalm 23:6

Many times over the last year of Mama's life the family didn't think she would make it. She had been fighting a terminal illness for about three years. The final week of her life was a long one. She seemed to be clinging to life for some unknown reason. Some felt it was just the process of the body shutting down.

As I read my *Daily Bread* on the morning of her funeral, it was as though it was speaking directly to me and my family. I turned back the pages a couple of days and read the devotions again. Mama died on a Sunday and the devotion was "Child of God", it was about labels we place on people seeing perhaps only the bad. It spoke of focusing on the whole person and seeing each one as a child of God. An aunt came to Mama's bedside about two hours before she died. They had been friends when Mama and Daddy had married more than forty-one years before. Conflict and hard feelings had developed over the years between them, and they were not the best of friends. But my aunt had had a dream the night before, and felt the urgent need to come see her. As she stood at her bedside and talked to her, she made peace; she looked at her and spoke with compassion and Christ-like love.

The next day's devotion, "Dependence on God," was about trusting God to carry us through when we face situations we cannot handle alone—trusting God's expanded vision and proven faithfulness. Truly it was

God who carried us through that dark day as we made funeral arrangements.

The morning of the funeral I was reading the devotion, "Joyful Recognition." I thought of her struggle the last few days of her life and then the final letting go of this earthly tabernacle. I visualized her entrance into eternal life held within the arms of God—arms that may have felt strange at first—and then the joy of knowing that she had returned home.

Sing for Peace: No. 10, "God of Grace and God of Laughter," verses 2 and 3

Prayer Thought: Lord, we thank you for your presence and the comforting assurance you give us just when we need it most. May we come to realize how very much you love each one of your children.

Tuesday **2** November	**Little Annoyances** By Ferryl Cash Troy, Kansas	

"I waited patiently for the Lord; he turned to me and heard my cry. He lifted me out of the slimy pit, out of the mud and mire; he set my feet on a rock and gave me a firm place to stand. He put a new song in my heart."

—Psalm 40:1–3 NIV

September 1999 brought many problems in our busy, hectic lifestyle. The microwave quit and had to be replaced. The family car wasn't working properly and needed to be repaired. I had to drive my husband's car and didn't know where any of the buttons and gadgets were that worked the lights, the windshield wipers, the air conditioner. The dryer had broken down and needed a new part.

Finding time to get all these things fixed was also difficult because my husband taught school during the day and coached football until 6:00 p.m. I worked during the day, also, and taught piano lessons after school every night. On many nights I had volleyball matches, took my daughter to dance classes, and had high school football games to attend. Feeling much stress and frustration was normal, but all of this on top of everything else was setting me on edge.

I had to remind myself how truly wonderful life is and how blessed I really was—all of these breakdowns were just "little annoyances." These would all pass and could be easily remedied. I had to look at the positive. I had another car to drive. It was only a part on the dryer, not the whole thing that needed to be replaced, so it would be less expensive. The microwave could be replaced. I really had nothing to complain about. I just had to remember to keep all things in perspective. Life truly was good!

Sing a New Song: No. 1, "Sing a New Song!"

Prayer Thought: We praise you for the strength and help you give us daily, almighty God. Grant us perspective when we dwell on our "troubles," and shift our focus to more positive thinking.

| Wednesday 3 November | **New Avenues for Blessing** By Dianne Lyell Guinn Paris, Tennessee | |

"Be steadfast and trust in the instructions which have been given for your guidance. I will be with you and strengthen you for the tasks that lie ahead if you will continue to be faithful and commit yourselves without reservation to the building of my kingdom."
—Doctrine and Covenants 153:9c.

I had worked for twenty-seven years as a secretary in a manufacturing facility office. The job had been very good to me and provided me many opportunities. After the loss of my husband, working through the grief, and remarriage I had decided to retire in a couple of years. I was making plans but they were "down the road a bit" when the company decided to reduce their salaried employees by 10 percent company wide. I was given a wonderful opportunity to retire early with extra years added to my pension plan if I retired in the year 2001. Yes! It was a "no-brainer."

After tackling the chores around the house that I'd put off for lack of time I began to think in terms of how I could give back to someone else. One day I picked up the local newspaper and read an article asking for mentors to spend one hour a week in the school system with a child who needed someone to make a difference in his or her life. I tucked the paper away and thought I'd call "later." But it kept coming back to mind. The Spirit's prompting led me to the phone to call the Family Resource Center and volunteer.

After turning in my application I was told that I would have to be checked out by my references to be approved. During this time I asked God to lead me to someone I could help and to give me strength for the task. I was given a blond-haired boy of eight in second grade. He is a precious child! He is one of four boys being raised by a single father. I now go one day each week to have lunch with him at school. We then spend the remainder of time reading together.

My life is so richly blessed. My "thank you" to God for my blessings turned out to be just another avenue for him to bless me again.

Hymns of the Saints: No. 377, "Let Your Heart Be Broken"

Prayer Thought: Loving God, thank you for the many opportunities you give us daily. May we always remember that we are "blessed to be a blessing."

<table>
<tr><td>Thursday
4
November</td><td>**Gracious Receiver**
By Florence King
Feilding, New Zealand</td><td></td></tr>
</table>

"Let us search and try our ways, and turn again to the Lord. Let us lift up our heart with our hands unto God in the heavens."—Lamentations 3:40–41

Several years ago I was hit by a car, receiving a fracture just below my left knee. It didn't heal properly and I was told it would get worse as I grew older. This has happened. I have trouble walking on flat ground or going upstairs, but as soon as I am on uneven ground or going downhill or downstairs, I find I need something to hold onto. Quite often this hasn't always been available.

One day recently, I was crossing the main street in Feilding—two wide roadways with a grassy verge between them. About two months ago, major road works were started, causing problems for both motorists and pedestrians. I had crossed one road and was on the grassy verge. As I tried to step down, my leg gave out, causing me to be unable to move. A young woman pushing a pushchair with a little boy inside stood beside me. I asked her for help, and she helped me, with a smile. I have had to ask for help several times, and have never been refused. And I've always been helped with a smile.

Although we've been told it's more blessed to give than receive, if we were all givers, who would be the receivers? Some receive as if it were their right to do so, while others receive graciously. When someone offers us a compliment, how good it makes the giver feel if we simply say thank you with a smile, accepting the gift of their compliment. It is likewise with God's gifts to us. Let us receive with thankful hearts.

Sing a New Song: No. 27, "Lay Your Hands"

Prayer Thought: Teach us to be gracious receivers, Lord, that others may find joy in the opportunity to give. We humbly receive with thanks all of your many gifts to us.

Friday **5** November	**"You Can Try"** By Melba Jean Dixon Farwell, Michigan	

"I press on toward the goal for the prize of the heavenly call of God in Christ Jesus.... Brothers and sisters, join in imitating me, and observe those who live according to the example you have in us."—Philippians 3:14, 17 NRSV

My dear friend Marge once shared an experience with me that I doubt I will ever forget. While in a time of prayer and meditation, Marge expressed her earnest desire to become like Christ. It was then that she heard a voice, perhaps not audible, but a clear and gentle voice that spoke to her heart, "You can try."

The apostle Paul addressed the church at Philippi in a spirit of love and joy, being confident that Christ, who had begun a good work in their lives, would continue to lead them toward the goal of their "heavenly call."

We experience trials and setbacks along the path of life. At times we nearly lose sight of the goal. Our will to do God's will is all-important.

"You can try." Three words, only three letters each, yet they sustain and encourage me in my own journey toward Christ—the Way, the Truth, and the Life.

Hymns of the Saints: No. 497, "With a Steadfast Faith"

Prayer Thought: Steadfast God, lead us forward each day toward the goal of imitating Jesus as an example for others.

| Saturday **6** November | **When You Are Smiling...** By Shirley S. Case Slater, Missouri | |

"Support one another in love, confident that my Spirit will be with you, even as I have gone before you and shown the way."—Doctrine and Covenants 154: 7b

My son Jimmy is known for his smiles. Anyone who encounters him comments on his gift of smiles. This evening I tried to get him to write an article for *Daily Bread*, as he also has a gift for writing, yet he wouldn't. But this is what he told me: "Write on smiling." When I inquired as to why, he said, "Because if you smile at someone they will smile back at you. It's kind of like that movie, *Pay It Forward*."

So why was I surprised at his suggestion? This is what Jimmy does! Countless times he has burst through the front door to holler, "I'm home!" And I'd look up at his 5'11" frame and he'd be smiling. Sometimes when he's been late, this has made me reconsider his punishment; I would realize he was OK and safely home.

I wonder if that's how God feels when we finally decide to "come home smiling." And somehow I can see God standing there with that same smile on his face.

Hymns of the Saints: No. 432, "If by Your Grace I Choose to Be"

Prayer Thought: Creator of all, thank you for the joy you put in the simple gentle curve of our mouths. Help us to remember to use it to help others feel your "Son" shine on them.

Sunday **7** November	**A Simple Street Corner** By Ruth Andrews Vreeland Albuquerque, New Mexico	

"O house of Jacob, come, let us walk in the light of the Lord!"—Isaiah 2:5 NRSV

I have a photo in the front pocket of my Bible cover. It wouldn't mean anything to anyone but me, and its importance would be unclear to anyone who didn't know me. But it's there to remind me that Jesus is my dearest friend, and walks with me wherever I go in life. It's a simple picture of the sidewalk and street corner at Woodrow and East San Gabriel, the street where I lived during early childhood.

I recently went "home" for my twenty-year high school reunion and stayed with a good friend for the weekend. I rented a car and planned to drive around my hometown for a bit on my own. My friend insisted on going with me, and I agreed, not knowing how I was going to react when we got to my old street. I parked across the street from the corner, and sat staring at it while tears began to run down my face. My friend was quiet, and then gently asked me to tell her what I was remembering. So I told her the story.

I was five years old and all my neighborhood playmates were enrolled in morning kindergarten. I was enrolled in the afternoon session, where I knew no one. I had no one to walk to school with, and was fearful about walking alone. My mother would walk with me from our house down to the street corner but could go no farther, as she had two small children to care for at home. Each time, she would remind me I was never really alone, because Jesus was walking beside me. I would tearfully let go of her hand and wave good-bye to walk the short distance to the school. As time went on that walk became easier and my faith became stronger. I was convinced Jesus *was* walking with me, and I would hold out my small hand and imagine he was holding onto it. He didn't let go until I was safely inside the kindergarten gate.

I sat in the rented car and stared at the street corner where my mother let go of my hand and Jesus took it in his, all those years ago. The memory came flooding back to my mind and I could *see* it all as clearly as I had seen it through my five-year-old eyes. I will always remember it that way, because it was truly how it happened. Jesus still walks beside me. I feel his nearness every day, and have felt his gentle guidance through the years. My mother was right: *I have never really been alone.*

Sing a New Song: No. 25, "Jesus, Name above All Names"

Prayer Thought: Holy Companion, we are so grateful for all the times you have held our hand when we have been afraid and faced new circumstances. We ask you to not let go of us.

<table>
<tr><td>Monday
8
November</td><td>**Instant Brothers and Sisters**
By Louita Clothier
Lamoni, Iowa</td><td></td></tr>
</table>

"There is no longer Jew or Greek, there is no longer slave or free, there is no longer male and female; for all of you are one in Christ Jesus."—Galatians 3:28 NRSV

The Community of Christ is made up of people with diverse beliefs, each seeking their own relationship with God. So what is it that unites us as a worldwide community, if not doctrine? It can only be an unmistakable special Spirit that gives a common commitment and makes us brothers and sisters instantly no matter where in the world we may be.

Our family certainly has found this true all of our lives as we have met church people throughout the world. After two minutes together, it seems we have always known each other. When our children travel cross-country alone, they always go armed with a church directory, knowing that in difficulty, this community cares for one another.

Before my retirement, I was a Suzuki-method violin teacher for thirty-five years. Several times I was privileged to travel to Central and South America to work with children and train Suzuki teachers. When there was a Comunidad de Cristo group in the city where I was to be, I insisted on having Sunday off to spend the day with my church people.

In Lima, Peru, I was staying with a Suzuki family who were Catholic. There was an atmosphere of terrorism all over Lima, and my host family felt responsible for my safety. They felt it was too dangerous for me to go to church alone by taxi and insisted on driving me many miles across the city to Eduardo and Cecile Dávila's home, where the largest church group met. They were understandably wary about me visiting someone I had never met before.

With some difficulty we found the house. My hosts nervously waited in the car to assure my safety. They simply could not comprehend it when my knock at the front gate was met by the Dávilas and others throwing their arms around me, as we all began chattering a thousand words a minute in true Community of Christ style. It was instant connection. I can't help laughing, remembering the amazement in the faces of my cautious friends observing that scene from their car.

What a privilege to be part of a worldwide circle of love and support.

Hymns of the Saints: No. 468, "Let Us Sing a Worldwide Anthem"

Prayer Thought: Gracious God, may your Spirit continue to bring us together as a worldwide church family, despite differences of culture, language, and lifestyle.

Tuesday **9** November	**God Is with Us Always** By Eileen Turner Portland, Oregon

"But mine eyes are unto thee, O God the Lord; in thee is my trust; leave not my soul destitute."—Psalm 141:8

It had been a very busy morning. I'd barely had time for a break at the hospital, where I'd spent the previous five hours with my students. On my way back to campus to teach my afternoon class, I decided to stop for a quick lunch at Wendy's.

Seated across from me in a booth were a grandmother, mother, daughter, and her infant. I was thinking how nice it was for the four generations to take time together to enjoy each other's companionship. Suddenly the grandmother slumped over, and the granddaughter jumped up, pulled out her cell phone, and dialed 911. I realized there was no time to wait for the paramedics, so I proceeded to get the grandmother to the floor, clear her airway, loosen her clothing, and check her status. About the time I had begun CPR, the paramedics arrived, and I was relieved while they defibrillated her and readied her for transport. I stayed with the daughter and granddaughter to ask where they would take her. She was enroute to the hospital I had just left a short time before, so I assured them she would be in good hands. But my thoughts were that she might not survive.

About six months later, I walked into a hospital room to respond to a patient's call light where my student was assigned. A woman sitting beside the bed of a patient gasped, pointed her finger straight at me, and exclaimed to the patient, "That's her! She's the one who saved your life!" I was stunned to find this same grandmother and her daughter here. We spent some beautiful moments reminiscing about that unfortunate event and being grateful for the way it had turned out.

This wasn't the first time I had performed CPR, but it was one in which the outcome was good. There have been many instances when I have felt the Lord placed me in just the right place at the right time, or helped me follow my intuition and make a decision that was the correct one.

If we trust in the Lord, he will not let us fail. Together we can accomplish great things.

Hymns of the Saints: No. 127, "I Am Trusting Thee, Lord Jesus"

Prayer Thought: Lord, guide us in our actions and decisions, that we might bring help and blessing wherever we may be.

Precious Gift Lost
By Marlene Brunner
Yuma, Colorado

"Every good gift and every perfect gift is from above, and cometh down from the Father of lights, with whom is no variableness, neither shadow of turning."—James 1:17

For a couple of years I served as a volunteer with the HOSTS (Help One Student to Succeed) program in one of our elementary schools. It was my responsibility to go in for one hour every Monday morning and assist one specific second-grade girl to learn good reading skills. It was so rewarding to watch this young girl make progress.

At the end of the school year, all the volunteers were honored at an assembly of parents and students, and each volunteer was presented with a beautiful impatiens plant.

I took my plant with the beautiful blossoms on it home and set it in my bay window. I watered it and cared for it as best I could. However, each day more blossoms fell off. New buds would set on but they wouldn't stay on long enough to open. I tried to replant it in a different pot, but that didn't help. I even talked to the florist about it. No matter what I tried to do for it, nothing seemed to help. Finally it died.

Could this possibly be what happens to all the beautiful talents with which God blesses us? We have each been given gifts and talents in abundance, but we sometimes try to find and use them on our own without asking for God's help in the process. God knows what each of us has to work with and for what purpose he expects us to develop our gifts. We then need to follow God's guidance to grow into the beautiful people he has designed us to be.

Prayer Thought: Creator and giver of all our abilities, remind us to turn to you in our journey of discovery. Reveal our hidden talents to us and nudge us in the direction we should go to develop them.

| Thursday **11** November | **Con Game** By Diane F. Schwartz Las Vegas, Nevada | |

"Heal the sick; cleanse the lepers; raise the dead; cast out devils; freely ye have received, freely give."
—Matthew 10:7 IV

I never know what's going to happen to "make my day," to borrow a phrase from Clint Eastwood. One hot day last summer I stopped in a small shopping center and was immediately approached and asked for a dollar. I quite often give people money, but the man wasn't dirty, his clothes looked good, and he wasn't ill fed, so I said, "Not right now." Then he said, "How about when you come out?" I said, "We'll see."

I knew he would be waiting, so I made sure I had a dollar in my hand when I left the store. At first I thought he had gone, but he had only moved down about three storefronts. As soon as he saw my bright yellow T-shirt, he started waving his arms and yelling, "Here I am lady, I'm coming. I'll be right there." I thought he should earn his money, so I started to the car but he cut me off. He then told me that he could get arrested, because he wasn't supposed to ask people for money. I handed him his dollar anyway, and away he went.

How ironic! Here he was asking for money, all the while telling me he'd be in trouble if they caught him. I grinned all the way home. You never know when God's going to give you an opportunity to grow. Some people would have been angry, and maybe at another time I might have been. But I'm so glad he picked me to ask for a dollar. I knew I was being conned; he certainly knew he was conning me; and of course God knew but no doubt hoped I'd do the right thing.

Sing for Peace: No. 36, "Called by Christ to Love Each Other"

Prayer Thought: God of us all, grant us your insight when we are confronted with a difficult situation and must decide quickly what to do. Be present with us.

| Friday **12** November | **Quiet Servant** By Roberta Dieterman Caledonia, Michigan | |

"Fear ye not therefore, ye are of more value than many sparrows."—Matthew 10:31 KJV

The secretary in the office where I volunteer suddenly became very ill. She was in the hospital for one month and underwent two surgeries, and then she was in rehabilitation for a few more weeks before she went home to finish her recovery.

She was one of those quiet people who do their job and a lot of extra things we tend not to be aware of. As the days of her absence increased, so did the pile of work on her desk. It seemed no one could keep up with all those things she did so effortlessly.

I went to see her one day when she was in the hospital and was surprised at how very frail she appeared. She was a far cry from the energetic woman who had greeted us in the volunteer office, always filled with such a sheer joy of life. She said she would be back to work as soon as she was able, and that she knew she was in God's hands. I told her we would pray for her, and she said she knew our prayers would be answered. She was back on the job three months after her hospitalization.

It made me aware of those people all around me who go about their work with quiet grace, never calling attention to themselves. I'm sure many times I take these people for granted, until they are no longer there. Sometimes I take my faith for granted too. I don't realize how much my church and its people mean to me. God has blessed us with those believers among us who guide us daily with their energy and loving spirit.

Hymns of the Saints: No. 462, "O Master, Let Me Walk with Thee"

Prayer Thought: May we see in a new light, Lord, those around us who quietly serve, and may we show our appreciation for the dedication of so many.

Saturday **13** November	**Daily Reasons for Thanks** By Doris Hillyard Toronto, Ontario, Canada	

"Speaking to yourselves in psalms and hymns and spiritual songs... giving thanks always for all things unto God and the Father in the name of our Lord Jesus Christ."
—Ephesians 5:19–20

Although I have read and enjoyed *Daily Bread* for many years, the 2002 issue seemed extra special to me. Perhaps because my need was greater, but the scripture readings, testimonies, and prayer thoughts centered so pointedly for my benefit and support. On some occasions after reading, even if a little down, I had to smile and was encouraged the way God answered my need through them. I could mention many articles but three were most direct.

Early last summer, while helping a friend out of town, I had a minor car accident. Although it caused no bodily injury, it did cause mental anguish to me, and much inconvenience. On returning home, I read "Have Faith in God" (May 29), the testimony for the day of the accident, and I was uplifted and strengthened. "Challenging Summer" (June 7) made me smile, and I was encouraged, as I too was experiencing quite a different kind of summer. The June 14 reading, "Joyful Occasion," was a highlight, as I remembered my own baptism on June 14, 1940, more than sixty years ago.

The scriptures say, "In all things, give thanks," and I do thank God for blessings received and the wondrous ways they come to me.

Sing a New Song: No. 22, "Jesus"

Prayer Thought: We offer our thanks, Lord, for the many ways you reach us daily at our point of need. Keep us seeking your Spirit through the testimonies of others.

| Sunday **14** November | **Enriched by Youthful Energy**
By Peggy Michael
Cantonment, Florida | |

"As you do not know the path of the wind, or how the body is formed in a mother's womb, so you cannot understand the work of God, the Maker of all things."
—Ecclesiastes 11:5 NIV

When Tammy moved into my mobile home, I traded unused space for laughter, beauty, and kindness. After graduating from Graceland University, she needed a place to live while she continued her education. I still had much dismantling to do, for I had lived in my house for more than forty years. How we enjoyed our time of transition!

Though I knew Tammy and her family well, she became like a granddaughter to me. We gardened and shared a good movie every now and then. Often she put an extra piece of chicken on the grill. When she went home on the weekend, she brought back specimen roses from her mother's garden. The rest of her family is as special as she is.

The highlight of her stay was spring break. She asked me if some of her Graceland friends could visit. Of course they could—all the extra friends she could pack into the mobile home. The time came when a vanload of energy spilled out, and the celebration began. They shared their joy with me. Some even came back the following year.

My house is sold now, and Tammy lives half a continent away, but her touch on my life shall remain a part of my happiness.

Hymns of the Saints: No. 154, "Sometimes a Light Surprises"

Prayer Thought: Most gracious God, we offer our thanks for the encounters and relationships that have blessed our lives in times of special need.

| Monday **15** November | **Midnight Encouragement** By Geraldine Billings Greer Mesa, Arizona | |

"And let us not be weary in well doing; for in due season we shall reap, if we faint not. As we have therefore opportunity, let us do good unto all men, especially unto them who are of the household of faith."—Galatians 6:9–10

About a year ago I received a letter from a girl who was in my college prep English class during the 1964–1965 school year. In the letter she thanked me for the information she had learned in my class. She said that she had used this information during her college years and was now teaching it to her daughters, who were in college.

I was grateful to learn that some of my teaching was appreciated. I was also reminded that my grandmother had told us that we would reap what we sow. We need to keep this in mind when teaching our church school classes. We never know how much of the information the little ones will remember and use.

Hymns of the Saints: No. 439, "Teach Me, My God and King"

Prayer Thought: Eternal God, remind us that what we teach today may be used by others tomorrow, and therefore to offer our very best.

<table>
<tr><td>Tuesday
16
November</td><td>**An Angelic Smile**
By Charles Kornman
Grand Junction, Colorado</td><td></td></tr>
</table>

"I am the Lord your God.... I have put my words in your mouth."—Isaiah 51:15–16 NIV

Pop Korn (a clown) visited children at a Shriners hospital. He walked through the wards doing what a clown does—reaching out in love to everyone. Some children looked at him through pain-filled eyes. Some, in body casts, radiated big wide-eyed joy. And some would shrink back in their cribs, afraid of God knows what terror.

Pop Korn taught them how to kiss a goose (think like a fish and chew like a camel), how to sew their fingers together with a hair from his head, and whatever else seemed appropriate. He even proposed to a nurse—this brought howls of laughter. The children radiated love to Pop Korn.

One little girl (from Greece, as I recall now twenty years later) had an enlarged head and badly deformed limbs. Pop Korn spent a little more time with her than the others. He had to communicate through an interpreter but that wasn't the reason for the extra time. Pop Korn needed something that she could give. As he turned to leave she said something through the nurse interpreter that stopped him dead in his tracks: "Can you make the hurt go away?"

I walked back to that bed with "God, please help me" in my heart. I don't remember the story that I told her—probably something like Fearless Freddy the Fish, who experimented with blowing bubbles under water. As I told the story through the interpreter I massaged her pencil-thin legs and arms with "Please, please, please" in my heart. As I left she smiled an angelic smile as the interpreter told me, "She said to tell you that it doesn't hurt anymore!"

How does one say, "Thank you, God!" for such blessings?

Sing a New Song: No. 35, "Make Me a Servant"

Prayer Thought: God of mercy, we ask you to work through our efforts to bless those who suffer, whether we are doctor, nurse, clown, or friend. Touch those in pain with release and healing rest.

| Wednesday **17** November | **The Cardinal** By Jim Chalou Bay Port, Michigan | |

"Could you say, if you were called to die at this time, within yourselves that you have been sufficiently humble, that your garments have been cleansed and made white, through the blood of Christ, who will come to redeem his people from their sins?"—Alma 3:48–49

I love to deer hunt, or so it seems the last few years, to "deer watch." This particular day the weather was too nice and nothing was moving, so I went back to the house for lunch. Not one to waste a vacation day, I went back out and took a large pail of screenings. That's what is left after grain is cleaned—mostly weed seeds, and enjoyed by most birds. I poured the pail over a stump, and in about half an hour there were maybe thirty birds chirping and fighting over the seeds.

Then a beautiful red cardinal landed on the stump, sitting in a ray of sunshine. Almost at once the birds became quiet and stopped fighting, and all ate together.

That brilliant red bird made me think of the blood of Jesus that was spilled for our sins, and how important it is to take that blood along whenever we are called to facilitate peace in a world of conflict.

Hymns of the Saints: No. 441, "In Nature's Voice We Hear You, Lord"

Prayer Thought: Maker of all creatures, we thank you for speaking to us through the lessons of nature—through mysteries of sharing, and colored feathers that remind us of Christ's sacrifice. May Christ abide in us.

| Thursday **18** November | **The Spirit's Presence** By Carol Smith Barnes Sedalia, Missouri | |

"I will sing to the Lord as long as I live; I will sing praise to my God while I have being."—Psalm 104:33 NRSV

One morning I awakened from a spiritual dream shedding tears of joy. My grandmother, who had passed away some years before, had appeared from celestial realms to embrace me. Her smile was all-knowing and loving, from a glowing face. We didn't say a word to each other, for our love transcended words.

My husband was preparing for work and didn't know what to make of me as I jumped out of bed, threw my arms around him, and sobbed profusely. I gained my composure enough to relate my dream to him, while assuring him I was all right. The Holy Spirit remained with me in greater power than usual as I went about my work. I felt such wonderful peace and energy.

I thanked God for this experience. He knew how much I missed my Grandmother Smith. She was a wonderful, stabilizing influence in my life. Granddad

Smith had passed away when I was nine, and afterward I became Grandmother's companion in many ways. My parents had agreed to let me stay with her a while until she adjusted to being alone. She was a caring, soft-hearted individual with a great missionary zeal. When I was in college she continued to keep in touch by sending me issues of the *Saints' Herald*, and always marked the articles she thought I should read.

The morning after my experience, a church friend called to ask if we could change the time for our trio practice for Sunday's worship service. Her father was close to death, and she was afraid that if we waited, she wouldn't be able to make the rehearsal. We agreed to practice later that morning. Jennie and her daughter, Brenda, arrived as I was playing through our number. I continued to marvel at the sweet spirit that remained with me.

After our rehearsal, we visited about the seriousness of her father's condition. The Spirit led me into a message of comfort for Jennie as I related my dream. I told her of the happiness that shone from my grandmother's face and how she looked as if she were in the prime of life, although I had never known her at that age. I reminded Jennie of how tired her father was and urged her to accept his passing with joy, as he was waiting for her to be at peace. Later that day, I received a phone call from Brenda that her granddad had passed quietly as Jennie held him in her arms.

I am sure my experience came for the sake of my friend. The Spirit, which had stayed with me in power, subsided after I received word. That Spirit has returned many times as I have shared this spiritual experience with those who are grieving. As the years have passed, I have learned to expect special purposes in every blessing I receive—even to watch for them.

Sing a New Song: No. 39, "Mourning into Dancing"

Prayer Thought: We rejoice, merciful God, when you comfort us through the power of your Spirit and remind us that there are realms beyond this earthly life.

| Friday **19** November | **Blessed with New Life**
By Ellen L. Wang
Colville, Washington | |

"For this cause I bow my knees unto the Father of our Lord Jesus Christ, of whom the whole family in heaven and earth is named."—Ephesians 3:14–15

Two new special "bundles of joy" were added to our family in 2002. Another granddaughter was born August 2, and our first great-granddaughter arrived on December 7. It was a time of reflection for us as we shared in these special events, and even now, as we continue to become acquainted with these newest members of our family.

We have been truly blessed to have our children, grandchildren, and now great-granddaughter as a daily presence in our lives. Such joy we have received! It is so healing, especially during times of trial and tribulation, to be around young, vibrant members of our family.

Life happens and continues to do so, and God has sent many messages and lessons through the youngest members of our family. They are a big part of our on-going growth in this life.

Sing for Peace: No. 3, "Gather Your Children"

Prayer Thought: Lord, connect us across the generations in our families, that the young may learn from the old, and that the old may be given new vision.

Saturday **20** November	**Acknowledging God's Greatness** By Mildred Finger Fresno, California	

"Let everything that has breath praise the Lord."
—Psalm 150:6 NIV

Few people are gifted to glorify God so beautifully and majestically as did Handel in his music. Yet from the mouth of every believer in Jesus Christ can come praises and adoration for the King of Kings.

A number of years ago, on an early morning walk, I stopped to notice the beauty of God's creation. Feeling grateful within, I began to sing one of our beautiful hymns of praise. Knowing my limitations, I changed and hummed softly. As I did, it seemed as if my whole being was immersed in praise. I wanted to lift up praise to God, and I did with each footstep I took. John Wesley once said that a Christian's life ought to be a perpetual benediction.

We praise God in our sanctuaries when we meet to worship. We praise God because his glory is above the earth and beyond the heavens and his greatness is unsearchable. We praise God for sending Jesus, and the promise he gave with it, for Jesus is the King of Kings. What could delight God any more than our praise, acknowledging that God is greater than our understanding?

Hymns of the Saints: No. 192, "God of Eternity"

Prayer Thought: Living God, we offer our praise to you for your mercy and love, for your creative power, for your blessing to us of salvation through Christ.

Love Remembered

By Shirley Dauzvardis
Blue Springs, Missouri

"Beloved, I pray that all may go well with you and that you may be in good health, just as it is well with your soul."
—III John 2 NRSV

Several years ago, I was doing an internship in a nursing home when I noticed an elderly female resident sitting mutely in her wheelchair near the nurse's station. Every day after bath time, "Sarah" was wheeled there in hopes that this busy environment would be therapeutic for her. Sarah seemed to have forgotten everything she had learned in life, including words of speech. Nothing was expected of her and no one spoke to her. She was equally quiet and appeared to be unmoved by all the hustle and bustle.

One day I decided to try communicating with her. I leaned down closely, called her by name, kissed her cheek, and gave her a little hug. To my surprise, she responded by laying her head on my shoulder, and for a brief second, she smiled. Sarah still responded to love and affection.

Love is powerful, and it appears to outlast every other behavior. God's love for us is like that too; it never wanes and never leaves us alone.

Sing for Peace: No. 12, "Of All the Spirit's Gifts to Me"

Prayer Thought: Savior who offered your healing, loving touch, teach us how to communicate your love for all people, no matter their condition.

"If then God so clothe the grass, which is today in the field, and tomorrow is cast in the oven; how much more will he provide for you, if ye are not of little faith?"
—Luke 12:30 IV

One day as a friend visited me, I shared with her, "When the service man plugged my alternating air flow mattress into the electrical outlet, it sparked."

"Let me investigate," she replied. "Look, here's the problem. See these small nicks in the insulation? It looks like teeth marks; a mouse probably chewed on the wires. The protection is completely gone from some of the areas, exposing the wires. If either of these two bare wires had touched each other, there would have been a fire. God is watching out for you. I have a friend who owns a contracting business. His electrician can repair this for you. I'll call right now."

On their arrival, I asked them to check all the wiring in our home. In the basement, they found the bottom of the forty-four-year-old fuse box jutting out from the wall and open to the air. A thick layer of dust covered everything—another potential fire discovered. And the dining room ceiling light had a short in it.

Since the building of our house, the city's electrical codes had changed. We didn't have the special safety breaker outlets in the bathroom or kitchen that automatically shut off the electricity wherever any in-use equipment falls into water. When they finished inspecting our residence many things needed fixing. I was astonished at all the dangers that surrounded us. I felt like I was living in a firetrap. It would cost $3,500 to fix our place.

As my daughter sought a loan to pay for the needed repairs, I received a call from my brother. "Happy birthday, Sis. How are things going?" After I explained our predicament he replied, "I know where you can get a twenty-four-month loan interest free."

"Where?"

"You're talking to him," he answered. Four days later I received a check in the mail for $3,500. I called the contractor. "We have the money," I told him. "When can you start?" I asked.

"We'll start tomorrow," he replied.

The work took several days to finish. At last I could live from my wheelchair unafraid. Our abode was now electrically safe. God protected us from the unknown dangers. When they were detected, God provided the means, both money and people, by which these hazards could be corrected. "Thanks, God! How wonderful you are."

Hymns of the Saints: No. 137, "My Times Are in Thy Hand"

Prayer Thought: We are grateful, Lord, when we are living with unseen dangers, for warnings that may come our way and for the means to fix the problems.

| Tuesday **23** November | **Rigid or Resilient?** By Dorene Kilburn St. Paul's Station, Ontario, Canada | |

*"Let the morning bring me word of your unfailing love....
Teach me to do your will, for you are my God; may your
good Spirit lead me on level ground."*
—Psalm 143:8, 10 NIV

Weather patterns in recent years have seemed to bring drastically big surprises at times! In late March the expected signs of spring began to show where we live—budding trees, daffodils pushing through the earth. Then on April 4, we awoke to ice everywhere, hanging from the eaves, covering hydro wires and tree branches. It had rained heavily in the night, and the temperature had dropped a few degrees below freezing. Huge branches of a big old Manitoba maple tree had broken off under the weight of the ice and were strewn across the ground. This tree is considered by many to be a "weed" tree, not to have a long, healthy life span—very rigid and unbending. Several of our tall, slim cedars had branches bent right over to the ground from the heavy ice hanging on them. The temperature remained below freezing for two more days, and we feared the damage to our beautiful cedars would be irreparable. But cedars are different from maples. The branches are flexible, and when the ice melted, it only took a few days for them to return to their proper form.

Are we like maples or cedars? Are we rigid or resilient? We face the possibility of necessary change all through our lives. Change is difficult. We prefer to hang onto long-held views and habits. But sometimes the Lord asks us to be more flexible. A major example of this was changing the name of our church, of letting go of the old and embracing the new. Not easy for many people! I think we can see that much good has come from the change. We have been called to take a much more thoughtful look at the meaning of true community and making sure that Christ is the center of that community. May we always be willing to bend to new insights and new challenges that we feel are God directed.

Hymns of the Saints: No. 182, "Make Room Within My Heart, O God"

Prayer Thought: Assure us that you are directing us, Lord, when we are called to change our attitudes and actions. May we trust in you when we need to let go of the old and take a new path.

Wednesday **24** November	**A Richer Ministry to Offer** By Jane Miller Berryville, Arkansas	

"I will lift up mine eyes unto the hills, from whence cometh my help. My help cometh from the Lord...."

—Psalm 121:1

Once in a while I look back on my life and all the twists and turns that have brought me to where I am now. The pain of my sorrows floods over me and they are fresh again. I have been down many dark paths and through many stormy days. To dwell too long on these thoughts would be a mistake, but to forget them would also be a mistake because the lessons learned would be wasted.

Each of my experiences, the good and the painful, has taught me to be strong and to rely on my faith in God. Because of these sorrows, and also the joys of my life, I have a stronger and more knowledgeable ministry to

419

offer. I can see the pitfalls and feel the pain of those I try to help. I can point them to the same Source of strength that has brought me to where I am now.

Hymns of the Saints: No. 150, "Lord, in This Hour"

Prayer Thought: Gracious God, may we learn from life's lessons to rely on you for our strength. May what we have learned help us better understand the problems of others.

| Thursday **25** November | **Keepers of the Flame** By Bonnie Fannin Portsmouth, Ohio | |

"But they that wait upon the Lord shall renew their strength; they shall mount up with wings as eagles; they shall run, and not be weary; and they shall walk, and not faint."—Isaiah 40:31

The morning of Thanksgiving 2002 (in late November in the United States) I awoke thinking of my many blessings. My husband and children came to mind first, of course; then came health and home. As I lay there thinking of my childhood I thought how fortunate my sister and I were as children. Dad and Mom never made big money, but we always seemed to have all we needed while growing up. My parents have been members of Community of Christ all their adult lives (they are seventy-eight) and have tried to be good stewards. They are always willing to help others and the church without putting themselves first. This is perhaps the reason that many blessings have been given to our family.

I truly feel in my heart that we are put on this earth for a purpose. Maybe just to try to live a good life as an example to others, or maybe to see others who don't live such a good life be examples for us. I believe that making mistakes isn't all bad, as long as we learn from those mistakes. We only get one chance in this lifetime, so may we leave a legacy of good that can influence others. As it says in the hymn "The Bread That Giveth Strength," we shall never again pass this way.

There have been many who have influenced my sister and me, but none has set the example of our beloved parents. Mom and Dad have been married for sixty years, for which we are very thankful.

Hymns of the Saints: No. 423, "The Bread That Giveth Strength"

Prayer Thought: Faithful God, may we learn to be faithful examples to others, helping them find a better quality of life in your service.

Friday **26** November	**Keep on Being Thankful** By Barrie Fox Kirkby in Ashfield, England	

"For I tell you, that many prophets and kings have desired to see those things which ye see, and have not seen them; and to hear those things which ye hear, and have not heard them."—Luke 10:24 KJV

I read of an Anglican Church bishop saying how delighted he was to have been invited to walk in a procession of Afro-Caribbeans who were welcoming and taking their new minister to their church in a London suburb. The bishop went on to say that as he began the walk, he initially felt himself to be somewhat disturbed to see the processional cross, which was some way ahead of him in the procession, drifting from side to side and appearing to be carried with undo care. He quickly realized, however, that the cross was actually being carried by a severely disabled young woman who was being pushed along in a wheelchair. He commented that, on realizing the endeavor she was making, his attitude quickly changed. I was moved as I read this and was caused to reflect on the wonderful contribution that some of our disabled associates do make.

I am reminded that one of God's miracles is the way some people are undoubtedly empowered to work in their Christian endeavors so positively and so meaningfully, despite their difficulties and problems. Prayer has been called the language of faith, and I am most thankful to be able to continue to say that I believe God hears our prayers, communicates with us in various ways, and encourages us to be part of the Christian endeavors with which we associate ourselves.

Hymns of the Saints: No. 61, "My Soul, Praise the Lord"

Prayer Thought: Heavenly Father, grant us strength and determination as we endeavor to participate in Christian causes despite personal difficulties, whatever they may be.

| Saturday **27** November | **A Clear Mind** By Mildred Jordan Houghton Lake, Michigan | |

"So built we the wall; and all the wall was joined together unto the half thereof; for the people had a mind to work."
—Nehemiah 4:6

For some time two large, dead limbs on a big oak tree overhung the power lines and phone lines leading to my house. I knew, as others had told me, that a thunderstorm with strong winds could cause a lot of problems for my neighbors and me. So I called the power company, and they came and soon remedied the problem. That night it stormed, but I slept serenely through it, for the threat had been removed.

Some things in life do pose a threat. I think of young people growing up and the things they are exposed to. A good family background can help them deal wisely in facing life's problems and temptations, but sadly many children are not that fortunate.

In this fast-moving age we face the threat of distracted drivers, often using mobile phones, juggling a drink, or fiddling with the radio or tape players. It doesn't take much to cause a car to swerve, and that can be deadly. Lives are valuable. Of course we don't want to cause someone's death or our own either. Accidents can happen at any time. By keeping our minds clear and on what we are doing, we will usually be able to avoid trouble.

Sometimes we must make difficult decisions. We often ask, "What if...?" and then worry, over and over. Let's take our worries to our Maker and leave them there. Trusting in God's capable, all-knowing wisdom truly works.

Hymns of the Saints: No. 152, "Beyond the Mist and Doubt"

Prayer Thought: Lord, may we learn to do all we can to solve or prevent problems but may we ultimately trust in you for answers.

Sunday **28** November	**Uplifted Hearts through Song** By Neva Minthorn Nelsen Beaverton, Oregon	

"Sing forth the honor of his name; make his praise glorious."—Psalm 66:2

I have some favorite songs I like to play on the piano, and sometimes I sing along, too. There are hymns from the many church books I have collected that I play for hours, so when it's my turn to play for morning worship, I can always find music to fit the theme.

We are so blessed to have this music to share. Men and women who have written these hymns have left us a great legacy. The old hymns uplift me because they remind me of my younger days or of important events in my life. Many newer hymns uplift me also as I learn their words and gain a new perspective.

Perhaps when our time on this earth is over and we gather with loved ones to meet the Lord, we will rejoice in song. We may sing a new song of love and praise for God's goodness and mercy.

Sing a New Song: No. 2, "As the Deer"

Prayer Thought: Draw us together, Lord, through the beauty of music, whether through the melodies or words, that we may have new insight and discover deeper praise.

Monday **29** November	**Strength through Adversity** By Janie S. Qualls Lake City, Arkansas	

"I have said this to you, so that in me you may have peace. In the world you face persecution. But take courage; I have conquered the world!"—John 16:33 NRSV

Two pine trees stand side by side on the edge of the yard. One, ravaged by disease and insects, is covered with pine cones. The other is healthy and has never lost a limb to anything, but it only has a few cones. It seems that the one that has suffered the most is bearing the most fruit.

In my life, it appears that the times when I have been broken by pain or trials have been the most productive for me spiritually. The storms of life seem to make me stronger.

Hymns of the Saints: No. 284, "Gracious Spirit, Dwell with Me"

Prayer Thought: Creator, we know that storms and all manner of adversity strengthen the trees even as exercise strengthens the human body. May we look for ways our troubles have increased our value in ministry through knowledge gained.

Hugging a Tree
By Shirley Vallier Remmenga
Fort Collins, Colorado

"Bear the burdens of body of which the Spirit of healing from the Lord in faith, or the use of that which wisdom directs does not relieve or remove, and in cheerfulness do whatever may be permitted you to perform that the blessing of peace may be upon all."
—Doctrine and Covenants 119:9c

My heart was sad and heavy when Elmer and I returned from our ten-day vacation in Grand Cayman. My brother Kent had died while we were there, and circumstances were such that it was impossible for us to attend his memorial service or to give any personal support to his family as I desired to do.

This heaviness persisted for another couple of weeks even though I had been able to contact my brother's family and to set up a time to fly to Alabama and visit them. So when I woke up this particular Saturday morning, I decided to take a long walk and talk it out with the Lord. The day was beautiful and the road I took along the irrigation ditch was mine alone. I began to express my feelings to the Lord aloud as I walked along. I became aware of a big cottonwood tree ahead of me and decided that I would turn around there, for I had been walking for about forty-five minutes by then.

When I reached it, I suddenly had an urge to put my arms around that big old tree and just hug it for a while. As I spread my arms and pressed my chest and face into its rough bark, I began to feel my sadness flow out of me and into the tree. I probably didn't stand there for more than three or four minutes, but it was long enough for me to receive a healing of the spirit. As I released my hold on the tree trunk, I knew that God had lifted my burden and had set me free. Was there some kind of magic in that tree? No, not that. The healing came from God, and the tree was the means through which God had blessed me.

Hymns of the Saints: No. 287, "Holy Spirit, Come with Power"

Prayer Thought: Most gracious God, we thank you for the healing power of your Spirit, which you so generously share with your children. Make us whole, and free us from those burdens that hold back the good we can do.

December 2004

S	M	T	W	T	F	S
			1	2	3	4
5	6	7	8	9	10	11
12	13	14	15	16	17	18
19	20	21	22	23	24	25
26	27	28	29	30	31	

<table>
<tr><td>Wednesday
1
December</td><td>**Deliverance**
By Alma J. V. Leeder
Wiarton, Ontario, Canada</td><td></td></tr>
</table>

"I will not leave you comfortless; I will come to you."
—John 14:18

As a "minister of blessing," I have often found myself in need of uplift. Such a time occurred some years ago when my wife Shirley's father passed away. The family asked me to take charge of the funeral service, and I agreed to do so. His passing, at age ninety-five, wasn't unexpected. In many ways he had lived an exemplary life, so it was really a time of celebration.

Several days later, I officiated at the wedding of my niece, which was a happy occasion. However, at the reception following the ceremony, I was summoned to the telephone and received word that Shirley's brother had been killed in a farm accident. We drove homeward with grieving hearts, and I was faced with another funeral requiring healing ministry.

Our home became the family gathering place, and I could find no time or place to prepare a message or to settle my own feelings. On the morning of the funeral, I awoke early and went quickly to my study area. As fast as I could write, the message flowed through my pen, and I was delivered from personal anxiety to provide healing ministry to our sorrowing family. I know that there is a Comforter; its influence has sustained me when nothing else could.

Hymns of the Saints: No. 159, "Oh, for a Faith That Will Not Shrink"

Prayer Thought: All-gracious Lord, may we receive your loving support in those times when our own words and strength fail us or are not sufficient. Let your message flow through us when we are called on to bring ministry.

Thursday **2** December	**Everlasting Arms** By Mark E. Megee East Windsor, New Jersey

"The eternal God is your refuge, and underneath are the everlasting arms...."—Deuteronomy 33:27 NIV

Being with our heavenly Father is comforting. We seek him in our moments of need and in our darkest hours. One night I was just sitting around the house. My daughter had gone to a Rainbow Girls meeting, my step-children were out of the house, and it was just me and my son, Sean Patric. The two of us had always looked forward to our nights together. We would play and laugh, and maybe even share some popcorn.

After some homework and playtime, Sean wanted just to sit on the couch and be together. We sat down, and he put my arm around him. He then thanked me for being his dad and for being there whenever he needed me. He didn't want to play. He didn't want to talk about it. He just wanted his father's loving arms around him—the same thing we are looking for at times as adults.

Hymns of the Saints: No. 193, "My God, How Wonderful Thou Art"

Prayer Thought: Heavenly Parent, sometimes we simply need the warm embrace of your arms, assuring us of your presence and loving acceptance. Once we are loved, then we can receive instruction.

Words that Uplift

By Shirley Botting
Wiarton, Ontario, Canada

"The Lord is my shepherd; I shall not want. He maketh me to lie down in green pastures; he leadeth me beside the still waters…. Surely goodness and mercy shall follow me all the days of my life and I will dwell in the house of the Lord forever."—Psalm 23:1–2, 6

I love this scripture. It has such a calming effect on me. When I was very young my health was not good. My mother wrote to the *Saints' Herald* asking for prayers for me. A woman answered and told my mother to send me out by the lake, as she was given to know we lived by the water. I was to walk along the shore two times a day; she said I needed the quietness. So I remember doing this one summer, until in the fall I could see the ice coming along the shore. I was happy. God blessed me, as my health did become better.

This scripture gives me peace of mind, but many times I don't take time to study the scriptures, which also help us come close to God. They were written and preserved by godly people, and contain much counsel; if we heed the counsel, it will bring us spiritual comfort. Life brings difficult experiences to all of us, but reading devotions, along with prayer every day, will allow God to lead us in the right way.

Hymns of the Saints: No. 183, "Lord, Lead Me by Your Spirit"

Prayer Thought: God of the ages, we offer our thanks for all that has been written to uplift us—scriptures, hymns, and daily devotionals—and for those whose minds you have inspired to write or compose.

<table>
<tr><td>Saturday
4
December</td><td>**Seeking God through Prayer**
By Paul McCain
Oklahoma City, Oklahoma</td><td></td></tr>
</table>

"Search diligently, pray always, and be believing, and all things shall work together for your good, if ye walk uprightly, and remember the covenant wherewith ye have covenanted one with another."

—Doctrine and Covenants 87:6e

In April 1968 I was sent overseas on temporary duty with the United States Air Force. Although we expected our lives to be interrupted by my service duty, my wife and I decided to start a family. I was again sent overseas in April 1969. My wife was expecting, and with her being diabetic we had some apprehension because of the difficulties diabetic mothers have. Her difficulties increased to the point that the doctor requested I return home. I arrived home in July and was home one week when the baby was born prematurely and lived only six hours. We had called upon the Lord many times to strengthen us in this situation, and my wife had been administered to before the birth.

I remained with my wife long enough for her to regain her strength and then finished my overseas tour of duty. As soon as I returned home in October we started proceedings to adopt a child, thinking it better to adopt than to risk childbirth again. Through a close friend, the medical staff secretary for a hospital in Tulsa, we made connections and found a child who had just been born who would have been turned over to an adoption agency. Five days after Julianne was born, she went home with us.

About a month later I was transferred to Indiana. We had pretty much given up the idea of having children but were persuaded otherwise by a doctor with exceptional qualifications who, after many serious discussions, encouraged us to try again. We prayed about the matter and decided to go ahead. Shortly thereafter my wife became pregnant, yet despite our efforts, we became apprehensive. After about seven months the anxiety seemed too much to bear. We turned to God in special prayer and asked for God's help.

I recall going to the trouble to outline what we wanted to be assured of: (1) that the child would live; and (2) that the child would be whole. I prayed directly and concisely, ended the prayer, and with only a few moments' hesitation felt strongly that God had something to say. The words God gave to us were even more than expected. He assured us that the baby would live and would be whole. We were also told two things that we really didn't ask for: the prayer was answered because of our faith, and there was a work for the child to do.

God continues to bless us in the lives of our two beautiful children, grown now, both of whom were given to us in a special way, and I know beyond a shadow of doubt that God is alive today and concerned about individuals.

Hymns of the Saints: No. 141, "Father, in Thy Mysterious Presence"

Prayer Thought: Teach us to seek your guiding presence in all things, Lord, and to trust in your answers as you respond to our cries for help.

Renewed Desire for the Season

By Helen L. Lynn
Carlsbad, New Mexico

"Do not neglect to do good and to share what you have, for such sacrifices are pleasing to God."
—Hebrews 13:16 NRSV

It was difficult to believe another Christmas was so near! The year had simply flown by so quickly. It seemed like I had only put the previous year's holiday things away a short time ago. I thought maybe I could just ignore the whole thing, since I didn't have any family nearby. Being alone I couldn't handle the pretty lights and decorations. Maybe I could just enjoy the neighbors' decorations and let it go at that. Gift shopping had no appeal either because it was all I could do to pay the mounting medical bills for my very ill husband. Besides, everyone I knew had everything they wanted and needed, so what could I give them? Bah! Humbug! I thought. Mr. Scrooge had the right idea. Forgive me, Jesus, for such negative thoughts about your birthday.

Still, I do enjoy all the holiday mail and never wanted to give up sending and receiving Christmas cards and letters. That correspondence was too important. Gifts started coming in the mail and from nearby friends— homemade fudge, inspirational books, and offers for meals out. The nursing home where John is was having a Christmas party with gift exchanges. In the midst of all this generosity how could I not have at least a tiny bit of the holiday spirit?

Just a few days before Christmas I awoke one morning aware that I wanted to share the joy of giving as well as receiving. I knew I'd better get busy! That was one of the best Christmases I've ever had.

Hymns of the Saints: No. 235, "O Thou Joyful, O Thou Wonderful"

Prayer Thought: Redeeming Lord, lift our spirits at this special, yet often difficult time of year that we might discover joy and share it with someone else.

Monday **6** December	**"Widows' Might" Surprise** By Marlene Brunner Yuma, Colorado	

"For there is a God, and he has created all things, both the heavens and the earth, and all things that are in them; both things to act, and things to be acted upon."

—II Nephi 1:95

In our congregation we have a functioning support group for widows called The Widows' Might, which was started in 1998 as a congregational model. We meet once a month for devotions and to share in varied activities. Some are: JOY boxes for people who are terminally ill or experiencing extended rehabilitation; cookies for widowers; guest speakers; and other types of fellowship.

One activity our widows enjoyed very much was a surprise that I planned for them. We drove to someone's house to see her collection of Shirley Temple dolls and other memorabilia. While we were there, a caterer prepared a luncheon for the women at the church. When we returned to the church, they were so surprised and thrilled to see what was prepared and waiting for them. It was such a joy to see their joy and excitement.

It made me think about what God has prepared for us in the hereafter, if we remain faithful. The scriptures tell us that we cannot begin to comprehend what wonderful things God has in store for those who keep his commandments and remain faithful throughout life. Oh my, what wonderful things await us!

Hymns of the Saints: No. 322, "O How Blessed Are the Poor in Spirit"

Prayer Thought: Surprise us daily, Lord, when we need it the most, with a loving gift of uplift from your Spirit—an invitation, a letter, a phone call, a hug from someone—and may you use us to bring a surprise blessing to another.

| Tuesday **7** December | **Old Faithful** By Shirley McCarty Port Elgin, Ontario, Canada | |

"Thus saith the Lord; I am returned unto Zion, and will dwell in the midst of Jerusalem; and Jerusalem shall be called a city of truth; and the mountain of the Lord of hosts, the holy mountain.... There shall yet old men and old women dwell in the streets of Jerusalem...."
—Zechariah 8:3–4

My husband and I recently returned from "Mission 2003: Launch Out" at church headquarters. During our travel home, I reflected on the words of President Grant McMurray at the last morning session. He had emphatically stressed that we, as a church, should stop making excuses that we are too small or too old to launch out.

I thought of our ninety-five-year-old member who felt she could not contribute any longer but who sells more tickets than anyone to our annual fund-raising dinner to give a $500 peace award to a graduating high school senior. Our ninety-one-year-old member makes jams from her garden for neighbors and friends and offers flowers from her garden to decorate our worship centers. Our legally blind eighty-six year old makes thirty to forty quilts every year for Blankets for Canada. Her eighty-nine-year-old husband faithfully helps her by threading all her needles. Some of the women are knitting pneumonia vests for the Honduran people. We also contributed sixteen quilts to the local police and fire department.

The average age of our congregation is seventy-two and the average attendance is twenty-five to twenty-seven—such dependability, dedication, and commitment. I am proud to be a part of such an active "older" congregation and pray that I will carry on their legacy.

Hymns of the Saints: No. 214, "There's a Spirit in the Air"

Prayer Thought: God who calls us to action, rally our spirits in your cause, so that even if we can but pray for others, we will commit ourselves to do so. Empower us to see no task as too small if it brings blessing to another human being.

Wednesday **8** December	**Mother's Hymn** By Geraldine Billings Greer Mesa, Arizona	

"Wherefore be ye not unwise, but understanding what is the will of the Lord.... Speak to yourselves in psalms and hymns and spiritual songs, singing and making melody in your heart to the Lord."—Ephesians 5:17, 19

A few months after my husband's stroke, I was feeling discouraged and very lonely. Then I remembered that when Mother was feeling low, she would sit at the piano and play and sing "What a Friend We Have in Jesus."

Suddenly I realized that I was singing that song. When I got to the second verse, all my problems seemed to vanish and a warm, comforting spirit enveloped me. Since then, whenever I begin to feel down, I sing my mother's hymn.

Music has always been such an important part of our worship services because it lifts our spirits and brings us together.

Hymns of the Saints: No. 86, "What a Friend We Have in Jesus"

Prayer Thought: Comforting Presence, when we are discouraged and our spirits are low, lead us to seek guidance and solace through the hymns of the church.

Thursday **9** December	**An Angel by What Name?** By Shirley S. Case Slater, Missouri	

"And there appeared an angel unto him from heaven, strengthening him."—Luke 22:43

Gwennie—isn't that a beautiful name for an angel? She's been a godsend in my life and in the lives of those around her. In December 2000 my mother died three days before Christmas. Gwennie was there. She held me as I cried and told me Mom's work on earth was through and that she'd been taken at this special time of year to sing with the angels and rejoice in the celebration of Christ's birth. She told me she would have been taken sooner but God had left her long enough so she could see me ordained a priest.

In January 2001 I was diagnosed with cancer. Gwennie was there. She smiled that big, beautiful smile of hers—that smile that reaches her eyes—and told me everything was going to be all right. She stands at prayer meetings and offers prayers for her children and grandchildren and for those in need in the world, trusting that God will take care of those needs. She has a pure heart and lots of humor. She's a beautician and ministers to those who come into her shop.

Gwennie witnesses of God's love and mercy every day. She wears bright colors and sparkly pins and earrings—she gives wonderful hugs and is always helping others. She is a blessing to our congregation and a very dear friend. And if you ask for an angel, God may send Gwennie.

Hymns of the Saints: No. 484, "Make Us, O God, a Church That Shares" (verses 1 and 2)

Prayer Thought: How grateful we are for your angels on earth, Lord. Show us how we, too, can bring such comforting ministry to others.

Friday **10** December	**A Firm Foundation** By Peggy Michael Cantonment, Florida	

"Remember, that it is upon the rock of our redeemer, who is Christ, the Son of God, that you must build your foundation:... a foundation whereon if men build, they cannot fail."—Helaman 2:74–75

For ten years I tried to keep the old house livable, but my efforts were no match for two hurricanes. They won. A huge oak in my neighbor's yard fell across the fence and filled one corner of the yard; a red cedar claimed the others. Branches ripped shingles from the roof and water came through the holes in torrents. The dining room ceiling fell and debris littered the ground. It's an understatement to say I faced a monumental task. Eventually I made the house livable until the family persuaded me to move. So we set a date for the bulldozer and put up a "Lot for Sale" sign.

One day a woman called and said, "I want to buy your place as is. Then she told me her story. She said she was driving by and felt as if a force had pulled her off the highway. The woman wasn't searching for property, and if she was, this wasn't too attractive. It was a good location, though, but that was about all. Still, she looked it over.

The house was set on a good foundation. Most of the floor was OK and the structure was sound. She insisted that the well-laid concrete block was there to stay. Then she went on to say, "As I stepped inside, a spirit seemed to welcome me." I admitted to the potential buyer that my husband and I had dedicated our home to the Lord long ago. We closed the deal a couple of weeks later. The new owner invited me to come by and see the transformation. When I saw her work, I almost wanted to buy it back. As I left I thought, *Don't write a house or a life off too easily.*

Sing a New Song: No. 10, "Firm Foundation"

Prayer Thought: May we look to the foundations of our lives, Lord, that we may be firmly grounded in you and able to withstand whatever life may send our way.

<table>
<tr><td>Saturday
11
December</td><td>**Never Say Impossible**
By Shirley E. Phillips
Independence, Missouri</td><td></td></tr>
</table>

"For with God nothing can be impossible."—Luke 1:37

Cybil, my daughter's little dog, a Pomeranian, jumps onto the bed. I awaken. "C'mere to Grandma," I call to her. Cybil crawls into my arms. We exchange "kisses." "Down, baby. Time to get dressed."

In sitting position, I bring my right knee to my chest, holding it there. I stretch for my foot. I take my left hand, sliding a white sock over my toes. I pull it up to my ankle. I switch positions, repeating the process.

I flip my green slacks across the bottom of the bed. Picking up one leg at a time, I poke them into my trousers. As I lie on my back, I roll from side to side and tug. Soon my pants glide over my hips, and I secure them around my waist.

"Cybil, come; I need a hug." Plop; I catch our dog and rub her back. "OK. Done resting." Cybil hops down. Slowly I raise myself, shoving my legs over the edge of the bed. Lifting one foot at a time by the sock, I push my feet into a pair of black tennies and fasten the Velcro. I smooth the quilt over the upper half of my bed. I lay the pillow on top of the spread. Now I am ready to get up.

The locked wheelchair stands next to the bed. I fold the arm back and check the brakes. I take one end of my sliding board and adjust it under my hips. I place the other end on the cushion of the chair. I make a right-handed fist and thrust it hard into the mattress. Push! I land on the seat. I remove the sliding board and clamp the arm of the chair in place. I hook the foot holders to the chair. Pulling on the cuffs of my slacks, I lift my legs, setting them on the footrests. From the foot of my bed

I finish straightening the other half of the spread. Bed's made. Off to the bathroom I go to wash and don the rest of my clothes.

"Cybil, where are you? Grandma's up." Cybil leaps into my lap. The two of us wheel into the family room. "What shall we do today? Sweep the floor, fix pudding, or cross stitch?" Cybil decides to watch me from her pillow on the floor and take a nap.

I pick up a pen and start writing. I thank the Lord for the motivation and strength he gives me each day. I thank him that I am able to adapt and never say, "Impossible."

Hymns of the Saints: No. 126, "I Know Not What the Future Hath"

Prayer Thought: God of all our days, strengthen our resolve to keep going, that no matter what befalls us we will not give up.

| Sunday **12** December | **Hallelujah!** By Ralph Holmes Sutton in Ashfield, Nottinghamshire, England | |

"And the glory of the Lord shall be revealed, and all flesh shall see it together; for the mouth of the Lord hath spoken it."—Isaiah 40:5

I was invited to conduct Handel's *Messiah* by a local church. Invitations were sent to all of the local choral societies and churches in the district to form an augmented choir. The soloists and organist were chosen and rehearsals were arranged. Most of the people who came to sing were ones who knew the work and had possibly sung it before. Many singers who made up the chorus of more than eighty voices attended local churches, while others were not practicing Christians.

I was allowed six rehearsals in which to coordinate the singers and produce an acceptable performance. It was not an easy task, but we had fun working together, as everyone was keen to give his or her best.

When conducting *Messiah* I look upon it as something more than a mere performance but rather an act of worship. By the final rehearsal it appeared that everything was going well. Toward the end of the rehearsal I felt a powerful urge to end with a prayer. My mind and heart were racing; I had some doubts: *Some may not be accustomed to this; how will they react?* Many had come to sing simply because they loved the music.

We ended with the "Amen" chorus. I made my comments and final arrangements for the performance, then said, "I think for the performance of such a work we need to ask God's blessing. Let us pray together." Every head immediately bowed. I offered the prayer and there was a quietness that followed which was unusual after a rehearsal.

I couldn't believe the number of people who came and thanked me for offering the prayer. The choir excelled; the press report was glowing. I take no credit for the result, for whatever we do in God's name will be acknowledged and blessed by him.

Hymns of the Saints: No. 472, "Unto God, Who Knows Our Every Weakness"

Prayer Thought: Thank you, Lord, for blessing us in times of weakness and uncertainty. May our faith be strengthened as we learn to place our trust in you.

Blessed by a Son
By Mary Twinn
Collinsville, Illinois

"For the Lord thy God blesseth thee, as he promised thee...."
—Deuteronomy 15:6

My apartment is so clean, uncluttered, and pretty, and so very quiet—so still and so lonely. My youngest son, Denny, left early this morning after having visited for a month. He is so neat and fastidious about his person, but his home definitely has a "lived in" look, as did my apartment while he was here.

I am reminded of a woman in my congregation many years ago whose son paid her an extended visit. She complained about "picking up" after him only to confess after he'd gone that she sorely missed him and wished he'd come back.

While my son was here he painted my apartment, fixed a ceiling fan, repaired a chair and a drooping drapery, and performed other tasks that needed to be done, all without me asking him or pointing out what needed doing. Then he presented me with a Mother's Day card that said, "Hope your Mother's Day is just like you. Simply wonderful, through and through." I knew he meant it.

What a blessed thing it is to be a parent.

Hymns of the Saints: No. 434, "When God Created Human Life"

Prayer Thought: We thank you, loving God, for the precious lives entrusted to our care and keeping. May our children never doubt that they are greatly loved and cherished.

Called to Shine
By Janie S. Qualls
Lake City, Arkansas

"For you were once darkness, but now you are light in the Lord. Live as children of light (for the fruit of the light consists in all goodness, righteousness and truth) and find out what pleases the Lord. Have nothing to do with the fruitless deeds of darkness, but rather expose them."
—Ephesians 5:8–12 NIV

During Advent, candles were called for as a regular part of our worship services. We used a butane lighter to light them, and although it appeared to be working fine, when the time came to light the candles, it balked. No amount of flicking could get it started.

I thought of how often I feel like the lighter, especially during the Christmas season. I get so caught up in the rush that I find my light has been extinguished and my testimony lacking. At those times I need to draw apart, be still, and let God heal my weariness.

Letting our light shine, if it is to be effective, requires a constant and steady connection to our Source of light.

Sing a New Song: No. 45, "Shine, Jesus, Shine"

Prayer Thought: Kindle the light of your Spirit within us, Lord, that your light might banish the darkness, both of our own lives and of those we encounter.

<table>
<tr><td>Wednesday
15
December</td><td>**The Right Power Source**
By Roberta Dieterman
Caledonia, Michigan</td></tr>
</table>

"And Jesus came and spake unto them, saying, All power is given unto me in heaven and earth."—Matthew 28:17 IV

While on a bus tour in Europe with friends, I became a topic of discussion because of my inability to use my electric converter. I had melted two curling irons on a previous trip. I was about to use my third one. I was sure I had the proper plug; however, as I watched my newest curling iron melt and drip down the counter, I knew I'd failed again! I still didn't know what I was doing wrong. My husband had no problem with his shaver; however, he had an electric outlet for shavers. How lucky!

Sometimes I find myself plugged into the wrong energy source, and a "meltdown" of my spirit happens. When I convert my energy from God's love into unselfish acts, the power generated is always just right. But when I misdirect that power into those things that separate me from God's love, there is a loss of energy.

That source of power we find in God's love is sufficient for all our needs. How wonderful life can be when we plug our lives into that most wonderful of power sources—God's love.

Hymns of the Saints: No. 406, "God, the Source of Light and Beauty"

Prayer Thought: Creator of light and energy, may we allow the energy that comes from your love to fill us and overflow in service to others.

A Guide for the Road
By Jean Webb
Ridgefield, Connecticut

"Praise is due to thee, O God, in Zion; and to thee shall vows be performed, O thou who hearest prayer!"
—Psalm 65:1–2 RSV

My husband and I enjoy visiting the national parks, so one September we drove from Glacier National Park in Montana to Yellowstone in Wyoming. We had been there one May, but the snow was still so deep that some roads were still closed.

The day after we arrived the weather was beautiful and warm. Our reservation was for the next night at the big lodge, so we drove on south to the Grand Tetons. The next morning, we tried to reenter Yellowstone, but there were ten inches of snow on the ground, so the rangers turned us away. The roads were treacherous. We were on the interstate (I-80) heading east. The roads were getting worse, and trucks and cars were lined up trying to get up the hills.

After a couple of hours, we pulled into a rest stop along with many others. People with campers said their water was frozen, and there wasn't any food at this stop. We made many calls trying to find a place to stay but were unable to find a vacancy. As we sat in our car thinking about our situation, we knew we might be spending the night there. We had two apples, a package of crackers, and one can of soda.

We decided to call one more place from our motor club book. The woman who answered said she would hold a room for us if we gave her a credit card number. This we did, and then had to ask the police where we could turn around because we had to go back forty miles. The officer said to leave quickly, because they were closing the road completely. It took one hour to go the forty miles.

When we arrived at the motel, we got the very last room. As we stood in this warm, dry room, we paused to offer a prayer of thanksgiving. The Holy Spirit was so strong around us that we weren't able to speak. We knew God had watched over us again. It wasn't our idea to make one more call; we knew the Spirit had inspired us to do it.

Whether at home or traveling, God never leaves us alone. All we have to do is listen and follow his lead.

Hymns of the Saints: No. 128, "Abide with Me"

Prayer Thought: Almighty God, our strength and guide, we offer our profound thanks for your care in times of great stress and worry and possible danger.

Friday 17 December

Firstfruits
By Charles Kornman
Grand Junction, Colorado

"Bring the best of the firstfruits of your soil to the house of the Lord your God."—Exodus 34:26 NIV

As I was eating breakfast the other morning, my imagination got the best of me. I looked at my toast and thought of wave after wave of wheat swaying in the wind. I could see the reapers moving down the field, capturing that wheat. I could see the grinding mills turning those kernels into cereal and flour.

I thought of gentle valleys on some tropical island where banana bunches hung from trees. I thought of people harvesting those bunches. In my imagination I watched those bananas being loaded into a boat and sent on their way to my table. I thought of peaches hanging from trees just east, over in the Palisade area. I remembered going out into the orchard and picking the peaches I was eating. I pictured myself freezing those peaches and anticipating when I would be eating them in the midst of winter.

I smiled as I thought of cows gently "mowing" the grass they would turn into milk. I thought of turkeys strutting around before they wound up in turkey bacon on my bread.

At lunchtime I pictured the green beans clustered on their vines. I could see ears of corn waiting to be harvested. I was almost back in the creamery churning cream into butter. My orange juice became golden oranges on green trees in Texas. The chicken drumsticks brought to mind how my sister used to like wings.

At the end of these meals I bowed my head in amazement that God could perform such miracles and bring them together on my table.

Hymns of the Saints: No. 76, "We Plow the Fields and Scatter"

Prayer Thought: Bounteous God, in much of the world, we take for granted the meals upon our tables. We thank you for every process of growth, harvest, and transport, and for every worker who labors for our benefit.

<table>
<tr><td>Saturday
18
December</td><td>**Hope in the Night**
By June Russell
Independence, Missouri</td><td></td></tr>
</table>

"Now the God of hope fill you with all joy and peace in believing, that ye may abound in hope, through the power of the Holy Ghost."—Romans 15:13

It was mid-December. I was sitting in my lounge chair listening to Christmas carols, but my mind was occupied with concerns about world conditions, security problems in our own country, a sagging economy, family members struggling to meet expectations and working under difficult conditions. Then, the music of one of my favorites, "O, Holy Night," soared, and as I thrilled to it, the words took on new meaning for me: "It is the night of the dear Savior's birth. Long lay the world in sin and error pining till he appeared and the soul felt its worth. The thrill of hope, the weary world rejoices, for yonder breaks a new and glorious morn..."

God's gift to the world on that long-ago Christmas brought hope to a war-torn and weary world in Jesus' day, and again brings hope to the war-torn, scary world of today, as it has to each generation of believers. Christ was called Immanuel—"God with us." He is with us today and every day as we look to him and listen for his voice of encouragement.

Yes, Hope came one holy night and comes for us every day if we will but be aware of his presence.

Hymns of the Saints: No. 250, "I Heard the Bells on Christmas Day"

Prayer Thought: Blessed Redeemer, as we remember your coming to this earth, even as one of us, may we look to you for our hope—that we may learn to practice what you lived as an example for us of love and gentleness.

<table>
<tr><td>Sunday
19
December</td><td>**Compassion**
By Olevia Huntsman
Bald Knob, Arkansas</td><td></td></tr>
</table>

"But the angel said to them, 'Do not be afraid, for see—I am bringing you good news of great joy for all the people: to you is born this day in the city of David a Savior, who is the Messiah, the Lord.'"—Luke 2:10–11 NRSV

Several churches in our area come together to present a Christmas cantata each year. There is much sacrifice of time for the many people who participate. The largest church hosts the event, with refreshments following the performance donated by individuals from all the churches. The choir director is from the Methodist church, the organist from Central Baptist, the pianist from Community of Christ. There is even a children's choir that includes about twenty-five students representing the local school. Their music teacher plays the bells with a group, and there are several band students who also assist with the music. This is a wonderful way for our community to draw together as one to worship and celebrate the birth of Christ.

This year one of the students, a nine-year-old boy, was singing with the children's choir but became ill and vomited on the stage. He ran from the stage with his mother at his heels and exited the room. The choir continued to perform. Near the end of the performance the choir director came to the microphone. She stated that she hadn't planned to make any remarks but that she wanted to thank the community for their support and the choir for their time and hard work. Then she

451

said that she wanted the young man who had become ill, and his family, to know that he had in no way spoiled the show. He simply had the flu, and it was flu season. She acknowledged the children's diligence in coming to practices and working so hard. She again thanked everyone for coming and then continued with the songs and prayers on the program.

I have three children, and in all their growing-up years they were fortunate enough to never have an embarrassing moment quite like that. The compassion shown by the choir director for the young man and his family was a gracious act of love. She was in tune with the pain of exposure this family experienced, and she wanted to ease that humiliation as much as possible. The scriptures tell us that God is love, and that when we have "done it unto the least of these, you have done it unto me." What a wonderful world this would be if we all took that to heart and let our lives reflect Christ in all we say and do.

Hymns of the Saints: No. 466, "We Are One in the Spirit"

Prayer Thought: Lord, help us to see the needs of those around us and to remember that it is in those needs that we have the opportunity to assist Christ's mission of building the kingdom.

Warmed and Comforted
By Margaret Gunderson Shupe
Loveland, Colorado

"And I will pray the Father, and he shall give you another Comforter, that he may abide with you forever."
—John 14:16

Several years ago, I went shopping with a friend, Karen, to help select the yarn she needed to knit an afghan for her "secret sister." I conscientiously helped, suggesting colors I liked. At the Christmas party where "secret sisters" were revealed, imagine my surprise when I realized the "sister" honored with the beautiful afghan was me.

Many hours I have sat bundled in that cozy gift, reading a good book or sharing *Fantasia* or a VeggieTale® movie with my grandchildren. Warmed and comforted by that wondrous labor of love I have experienced a spirit of friendship, not unlike the one promised to Christ's disciples before he left them.

Karen warms and comforts me with her afghan, but our sisterhood is more than an afghan. We journey together as neighbors and citizens of God's world, striving to bloom where we are planted.

God's gift of love, exemplified by Karen's gift, challenges me to open my mind, heart, and hands to share that hope with others. When I feel warmth and comfort, God rejoices with me! When others, too, feel warmth and comfort, God really rejoices.

Hymns of the Saints: No. 289, "Come Down, O Love Divine"

Prayer Thought: Comforting God, we thank you for the gift of the Holy Spirit, sent to comfort and strengthen us, and for the blessing of friends who do the same in their own way.

| Tuesday **21** December | **Feeling the Spirit** By Phyllis Elliott Florissant, Missouri | |

"There, ahead of them, went the star that they had seen rising, until it stopped over the place where the child was."
—Matthew 2:9 NRSV

At a church group meeting in our home recently, we discussed what things stirred a spiritual feeling or emotion in us. Some mentioned certain types of music, or sermons, or attending particular activities.

I remember several times when an activity was especially moving. The first I remember was a Christmas Eve church service. The choir entered a dimmed area where church members were already seated. They wore choir robes, and each carrying a lighted candle. They entered from the back at each side and proceeded down the side aisles to the front. The sight and feeling of that moment has stayed with me for twenty years.

Another experience that occurred years ago, also, was at a family activity night at the church. One of the teenage girls performed a ballet to the music of the Lord's Prayer. The dance was beautiful and spiritual, and very moving for me.

Other times, I have felt God's Spirit when speakers would read something I had written that was printed on the back of the bulletin. Each year as I am writing *Daily Bread* articles or reading the Bible and words to the hymns, I am aware of the Spirit with me.

People will feel the nearness of God's Spirit in their own way, because God works with us at a level suited to our needs.

Hymns of the Saints: No. 282, "When Kindled by Thy Spirit's Light"

Prayer Thought: Holy Lord, may we seek peace and quiet, that we may feel your Spirit with us.

Wednesday **22** December	**Unexpected Follow-up Note** By Charlotte Jones Sherman Oaks, California	

"I do not set aside the grace of God, for if righteousness could be gained through the law, Christ died for nothing."
—Galatians 2:21

The opportunity to share comes at unexpected times. I was touched by an unexpected note from a friend's daughter. At my friend's Christmas party, I had an opportunity to visit with her daughter. Her daughter had had difficult times, but along the way Christ had come into her life in a significant way. She was suffering a nervous breakdown, but still held onto her faith. Her mother had moved her from several states away to be with her for treatment. Because of a disappointment through a minister, her brother, my friend's son, had rejected religion in general, but her daughter had found strength in Christ.

At the party, we discussed some of the events in her life, and how Christ is always there to help us. I had known her since she was a baby. We felt close, but the Spirit of Christ brought us even closer.

The Spirit blessed our conversation and brought comfort to her, as she expressed in her note to me. It was such an unexpected joy to know comfort had come to her through our conversation.

Hymns of the Saints: No. 369, "Bear Each Other's Burdens"

Prayer Thought: Guiding Spirit, lead us in our conversations with others, whether to speak or just to listen, that we might in some measure bring peace to them.

<table>
<tr><td>Thursday
23
December</td><td>**Out of Film**
By Gerald John Kloss
Philadelphia, Pennsylvania</td><td></td></tr>
</table>

"When they saw the star, they rejoiced with exceeding great joy.... And when they had opened their treasures, they presented unto him gifts; gold, and frankincense, and myrrh."—Matthew 3:10–11 IV

It was Christmas morning and all was quiet in our house. Jerry Jr. had just turned three years old that November and we were as excited as he was about Christmas. Jerry awoke before his mother and I did and eagerly came in to wake us up after he spied the many gifts downstairs. We all went downstairs in our pajamas, and Jerry immediately began to open his gifts. As he tore off tons of wrapping paper I took picture after picture. Jerry was particularly delighted with one huge box that contained a Big Wheel for a three year old. After he opened this box we pulled the Big Wheel out, and he then continued on to open other gifts.

I thought I had only put in a roll of twenty-four exposures in my camera but noticed the counter was all the way up to thirty-two. I then looked at the back window of the camera and saw no number from film as I usually do and was aghast to discover I had neglected to put the film in.

By this time Jerry was fascinated with this large box and was climbing inside it. As I called to my wife and told her to quickly wrap everything back up so Jerry could unwrap it all again, she looked at me as if I had lost my mind and told me, "No way!"

As Jerry continued to play in the box, he kept calling me to come into the box with him and play garage. I did and soon realized that all of this stuff on the floor didn't mean as much to this child as having his dad with him in the box. I am thankful for the teaching of little children.

Hymns of the Saints: No. 247, "Newborn of God"

Prayer Thought: Heavenly Father, may we not be so busy filming life as living it.

<table>
<tr><td>Friday
24
December</td><td>**Brightest and Best**
By Janice Townsend
Spokane, Washington</td><td></td></tr>
</table>

"But in the gift of his Son has God prepared a more excellent way, and it is by faith that it has been fulfilled."
—Ether 5:12

The gift sat beneath the tree, bigger and brighter and surely better than any of the rest. My twelve-year-old heart rejoiced in the knowledge that this special present was meant for me. As the days before Christmas passed, I spent more and more time looking at that gift, admiring its size and beautiful wrappings, fantasizing about what it might contain. And when the time came for it to be opened, I was not disappointed. It was a special gift, and it was mine.

That was a long time ago, but I still get excited at Christmas. I still wait expectantly for the gift that is mine—the gift that is biggest and brightest and best. Only now I know that the magnificence of that gift cannot be found in boxes beneath a tree or contained by colorful paper and ribbon. The special gift that is meant for me—not just at Christmas, but every moment of every day—is the gift of Jesus.

I know that whoever believes in Jesus shall never perish, but will receive eternal life. Can there be any gift better than that? To me, Jesus is the brightest and best. He is the gift that never disappoints, given in love to every person and bringing all that is genuine and enduring.

Hymns of the Saints: No. 253, "Heir of All the Waiting Ages"

Prayer Thought: We offer our humblest thanks, gracious God, for the gift of Jesus. May we receive him gladly, rejoicing in the power of your love.

Saturday **25** December	**My Patchwork Christmas Tree** By Karen Anne Smith Ludington, Michigan

"'Look, the virgin shall conceive and bear a son, and they shall name him Emmanuel,' which means, 'God is with us.'"—Matthew 1:23 NRSV

I've seen many beautiful, tasteful Christmas trees this season. Some were color-coordinated in purple hues and some were dressed in gold. Many trees were decorated according to themes such as an old-fashioned Christmas or a storybook tree. But that's not my tree.

Like an old pair of blue jeans covered in patches, my Christmas tree is a crazy patchwork of homemade ornaments that my boys have brought home from school. Here hangs a Styrofoam snowman and a red Popsicle-stick sled. There are paper pinwheels and a reindeer made from corks. I also have two wooden unicorns, gifts from my kid brother, and a Marvin the Martian that was cross-stitched by an Army sergeant now stationed in Korea.

One very special ornament is a white porcelain angel. Something is different about this angel—his halo is askew and a tennis shoe peeks from under his robe. This angel comes from an autism society in Canada, a guardian angel of children with autism.

Yes, my Christmas tree is quite an eclectic collection of mismatched ornaments, but I love it. Each ornament tells a story. Every ornament represents a loved one. Even the crocheted angel on top and the white baby blanket that nestles around the tree trunk were gifts from dear sisters in Christ.

How precious it is, when we share our visions and work together to create something beautiful, something that no one person may achieve alone. How beautiful it is when we come together as a Community of Christ.

Hymns of the Saints: No. 259, "Jesus, Good Above All Other"

Prayer Thought: Lord of all time, help us to embrace our diversity and learn and grow together. May we support each other in love, that together, and with Christ, we may create something beautiful—your kingdom on earth.

Sunday **26** December	**Something Anyone Can Do** By Shirley Vallier Remmenga Fort Collins, Colorado	

"Continue your love to those who know you, your righteousness to the upright in heart."—Psalm 36:10 NIV

She was sitting on one of the stairs leading down to the lower floor of the church. She had her head in her hands and was softly crying. We were at a senior high retreat and I thought it had been going well. However, it wasn't so with her. I had no idea what was wrong, but I knew I needed to go to her.

I didn't say anything to her as I sat down beside her, put my arm around her shoulders, and just held her. She began to sob and shake. I hugged her a little tighter. Gradually, her grief subsided and her tears stopped. We continued to sit there like that until she looked up and smiled at me. It wasn't long before I lowered my arm and she stood up. When both of us were on our feet, we hugged each other and then she went down the stairs to join the rest of the teenagers. She never told me what had been bothering her and I didn't ask. Somehow, by just being there with her and for her made a difference that night. Out of that experience a bond was formed between us, a bond that still exists even though we rarely see each other.

Sometimes the best thing we can do for others is to be there for them when they need a friend. It seems like such an insignificant thing, but it is so important. Anyone can do it. The only requirement is a loving heart.

Sing for Peace: No. 15, "Put Peace into Each Other's Hands"

Prayer Thought: Help us, God, to be there for others as you are always there for us.

Monday **27** December	**Become as a Child** By Ardith Lancaster Paisley, Florida	

"And as they looked to behold, they cast their eyes toward heaven, and they saw the heavens open, and they saw angels descending out of heaven, as it were in the midst of fire; and they came down and encircled those little ones...and the angels ministered to them."—III Nephi 8:25–26

"Read me a 'tory! Read me a 'tory!" one of my young neighbors called to me over the fence. The call from an older brother followed: "Hi, Ard, can you come over?"

The presence of young children in my neighborhood is such a delight to me. Their natures are so generous, and their curiosity is ever-present: "Where are you going?" "What are you doing?" "Can I help?" Children have the ability to be disarming and at the same time so warm and openly loving and helpful.

We need to further explore the Lord's injunction to "become as a little child" if we are to identify those characteristics he was holding up for us to emulate.

Hymns of the Saints: No. 225, "When, His Salvation Bringing"

Prayer Thought: Welcoming Lord, we picture you with open arms waiting to embrace the children, and we long to be among them. May we rediscover how to be like them—inquisitive, helpful, and nonjudgmental.

"Some trust in chariots, and some in horses; but we will remember the name of the Lord our God. They are brought down and fallen; but we are risen, and stand upright."
—Psalm 20:7–8

I am thankful for all those who are praying for me today. I am also honored to pray for others. Prayer is a way we share our faith in God and our love for one another.

Over the past ten years, my big sister, Jeanie, has faced a daily battle with cancer. She could allow herself to become depressed and engulfed in self-pity, yet she chooses to be an avid reader, aware of current events and mindful of everyone else's needs. She often prays herself to sleep holding up family members and friends.

What a blessing to us all that she chooses to find this healing peace in the loving arms of God. Our strength and faith are renewed through her daily example.

Sing a New Song: No. 34, "Make Me a Channel of Your Peace"

Prayer Thought: Draw our hearts to you daily, Lord, on behalf of others, and teach us to focus on the power of your Spirit to overcome our struggles.

Wednesday **29** December	**Fellowship of Love** By Barrie Fox Kirkby in Ashfield, England	

"I was made a minister, according to the gift of the grace of God given unto me by the effectual working of his power."
—Ephesians 3:7

From time to time, as I visit various congregations, I am truly concerned about the small percentage of the membership present at their services. Among the words we find for "fellowship" in a thesaurus are "companionship," "association," and "fraternity"—words that bring to mind the fact that we are, in our congregations, called to be companions, colleagues, and co-workers in the fellowship of the Community of Christ.

As I think about some of the empty seats, I am reminded of the old "conscience" verse that goes something like this: "Occasionally I do think of church and pop in for a visit, so that when the day comes that I'm carried in, the Lord won't say, 'Who is this?'"

As I get older, I seem to become more and more aware that there are indeed two ways of standing between God and people—we can shed light or cast a shadow, promote a link or become a barrier. May I then beware of writing off too quickly these non-attending members in my congregation and may they remain in my thoughts and prayers.

Hymns of the Saints: No. 485, "Blest Be the Tie that Binds"

Prayer Thought: God who calls us, may it be our special mission to reach out to those who have drifted away from us. Enable us to bring healing and renewed interest in fellowship.

Thursday **30** December	**Cultivate Humility** By Dorene Kilburn St. Paul's Station, Ontario, Canada	

"Do nothing from selfish ambition or conceit, but in humility regard others as better than yourselves. Let each of you look not to your own interests, but to the interest of others. Let the same mind be in you that was in Christ Jesus."
—Philippians 2:3–5 NRSV

Some years ago, when I was reading a book, I came across the word "hubris," and I thought, now that's an odd word. As is so often the case, after a word catches our attention, it seems to pop up again and again in the written and spoken word. The word "hubris" is heard quite often when there is discussion in the media about people in the public eye. The dictionary defines it as "excessive pride and self-confidence; arrogance." It comes from Greek, so that's why it sounds rather odd.

There is a fine line between healthy self-confidence and arrogance. I am embarrassed now at how I viewed Jesus when I was very young. Among those short scriptures we memorized as children was "I am the light of the world." I remember thinking that this statement attributed to Jesus sounded rather conceited. That was my immature understanding of it at the time. I would later learn that Jesus spoke those words because he trusted God and was committed to the mission for which he was sent—to be the light of the world. He was not simply puffed up with his own importance!

We have all seen people raised from obscurity and placed on a pedestal because of extraordinary gifts: music, art, public speaking, for example. Some remain humble and some become overly self-confident to the point of arrogance and become totally focused on themselves.

Because we are human, it is possible to become too confident, even when we are doing the Lord's work. When we get compliments because we use our particular gifts in service, we must never forget that it is God who has placed those gifts in us. The glory must be God's, when we use them effectively in ministry.

Hymns of the Saints: No. 487, "Be with Me, Lord, Where'er I Go"

Prayer Thought: God of compassion, who understands each one of us in our humanness, help us remain humble and always remember that whatever good we can accomplish for you is the result of the gifts you have placed in us.

| Friday
31
December | **Prepare to Weave**
By Cheryll Peterman
Independence, Missouri | |

"Trust in the Lord with all your heart, and do not rely on your own insight."—Proverbs 3:6 NRSV

As an employee of Herald House and church headquarters, I work at the Temple, in Communications. The chaplains who volunteer here make regular rounds to visit briefly with all employees, and on many Tuesdays, I am visited by my friend Helen. She has a gentle spirit, a positive outlook, and years of wisdom behind her, and she always has tucked in her hand a printed thought for the day. In the spring of 2002, she shared one with me that gave me courage for the year ahead: "Prepare to weave, and God will give you the thread." I don't remember the source of the quote, but how true it has proved to be.

I have had many responsibilities these past few years, in particular, caring for my increasingly ailing mother and a dependent adult brother. They lived in a duplex one block from us for about five years until Mother could no longer care for herself following back surgery. When she went into a nursing home, my brother slept at their duplex at night but spent the rest of his time at our house. Our son was in the midst of a long-distance divorce, and with him and his large dog living with us, our small house was completely full. When we realized that Mother would not be coming home, my husband and I decided that we needed a different housing arrangement.

Our house was paid for, and the thought of starting over in our late fifties was not attractive, but neither was going on as we were. Helen's thought-for-the-day that particular Tuesday in May settled deeply in my mind, and we began to look at possible new places to accommodate us all. As we searched for someplace closer to work for me and with certain requirements for my brother (a walkout lower level, for instance), I made our needs a matter of prayer, and we prepared our house for sale. One early July weekend, we found our answer in a new housing development for older adults, and we built a new home that has worked wonderfully for us. I am closer to work; we live by a small lake with sounds and views of wildlife; our house exterior is maintenance free; and yard care is provided for a reasonable monthly fee.

I remember how excited yet afraid I felt as the foundation went in and as lumber was delivered; we called it "our commitment." We could scarcely believe that we would one day live in this house. But I kept remembering Helen's words and knew that God indeed knew our needs and was gently leading us to trust that it would all work out.

In so many ways it has worked out beautifully, and I am now less stressed. We have been led through selling

466

one house, building another, and all that goes with it. Indeed, God will lead us if we have courage to pursue the answer. May we all look to the year ahead with our hand in God's, listening for his whisper to us.

Hymns of the Saints: No. 302, "O God, Our Source of Truth"

Prayer Thought: Eternal God, may we always seek your wisdom in our decisions and trust you when we sense you are leading us. Grant us courage to follow.

Author Index

Dauzvardis, Shirley	Jan. 10, Nov. 21
Davis, Anna	Feb. 7
Dayton, Lois	Jun. 29, Jul. 18, Oct. 18
DeBarthe, Enid Stubbart	Apr. 15, Sep. 4
Dickerson, Genie	Jul. 15
Dieterman, Roberta	Mar. 9, May 31, Jun. 25, Aug. 8, Sep. 22, Oct. 8, Nov. 12, Dec. 15
Dinger, Bridget	Jan. 14
Dixon, Melba Jean	Jan. 7, Apr. 7, Jun. 13, Sep. 19, Nov. 5
Edwards, Jim	Jul. 28
Elliott, Phyllis	Jan. 25, Aug. 31, Dec. 21
Fannin, Bonnie	Nov. 25
Fant, Constance	Jul. 3
Fehrenbacher, Janie	Jun. 21, Sep. 18
Finger, Mildred	Nov. 20
Fleming, Cheryl	Jan. 29
Foster, Beulah	Feb. 26, Apr. 29
Fox, Barrie	Mar. 26, May 11, Jul. 21, Sep. 14, Nov. 26, Dec. 29
French, Linda	Mar. 25
Frey, Willa	Mar. 24, Jul. 17, Oct. 3
Fultz, Henry	Jan. 19
Green, Helen M.	Apr. 5, May 7, Jun. 16, Aug. 1, Sep. 3, Oct. 30
Greer, Geraldine Billings	Mar. 8, Sep. 7, Nov. 15, Dec. 8
Grewal, Dennis D.	Sep. 23
Griffin, Bill	Jan. 20, Apr. 13, Jul. 5
Grinnell, Russell	Apr. 22, May 23, Jul. 19
Guinn, Dianne Lyell	Feb. 1, May 6, Nov. 3
Hall, Ken	Apr. 26
Harrison, Martha	May 1

Henson, Jane	Feb. 17, Jun. 2
Hillyard, Doris	Nov. 13
Holman, Norma	Feb. 11, Jun. 27, Oct. 9
Holmes, Ralph	Feb. 16, Jul. 24, Dec. 12
Huntsman, Olevia	Jan. 22, Apr. 2, Aug. 11, Oct. 28, Dec. 19
Hyden, Carol	May 13
Jones, Charlotte	Mar. 27, Apr. 17, May 18, Aug. 29, Sep. 29, Oct. 26, Dec. 22
Jones, Diane Brunner	Jan. 18
Jordan, Mildred	Nov. 27
Kilburn, Dorene	Jan. 13, Mar. 6, Apr. 8, May 8, Aug. 2, Oct. 24, Nov. 23, Dec. 30
King, Florence	Feb. 24, May 2, Jul. 20, Sep. 6, Nov. 4
Kirby, Lillian Bayless	Feb. 6, May 17, Aug. 14, Oct. 13
Kloss, Gerald John	Feb. 2, Mar. 14, Apr. 1, Jun. 12, Jul. 6, Aug. 26, Sep. 8, Oct. 29, Dec. 23
Knackstedt, Ethel	Apr. 10, Jul. 29, Sep. 25
Korf, Cindy	Feb. 18
Kornman, Charles	Feb. 13, May 12, Oct. 10, Nov. 16, Dec. 17
Kuppart, Eva Mildred	Jun. 7
Lancaster, Ardith	Apr. 25, Aug. 27, Dec. 27
Landsdown, Larry	Mar. 22, May 21, Jul. 1
Landsdown, Myrna	May 30
Leeder, Alma J. V.	Apr. 11, Dec. 1
Lents, Helen	Sept. 26
Linne, Elaine	Feb. 28, Apr. 28
Locke, Annabelle Taylor	Feb. 15

Long, Carla	Mar. 1, Jun. 8
Loughran, Anne	Apr. 6, May 24
Luce, Deb	Mar. 30
Lynn, Helen L.	Aug. 24, Dec. 5
McCain, Paul	Jan. 26, Feb. 19, Mar. 13, Apr. 4, Jul. 16, Sep. 27, Oct. 22, Dec. 4
McCarty, Shirley	Dec. 7
McCurdy, Penny	Feb. 12, Aug. 9
McDonald, Jane	Oct. 31
McKain, Hal	Jan. 30, Apr. 16, Jul. 14, Oct. 25
Mallas, Shirley	May 5
Megee, Mark E.	Jan. 2, May 14, Aug. 16, Oct. 4, Dec. 2
Michael, Peggy	Feb. 10, Mar. 21, May 22, Jul. 2, Aug. 19, Nov. 14, Dec. 10
Miller, Jane	Jun. 26, Aug. 20, Nov. 24
Miller, Susan	Feb. 22, Aug. 3
Monroy, Bonnie	Apr. 23
Needham, Donna	Jan. 5, Jul. 7
Nelsen, Neta Minthorn	Jun. 19, Sep. 17, Nov. 28
Oetting, Judy	Jan. 17, May 28, Sep. 2
Olson, Elaine	Apr. 27
Osterhaus, Heather	Feb. 25, Jul. 4
Ourth, Florence	Mar. 29
Parker, Vivian	Nov. 1
Peabody, Sylvia Lenfestey	Mar. 15
Peterman, Cheryll	Dec. 31
Phillips, Shirley E.	May 10, Sep. 16, Nov. 22, Dec. 11
Premoe, Dorothy	May 4

Qualls, Janie S.   Mar. 16, Jun. 18, Aug. 7,
                                    Sep. 9, Nov. 29, Dec. 14

Remmenga, Shirley Vallier   Jan. 27, Apr. 19, May 27,
                                    Jul. 23, Aug. 15, Sep. 28,
                                    Nov. 30, Dec. 26
Richardson, Don   Jun. 20, Aug. 21, Sep. 20
Rotchford, Herbert W.   Sep. 24
Russell, June   Feb. 8, Sep. 21, Dec. 18

Saxton, Isabelle   Jul. 30
Schwartz, Diane F.   Jun. 11, Aug. 6, Oct. 6,
                                    Nov. 11

Serig, Ward   Apr. 14, Jun. 30, Oct. 23
Short, Merna   Jan. 23, Feb. 3, Mar. 12,
                                    Apr. 18, Jul. 11, Aug. 25,
                                    Sep. 10, Oct. 15

Shupe, Margaret Gunderson   Dec. 20
Smith, Karen Anne   Jan. 1, Mar. 11, Jun. 5,
                                    Aug. 12, Dec. 25

Southland, Sherry   Jan. 21, Jun. 14
Strickland, Emma   Jul. 31
Studer, Sonia J.   Mar. 19

Townsend, Janice   Jan. 3, Feb. 27, Mar. 20,
                                    Apr. 9, May 9, Jul. 22,
                                    Aug. 13, Oct. 20, Dec. 24

Townsend, Jo Ann   Jan. 31, Apr. 3, Jul. 8,
                                    Oct. 11

Troyer, Dorothy   Jan. 12
Turner, Eileen   Jan. 9, May 16, Jun. 10,
                                    Aug. 18, Sep. 15, Nov. 9

Twinn, Mary   Mar. 3, Sep. 12, Dec. 13

Van Eaton, Maurine   Mar. 23, Jun. 28
Van Eaton, Wallace   Oct. 14
Vreeland, Ruth Andrews   Jan. 15, Mar. 2, Jun. 9,
                                    Aug. 22, Nov. 7

Wang, Ellen L.	Apr. 30, Nov. 19
Webb, Jean	Dec. 16
West, Denzil J.	Feb. 21, Apr. 20, May 25, Jul. 12, Aug. 4, Oct. 19
Wilcox, L. Joyce	May 26, Oct. 12
Williams, Faye	Mar. 4, Jul. 27, Oct. 1
Williams, Ilean M.	Jun. 23
Yeager, Betty	Jun. 6

Scripture Index

147:18	April 19	57:15	July 19
150:1, 3, 4	March 10	64:8	August 19
150:4, 6	May 17		
150:6	November 20	*Jeremiah*	
		33:3	September 7
Proverbs			
3:5	September 25	*Lamentations*	
3:5–6	June 4	3:22–23	February 1
3:6	December 31	3:40–41	November 4
3:21, 23	October 8		
14:21	April 2	*Ezekiel*	
17:8	March 31	11:19–20	February 12
17:17	February 4	37:5	July 6
20:7	August 31		
22:6	May 13	*Daniel*	
28:20	July 30	9:3	July 9
31:10, 27–28	May 7	9:19	February 28
31:25, 27	September 1		
		Hosea	
Ecclesiastes		10:12	July 10
3:1	April 4	*Micah*	
7:8–9	August 20	6:8	June 3
11:1	October 14		
11:5	November 14	*Zechariah*	
11:9	July 23	8:3–4	December 7
		Malachi	
Isaiah		3:6	January 27
2:4	September 30	4:2	July 14
2:5	November 7	4:6	October 23
11:6	February 7		
12:2	June 8	*New Testament*	
12:5–6	October 9	*Matthew*	
14:31	June 29	1:23	December 25
30:17–18	March 7	2:9	December 21
40:1	May 29	3:10–11 IV	December 23
40:5	December 12	5:7–8	September 3
40:11	January 29	5:10 IV	August 3
40:31	January 21	5:14	October 24
	November 25	5:14–16	March 20
41:10	August 29	5:24 IV	April 11
42:6	September 27	5:31 IV	June 28
42:16	June 21	5:44 IV	August 14
43:18–19	May 24	6:19	October 27
51:15–16	November 16	6:26	September 20

475

6:29 IV	July 8	22:44	February 14
6:37 IV	May 23		
7:31 IV	January 25	*John*	
10:7 IV	November 11	2:18–19	April 5
10:31	November 12	3:8	April 28
11:28–30	August 27	3:14–15	April 8
13:19 IV	March 23	4:16 IV	June 22
18:2	February 16	4:26 IV	April 10
18:20	October 26	8:10–11	June 9
20:16	July 15	8:31–32	January 3
23:21 IV	June 16	10:27–28	January 24
25:41 IV	February 21	13:34	October 6
28:17 IV	December 15	14:16	December 20
		14:18	December 1
Mark		14:27	January 10
1:15 IV	February 17	15:15	March 2
6:43–44 IV	May 10	16:33	November 29
10:6	June 11	17:22–23	March 27
10:12 IV	June 23		
10:14	September 4	*Acts*	
10:51–52	March 6	1:8	July 24
11:22–24	January 15	2:28	August 1
12:35–36 IV	July 26	2:46–47	September 8
12:36 IV	August 30	3:6	May 31
		12:5	September 24
Luke		20:35	June 1
1:37	December 11		
2:10–11	December 19	*Romans*	
6:38	June 10	1:17	August 25
9:62	January 28	7:6	February 13
10:20	January 17	8:18	September 15
10:24	November 26	8:28	January 2
11:10 IV	July 20	12:9–10	June 24
11:14 IV	September 2	12:10	January 30
12:30 IV	November 22	12:10,12	September 26
12:48	January 26	13:8	May 5
13:24	February 19	15:13	December 18
15:22	July 16	*I Corinthians*	
15:24	April 24	12:4–6	July 11
18:15–16	August 4	12:8–10	March 25
18:17	May 4	12:24–25	March 8
20:23–25	August 23	12:27	January 19
22:26–27	March 16	13:4–7	April 27
22:43	December 9	13:6–8	May 9

476

II Corinthians
1:21–22	February 2
2:10	May 2
5:17–18	April 23
9:6	July 22
9:15	June 12
12: 4–6	July 11
13:11	March 18

Galatians
2:20	April 9
2:21	December 22
3:28	November 8
4:9	January 18
5:1	October 4
5:22–23	August 22
5:25	February 25
6:2	August 5
6:9–10	November 15

Ephesians
1:17–18	October 17
2:9–10	June 5
2:10	January 6
2:19	September 23
3:7	December 29
3:14–15	November 19
3:16–17	September 11
5:2	April 16
5:8–12	December 14
5:17, 19	December 8
5:19–20	November 13
5:20	August 6

Philippians
1:6	August 7
1:27	September 17
2:3–5	December 30
3:13–14	April 14
3:14, 17	November 5
4:6–7	October 11
4:8	January 9
4:8–9	August 18
4:13	January 16

Colossians
1:13–14	September 12
3:12, 17	May 8
3:16	February 11
3:17, 23	June 18
4:2–3	October 18

I Thessalonians
4:9–10	September 9
5:13	March 19
5:16–18	October 1
5:16–19	May 1
5:18	May 19

I Timothy
4:8	May 3
4:10	April 30
6:12	August 24

II Timothy
1:7	March 5

Titus
2:14	June 2

Hebrews
6:3	June 25
8:11	March 1
10:35–36	July 3
11:1, 3	June 14
11:13	April 12
12:1	April 20
12:1–2	June 6
13:1–2	January 11
13:2	September 5
13:5	March 29
13:8–9	February 20
13:16	December 5

James
1:17	January 22
	November 10
5:11	October 25
5:15–16	July 21
5:16	April 26

I Peter		13:27	October 16
1:8–9	April 17		
2:5–6	October 21	*Alma*	
4:9	September 16	3:48–49	November 17
4:10	January 8	14:82	June 30
5:6–7	October 2	14:88	August 13
		17:45	October 22
II Peter		17:68	August 17
1:5–7	August 15	19:78	September 27
1:19	October 10		
3:18	April 18	*Helaman*	
		2:31	January 20
I John		2:74–75	December 10
4:7	October 15		
4:9–10	January 14	*III Nephi*	
4:10–11	May 27	8:25–26	December 27
4:16	September 10	10:21	April 3
4:18	April 21	12:35	February 3
5:2	March 11		
5:3	July 12	*IV Nephi*	
5:9	June 7	1:17	January 7
III John		*Mormon*	
2	November 21	4:70	February 23
5–5	July 31	*Ether*	
		5:12	December 24
Revelation			
22:16	May 28	*Moroni*	
		10:13	June 17
		10:15	September 13

Book of Mormon

I Nephi		
1:1	May 6	

Doctrine and Covenants

II Nephi		*Section & Verse*	
1:95	December 6	3:15e	March 17
3:40–41	September 19	17:6e	February 6
3:61	February 26	17:12a	July 13
13:7	June 27	34:1a	March 30
13:29	March 21	38:2a–b	May 15
14:11	July 17	42:12d	May 26
15:4	August 8	59:2d	September 22
		60:3e	April 29
Mosiah		63:6b	February 9
1:49	June 20	68:4c	February 10
2:4	September 14	77:4b	July 5

478